T0291306

# Sustainable and Resilient Global Practices

# EMERALD STUDIES IN GLOBAL STRATEGIC RESPONSIVENESS

**Series Editor:** Torben Juul Andersen

**Recent Books in Series:**

*The Responsive Global Organization: New Insights from Global Strategy and International Business*
Edited by Torben Juul Andersen

*Strategic Responsiveness and Adaptive Organizations: New Research Frontiers in International Strategic Management*
Edited by Torben Juul Andersen, Simon Torp and Stefan Linder

*Adapting to Environmental Challenges: New Research in Strategy and International Business*
Edited by Torben Juul Andersen and Simon Sunn Torp

*Strategic Responses for a Sustainable Future: New Research in International Management*
Edited by Torben Juul Andersen

*Navigating Corporate Cultures from Within: Making Sense of Corporate Values Seen from an Employee Perspective*
By Michael Jakobsen and Verner D. Worm

*Responding to Uncertain Conditions: New Research on Strategic Adaptation*
By Torben Juul Andersen

*A Study of Risky Business Outcomes: Adapting to Strategic Disruption*
By Torben Juul Andersen

# Sustainable and Resilient Global Practices: Advances in Responsiveness and Adaptation

EDITED BY

## TORBEN JUUL ANDERSEN
*Copenhagen Business School, Denmark*

United Kingdom – North America – Japan – India – Malaysia – China

Emerald Publishing Limited
Emerald Publishing, Floor 5, Northspring, 21-23 Wellington Street, Leeds LS1 4DL.

First edition 2024
Editorial matter and selection © 2024 Torben Juul Andersen.

Individual chapters © 2024 The authors.
Published under exclusive licence by Emerald Publishing Limited.

**Reprints and permissions service**
Contact: www.copyright.com

**British Library Cataloguing in Publication Data**
A catalogue record for this book is available from the British Library

ISBN: 978-1-83797-612-6 (Print)
ISBN: 978-1-83797-611-9 (Online)
ISBN: 978-1-83797-613-3 (Epub)

Printed and bound by CPI Group (UK) Ltd, Croydon, CR0 4YY

INVESTOR IN PEOPLE

# Contents

List of Contributors                                                    *vii*

Preface                                                                 *ix*

**Chapter 1    Adaptive Strategy-making Processes for Long-term
Resilience and Sustainable Solutions**
*Torben Juul Andersen*                                                  *1*

**Chapter 2    Adaptation Strategies to Climate Change: Bibliometric
Analyses and Emerging Themes**
*Giuseppe Danese*                                                       *17*

**Chapter 3    Assessing Long-term Performance in Manufacturing
Companies Hit by a Natural Disaster: The Role of Organizational
Resilience and Human Capital**
*Elisa Martinelli, Elena Sarti and Giulia Tagliazucchi*                *37*

**Chapter 4    Environmental Sustainability Orientation, Dynamic
Capability, Entrepreneurial Orientation, and Green Innovation
in Small- and Medium-sized Enterprise**
*Kwadwo Asante, Petr Novak and Michael Adu Kwarteng*                   *55*

**Chapter 5    Supporting Green Business Growth: Towards a
Transformative Approach**
*Polina Baranova*                                                       *81*

**Chapter 6    Exploring Organizational Responses to Nonmarket
Institutional Pressures: The Case of the EU Taxonomy Regulation**
*Michelle Palharini, Matthias Fertig and Peter Wehnert*               *99*

**Chapter 7    Corporate Responsiveness and Sustainability Transition:
Insights from a Danish–Malaysian Palm Oil Multinational**
*Frederik Hejselbjerg Vagtborg*                                        *149*

**Chapter 8    When Supply Chain Sustainability Means Supply Chain Resilience: The Case of Dr. Bronner's**
*Hannah Stolze, Jon Kirchoff and Alexis Bateman*        *193*

**Chapter 9    Justice in a Cooperative Enterprise: The Case of Brazilian Justa Trama**
*Italo Anderson Taumaturgo dos Santos and*
*Victor Pessoa de Melo Gomes*        *217*

# List of Contributors

| | |
|---|---|
| *Torben Juul Andersen* | Copenhagen Business School, Denmark |
| *Kwadwo Asante* | Tomas Bata University, Czech Republic |
| *Polina Baranova* | University of Darby, UK |
| *Alexis Bateman* | Massachusetts Institute of Technology, USA |
| *Giuseppe Danese* | University of Padua, Italy |
| *Victor Pessoa de Melo Gomes* | University of São Paulo, Brazil |
| *Italo Anderson Taumaturgo dos Santos* | University of São Paulo, Brazil |
| *Matthias Fertig* | Friedrich-Alexander-Universität, Germany |
| *Jon Kirchoff* | East Carolina University, USA |
| *Michael Adu Kwarteng* | Tomas Bata University, Czech Republic |
| *Elisa Martinelli* | University of Modena and Reggio Emilia, Italy |
| *Petr Novak* | Tomas Bata University, Czech Republic |
| *Michelle Palharini* | Friedrich-Alexander-Universität, Germany |
| *Elena Sarti* | University of Modena and Reggio Emilia, Italy |
| *Hannah Stolze* | Baylor University, USA |
| *Giulia Tagliazucchi* | University of Modena and Reggio Emilia, Italy |
| *Frederik Hejselbjerg Vagtborg* | Copenhagen Business School, Denmark |
| *Peter Wehnert* | Friedrich-Alexander-Universität, Germany |

# Preface

Corporate exposures to environmental changes appear to have increased in size and intensity over past decades with many unexpected disruptive incidents with adverse effects on business activities, public services, and societal welfare. Operating in an integrated global economy increases the complexity of multinational enterprise where actions and reactions in different regions around the world intermingle as a mechanism to produce unprecedented events with potentially extreme outcomes. The many interdependent elements can create wicked problems that may seem impossible to resolve through conventional analytics calling for new approaches that engage diverse constituents in collaborative efforts to develop sustainable solutions. The ability to survive, persevere, and prosper under abrupt and uncertain conditions requires dynamic adaptive strategy-making processes that can facilitate organizational realignment of business activities in responsive initiatives to deal with environmental changes as they evolve.

However, the ability to advance organizational adaptability and gain resilient outcomes, that make the organization even stronger after responding to emergent events, is different when the implied exposures have systemic proportions. Here, the individual organizations are exposed to emergent developments, but so are many other private and public sector entities, which therefore calls for collaborative initiatives to generate responses that lead to durable outcomes. Operating in complex global contexts reflects conditions of radical uncertainty where exposures often are hard to identify and outline thus de facto constituting unmeasurable exposures. To a large extent, these exposures derive from, and are locked into, standard practices we have established to govern the global economic activities that create economic value for society and its constituents. When the connected cross-border activities are tightly coupled, say in optimized global value chains, it will have systemic repercussions when political and economic conditions undergo fundamental changes. This creates exposures for all internationally engaged organizations and calls for collaborative solutions that involve all businesses in joint policy efforts with exposed societies across the global economy.

That is, contemporary firms must continue to adapt their business activities to thrive where recent events, such as a pandemic and military conflict close to Europe, have shown how sudden unexpected environmental jolts can cause severe disruptions to the prevailing business conduct. Successful responses to such emergent changes rely on a collective ability to sense ongoing developments and consider coordinated responsive actions that engage businesses in proactive, timely, and meaningful initiatives where economic practices and standards coevolve going forward. It may entail joint reconnaissance involving internal and external stakeholders where organizational agents can take local responsive initiatives to explore for viable solutions that can generate new insights and inform forward-looking analyses for updated strategic direction and guidance as the context evolves.

We need to develop a better understanding of how to generate effective strategic adaptation in times of abrupt environmental changes where uncertainty and the unknown prevails. The interdependencies across specialized economic functions and regional market conditions require that business activities coevolve to gain lasting effects that permeate across all related business activities and public services on a global scale. Public policy and regulation can induce warranted change, but it will take corporate enterprise to effectuate the underlying economic transformation across interacting public–private relationships. Ideally, the public and private organizations should collaborate in the formation of viable and durable ecosystems that can form a sustainable economic path for the future. The ability to develop sustainable solutions thrives on innovation, experimentation, and learning across networks of collaborative institutional and individual relationships. We need to better understand how this can be established and managed.

This collection of chapter articles attempts to fill this void in our current knowledge by delving into the issues of effective responses, sustainable solutions, and long-term resilient outcomes from different perspectives and contexts.

Chapter 1 by Torben Juul Andersen argues for the need to develop *sustainable adaptive business practices* as a basis for long-term resilient outcomes. It argues that businesses operate in a complex dynamic world where human activities interfere with the natural environment in intricate ways that can lead to unforeseen potentially catastrophic outcomes that will affect all economic entities and therefore societies in general and particularly the most vulnerable communities. It argues that we must pay attention to uncertain and unknown factors that create our exposures although we as humans tend to ignore uncertainty and adopt control-based practices, thereby in reality creating a false sense of security, where in truth, we face more uncertainties than we realize. This reduces our ability to find ways to reduce the adverse outcomes caused by abrupt unexpected events and fail to address the underlying causes rooted in the way the global economic activities are structured. The related organizational exposures are only partially determined by enterprise governance but to a large extent derive from the prevailing structure of global business practices. So, effective responses must not only address local firm-specific conditions but should consider the systemic effects associated with the global business structure. Sustainable solutions must give thoughts to multinational enterprise risks as well as societal exposures around the world where they operate in public–private partnerships. The solutions to uncertain exposures and systemic risks will require experimentation that involves public and private organizations to generate new insights and engaged learning to identify viable solutions for a sustainable future.

In Chapter 2, Giuseppe Danese examines what is known about *business adaptation strategies* to deal with climate change conducting a systematic review of the extant literature. This review uncovers a hierarchical structure of significant predictors that map interdependent adaptation decisions and their impact on the environment. The author identifies nine predictors from a final set of records including institutional (regulatory), industry (e.g., tourism, insurance, and wine), interorganizational (horizontal and vertical linkages), and intra-organizational (e.g., capabilities, exposures, and firm-specific characteristics) influences, and effects. The author examines different choices, for example, adaptation versus mitigation, adaptation versus maladaptation, and active versus passive adaptive efforts. There appears to be infrequent recording and monitoring of long-term social and environmental impacts of these adaptive choices. To this effect, the study explores the links between interorganizational predictors and adaptive choices including the role of cognitive and behavioral biases.

In Chapter 3, Elisa Martinelli, Elena Sarti, and Giulia Tagliazucchi investigate how to sustain *economic activity after a natural catastrophe* and the role of human capital as a source of organizational resilience. The specific background is earthquake events that threaten the performance of businesses that operate in regions hit by natural disasters. The exposed organizations must adopt dynamic adaptive strategies to survive after a disaster that allow them to continue to generate revenue and build long-term resilience. This takes human capital, or individual engagement, to realign business activities and identify opportunities for business renewal. The study examines whether businesses that value their human capital respond better, gaining economic sustainability to natural disasters. This is analyzed based on corporate survey data and archival accounting information from 131 sampled firms that were hit by the Emilia earthquake in Italy in 2012. The sampled data were analyzed using partial least squares structural equation modeling (PLS-SEM). The results show the importance of human engagement to develop effective adaptive processes that generate more resilient outcomes to the adverse events. It was specifically identified that involvement of human capital creates valuable and organizational responsiveness. The study investigates how human capital affects long-run (6 years) business performance.

In the ensuing Chapter 4, Kwadwo Asante, Petr Novak, and Michael Adu Kwarteng study *environmental sustainability effects* in the hospitality industry and examine the role of dynamic capabilities and autonomy. They specifically investigate the relationship between the environmental sustainability orientation of the hotel management and the subsequent effects on green creativity within the hotel. They argue that combinations of green dynamic capabilities and green autonomy determine boundary conditions that affect the environmental sustainability orientation and the ability to enact green creativity within the hotel. The study integrates dynamic capability theory with the componential model of creativity and tests the relationships based on data from the hospitality industry in Ghana. The analysis is performed using symmetrical and asymmetrical approaches to uncover plausible configurations that lead to green creativity outcomes. The results provide evidence of firm-specific factors that drive an environmental sustainability orientation and enhance green creativity as guidance for hotel managers.

Chapter 5 by Polina Baranova develops a transformative approach to support the development and *growth of green business activities*. The study is based on analyses of survey data from 372 businesses operating in the British Midlands that show a trend toward increased focus on green business activities that will require development of green skills and environmental business support. The data show significant differences between large and small businesses and the way they engage in green business development. The characteristics of the business sector affect the growth potential where companies in manufacturing develop more sales from green products compared to service offerings. Manufacturing companies are found to be more proactive than service companies and are better at integrating the green ambitions into their business strategies. It appears that information gaps are major impediments to promote green business activities where business support agencies can provide useful pro-environmental enterprise support. Community policies can support development of green skills and capabilities to develop the green growth potential where enterprise support can catalyze business community contributions toward sustainable business development.

In Chapter 6, Michelle Palharini, Matthias Fertig, and Peter Wehnert examine the potential *effects of the EU Taxonomy Regulation* and identifies different organizational responses to these new hybrid practices imposed by forthcoming regulation. The study is focused on understanding firms' responses to the EU taxonomy, and whether they recognize value creation opportunities by aligning market and nonmarket strategies with the taxonomy goals. This regulatory initiative introduces hybrid practices that combine the logics of environmental considerations and financial return logics. Adopting a conceptual framework based on institutional theory, dynamic capabilities view and nonmarket strategy research, the authors examine how organizational structures and practices affect the way companies respond to the regulatory pressures. A study of companies located in several European Union (EU) countries find that most firms respond reactively, while firms with sustainability-driven business models tend to respond in an anticipatory way, and firms with high greenhouse gas (GHG) emissions and low taxonomy eligibility in a defensive way. They also find evidence for mimetic isomorphism related to the influence of consulting and auditing services. Further, high levels of uncertainty, ambiguity and lack of clarity has a great impact on firms' responses and motives. The study identifies different response types when companies are confronted with multiple logics of mandated hybrid practices and explains how organizational structures and practices linked to the different institutional logics determine the corporate responses.

Chapter 7 written by Frederik Hejselbjerg Vagtborg presents a case study of a Danish–Malaysian palm oil multinational and analyzes how the company *responded to new EU regulation* aimed to forge a sustainability transition. The study explores the strategic responses of a company operating in developing economies to the requirements imposed by the new EU sustainability regulation. It adopts a theory-guided approach and develops propositions that subsequently are investigated based on insights from the case study. The research uses data collected from interviews with senior and middle managers as well as external stakeholders cross-checked against archival data from corporate documents and public articles. The study finds that adherence to corporate social responsibility can enhance responsiveness to new regulatory demands particularly when combined with early signal scanning and real options reasoning. It shows how reputation, core values, and ethical concerns support stakeholder engagement and lever the ability to generate collaborative solutions that deal with the new regulation. The EU sustainability regulation has socioeconomic and political relevance and has not yet been studied from the perspective of commodity multinationals in developing countries. The study provides insights into how these companies can enhance responsiveness and adaptability to the uncertainties imposed by the changing regulatory environment.

In Chapter 8, Hannah Stolze, Jon Kirchoff, and Alexis Bateman present a case analysis of Dr. Bronner's as an example of an organization where *value-driven response capabilities* lead to more sustainable responses and resilient outcomes. The study investigates whether the use of sustainable strategies and responsive initiatives can help firms become more resilient in the face of disruptive incidents. Dr. Bronner's is a rapidly growing personal care products company with strong values that hone the engagement of their employees. The study explores the potential pathways to generate sustainable solutions and create resilient outcomes that resist disruptions and recover, even improve, operational capabilities after disruptions. It shows how sustainable responses can buttress and overcome the impact of emergent disruptions and build more robust long-term operations going forward.

Finally, Chapter 9 presents a case study by Italo Anderson Taumaturgo dos Santos and Victor Pessoa de Melo Gomes of the Brazilian company Justa Trama presenting the *effects of justice on sustainability* in a cooperative enterprise. The Sustainable Development Goal Number 16 established by the United Nations (UN) is about providing justice for all to build effective, accountable, and inclusive institutions. According to stakeholder theory, the perception of fair treatment implies that the organization incorporates fairness, impartiality, and morality as operating principles and core values. Hence, their study analyzes how justice influences organizational processes around an economic network of solidary cooperatives. They collect data from semi-structured interviews and archival information from formal documents made available by the involved members of the cooperative network. The study identifies how justice drives a series of corporate values and organizational processes applied across the production value chain. This develops relationships conceived as being fair, among organizations that pursue the same ideals, and thereby enhances more responsive actions with sustainable outcomes.

The chapters provide different perspectives to the issue of sustainable and resilient operating practices and the need for effective responses to deal with unpredictable, abrupt, and rapid changes in the global business environment. This search for sustainable solutions presents a diversity of methodological approaches including conceptual argumentation, theoretical modeling, systematic literature reviews, empirical examinations and data analyses, and several insightful case studies. These research chapter articles present current challenges of dealing with uncertain and unknown conditions, accumulating environmental degradation, extreme natural events, new evolving regulatory initiatives, green business opportunities, cooperative approaches, etc. We hope these diverse contributions can provide some inspiring reading to advance our thinking about how to generate sustainable and resilient practices for the benefit of future societies.

*Torben Juul Andersen*
Frederiksberg, September 30, 2023

# Chapter 1

# Adaptive Strategy-making Processes for Long-term Resilience and Sustainable Solutions

*Torben Juul Andersen*

*Copenhagen Business School, Denmark*

## Abstract

We operate in a complex dynamic world where human activities interfere with the environment in ways that may cause unpredictable extreme outcomes that reflect exposure to *uncertainty* and *unknown* factors as opposed to identifiable risk events. As humans, we tend to downplay the effects of uncertainty and create a false sense of security by adopting formal control-based management practices where we in truth face more uncertainties than we realize. Hence, we attempt to assess extreme disaster events to mitigate adverse effects but fail to address the underlying causes for the exposures rooted in the way we have organized global economic activities. Exposures partially derive from the way enterprises govern their economic assets while systemic exposures derive from the way we conduct our global business practices. Identified exposures are typically local whereas the systemic causes are global with collective societal effects. Therefore, mitigating enterprise exposures will not address the global systemic causes for the extreme societal effects. To reach more sustainable solutions we must involve businesses that operate the global economy as well as the societies they operate in around the world. Given the extreme uncertainty of systemic risks, grand solutions cannot be derived from computational analytics but require experimentation among engaged public and private organizations and open collaborative learning to identify viable solutions from diverse insights. We must embrace uncertainty to explore innovative opportunities for proposed solutions

Sustainable and Resilient Global Practices:
Advances in Responsiveness and Adaptation, 1–15
Copyright © 2024 by Torben Juul Andersen
Published under exclusive licence by Emerald Publishing Limited
doi:10.1108/978-1-83797-611-920241001

and implement them in gradual co-evolving progression to develop viable sustainable economic outcomes.

*Keywords*: Collaborative solutions; disaster events; experimentation; global economic infrastructure; systemic effects; resilience

## Introduction

Major risk incidents seem to increase in number and intensity including extreme weather events, drought, flooding, food restrictions, economic crises, cybercrime, political conflicts, pandemics, etc. (e.g., World Economic Forum, 2020, 2021, 2022). These events affect general economic activities but hit vulnerable developing economies disproportionately hard even though the underlying causes largely derive from systemic issues linked to global business practices endorsed by the "rich" countries retained through political and social mechanisms beyond the control of individual organizations. The economic exposures increase as populations grow and productive assets agglomerate around major urban centers often in exposed areas. The adverse effects of potential disasters affect people, businesses, and societies alike as a major challenge to achieve the goals of gaining sustainable prosperity reducing poverty by 2030 through active engagement of corporations and public entities (United Nations, 2015). Multilateral aid to support local crises is getting scarce as more societies are affected by disaster-like phenomena. In this situation, there is a need to consider alternative approaches and arrangements that can generate future solutions more effectively in collaborative efforts between public, private, and plural sector entities as integral parts of these global systemic phenomena. They should engage in open collaborative exploratory search for innovative solutions where conventional venture capitalists pursue projects that, each of them on their own, claim to have "the" solution to deal with a systemic exposure.

We observe increasing exposures to extreme phenomena caused by factors that are beyond the control of individual organizations and societies. The individual efforts to analyze potentially extreme events and their effects to mitigate adverse impacts are challenging and do not address the underlying factors rooted in the way we organize global economic activities that will have (severe) long-term climatic effects. The underlying systemic effects derive from global business practices that local actors cannot influence on their own – it will require collaborative efforts across sectors, institutions, and national borders (e.g., Andersen & Gatti, 2022). As the root cause is associated with the way we conduct global economic activities, the ability to generate sustainable solutions must rely on the engagement of the very business entities that conduct the economic activities around the world – it cannot be accomplished through public policy interventions alone. Public and plural sector organizations can provide needed regulation and expertise to address the systemic risk issues, but private enterprises must develop the viable business approaches and are therefore essential players.

The adoption of conventional control-based management approaches in response to complex systemic exposures attempting to quantify, analyze, and mitigate effects of local events will not deliver long-term resilient solutions that address the root causes for potentially extreme events. There is a tendency to commit resources that remedy (deficient) operations and improve the status quo as opposed to addressing the underlying sources by investing in experimentation and search for new sustainable approaches. The systemic exposures in a dynamic complex system are elusive and hard to quantify in meaningful ways. The future events are impossible to predict and describe in detail for practical planning purposes although we can make projections of potentially fatal outcomes. This means that it is harder to conceive of possible solutions that can be implemented in concrete efforts. The ability to foresee and respond effectively to emergent extreme events seem wanting partly because the economic ecosystem is optimized by forging dominant global standards with common practices and procedures that are exceedingly hard to change across the board (EURAM, 2023). It also relates to system-driven behaviors where business leaders must satisfy short-term demands for economic performance that makes it hard to endure current investments that reduce disaster effects in a distant future. Likewise, politicians often make short-term considerations to secure the next re-election where it is hard to promote long-term goals unless they have immediate positive effects. Hence, we arguably need plural sector engagement from "civil society" to change the way we organize economic activities.

The move toward more uncertain and unpredictable conditions can lead to poly-synchronous incidents with many simultaneous disruptions in related subsystems that require unconventional ways to be dealt with in these complex dynamic settings. We must distinguish between risk (*measurable uncertainty*), true uncertainty, and the unknown where we subconsciously rely on the risk concept paying less attention to the issues that are hard to measure. The highly complex systemic exposures defy simple description, are hard to quantify, and are therefore often dismissed or disregarded. We attempt to manage the systemic exposures through a risk lens, where the real exposures are linked to extreme uncertainty and unknown emergent conditions (Andersen, 2023; Andersen & Young, 2020). In this situation, we must embrace the uncertainty and use opportunities the changing circumstances may offer to form viable solutions and change the way we conduct business in the global economy. There is a need to explore through many small probing initiatives searching for approaches that can feed into more sustainable solutions for the future. These efforts should engage diverse institutions operating within the public, private, and plural sectors in collaborative exploration (Fig. 1.1) rather than society forging grand solutions that are unrealistic. Ongoing experimentation and learning as we walk the way outline a more sensible approach toward reaching viable, resilient, and sustainable solutions in small incremental steps rather than committing resources into large irreversible bets.

Systemic risk events relate to exposures that affect many, if not all, constituents in society including individuals, organizations, and communities, for example, caused by degrading business practices that increase the likelihood of major incidents as exposures build up over time in the absence of proper responses.

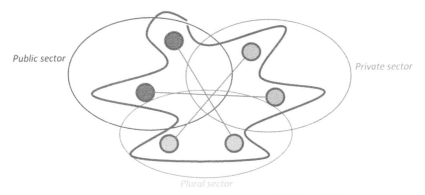

Involve Stakeholders in Exploratory Search Honing Their
Diverse Knowledge and Insights!

Fig. 1.1.   Engaging Public, Private, and Plural Sector Institutions in Collaborative Search:

The modeling of systemic risk effects in complex dynamic systems is intrinsically difficult as exposures are highly uncertain and defy meaningful quantification. Contemporary networked anthropogenic business activities operate in a complex system that is potentially unstable and uncontrollable where it is impossible to fully understand everything. The exposures in this environment are often expressed as probable downside losses to be mitigated whereas resilient adaptation (in principle) entails ongoing analysis of updated information to guide responsive actions that also take the upside potential of opportunities into account. To do this requires more organic structures where stakeholders can collaborate across public–private organizations to address the complex systemic challenges while honing the collective intelligence of individuals within these institutions.

## The Changing Risk Landscape

Most organizations are somehow connected globally with social links between individuals across borders with broad commercial, financial, and information flows facilitated by digital technologies that all contribute to adding complexity and uncertainty to the global business environment. It constitutes a complex dynamic system with many interacting elements where possible outcomes defeat simple prediction because each of the elements depends on the others in intricate nonlinear ways where developments in one location can have unexpected consequences elsewhere in the system. This makes it difficult to foresee developments and limits the ability to generate grand plans as viable responses but rather suggests that emergent exploration is appropriate to identify solutions.

   The "black swan" phenomenon reflects that extreme events are essential aspects of contemporary life that we tend to ignore because randomness and extremes contravene scientific norms that rely on large-scale analyses to identify prevailing probabilistic relationships (e.g., Taleb, 2007, 2013). But improbable events exert more influence on our lives than we care to realize and may be so impactful due to our ignorance that they often appear as "unexpected" events. So, our reliance on quantitative statistical analyses where data typically are assumed to display Gaussian properties is challenged where observed events constitute complex multilevel phenomena subjected to unruly influences of social and behavioral reactions. This renders a risk environment that increasingly implicates (potentially) large unpredictable effects where the context is moving from actuarial or probabilistic risks to uncertain conditions with many unknown factors (e.g., Andersen & Young, 2020). Hence, we see extreme events that often are international in scope where cross-border relations can induce self-reinforcing global systemic effects (Smith & Fischbacher, 2009) as, for example, observed in the 2007–2009 financial crises, the COVID-19 pandemic, and the evolving climatic effects. The risk landscape is changing from a modernist to a post-modernist frame (Miller, 2009), where conventional analytical techniques and control-based approaches fall short. Instead, there is a need to develop organizational systems where employees and managers are actively engaged to identify opportunities through collaborative efforts with a capacity to engage in experimental responses learning from the generated insights.

## Resilience, Agility, and Adaptation

Resilient organizations can deal effectively with events as they emerge making quick (local) responses to fend off immediate effects eventually finding actions that seem to work as a basis for broader applications across the entire organization. It requires more than standard procedures to gain resilience in organizations. A resilient organization as a social system relies on updated sensemaking, perceptual support, continuity, individual commitment, capabilities, active involvement, autonomy, creativity, innovation, resources, and structural flexibility to enable reconfiguration in the face of extreme events (e.g., Kantur & Isery-Say, 2012). A supportive organizational structure must have decision-making practices, information processing systems, and incentive schemes that are conducive to individual engagement and collaboration for a common outcome. This includes identification of emergent opportunities from exploratory efforts that may constitute viable solutions with upside potential that can generate resilient organizational outcomes (e.g., Taleb & Goldstein, 2012). Resilience reflects an ability to face disruption and unexpected developments adjusting to the changing conditions and making the organization stronger and more resourceful after extreme events than was the case before (Annarelli & Nonino, 2016; Vogus & Sutcliffe, 2007). Resilience relies on structures, processes, and practices underpinned by effective response capabilities. This entails that individual employees and managers display common values, emotional stability, self-efficacy, perseverance, big-picture thinking, support, participation, and collaboration (e.g., Abdullah et al., 2013).

When organizations face uncertain contexts with indeterminate or unknown outcomes, they perform better when they act through interdependent *causation* and *effectuation* processes (Packard et al., 2017), that is, responding, experimenting, and learning by doing as things evolve. Causation implies advanced conceptual thinking to analytically determine possible ways going forward in view of alternative opportunities. Effectuation implies that opportunities are identified and enacted by honing available resources and capabilities in responses to emerging developments. This means that initial attempts at updated consequential analyses of future scenarios are preceding a sensemaking process that guides the ongoing exploration for opportunities. Hence, causation and effectuation are not either-or propositions but should be pursued simultaneously in the form of central planning and decentralized emergence as a dynamic adaptive system (Andersen, 2013).

## Dealing with Wicked Problems

Rational decision-making implies a process of information collection to assess conditions and developing alternatives decision-makers can choose from. However, in the real world, incomplete information, complex interdependencies, and unknown factors create wicked problems without any obvious optimal solution. Wicked problems are difficult, even impossible, to resolve or optimize computationally because information is insufficient, possibly contradictory, and relationships are complex with frequent changes depicting truly turbulent conditions. This means that a problem cannot be analyzed based on a fixed dataset but considers a moving target with all parts in constant flux without a single (simple) solution. Hence, the term "wicked" depicts the conditions of flimsy data in changing states and does not reflect an "evil" force. In organizations, it refers to complex issues with many intricate relationships where all fixpoints are dynamic and change in an unstable system where attempting to modify some moving elements may cause effects elsewhere in the system that create new problems. The solutions to wicked organizational problems require collective cross-functional processes where individuals in the social system interact and exchange information possibly supported by digital technologies. Collaboration between many diverse individuals can improve the analytical accuracy and enhance the ability to generate viable solutions to wicked problems under the uncertain conditions of continuously changing environmental parameters.

Disruptive changes in the environment affect current business operations, and general market conditions, and may lead to changes in corporate value chains that condition the global economic ecosystem across different geographies around the world. Responding to these conditions requires a certain operational flexibility that allows adjustments to international production, sourcing, and distribution channels and building on speedy redesigns, market reallocations, workforce adjustments, etc. This points to a role for a central analytical function to evaluate, organize, and integrate built-in flexibilities in invested productive assets and coordinate ongoing adaptations to the operating structure that calls for dispersed response capabilities among individuals in the operating entities. Hence, studies in operations management find that central analytical coordination in combination with decentralized responses and sharing of information is the better way to deal with uncertain unpredictable contexts (Datta & Christopher, 2011). This resonates with the rationales arguing for interactive causation and effectuation processes as the more effective approach to handle value chain disruptions caused by complex dynamic conditions and extreme events in the global business environment.

## Effective Strategic Responses

Decentralization or delegation of decision power is the proposed cure to deal with uncertain conditions according to organization theory because it allows operating managers and employees that have insights, knowledge, and capabilities to make fast informed decisions in their local task environments (e.g., Child & McGrath, 2001). Yet, a robust integrated organization with an updated sense of direction informed by central analytical competencies is equally important for the responsive behaviors of individuals in a flexible agile operating structure. This depicts a combination of central integration and decentralized responsiveness in an ambidextrous structure that exploits the capacity of an existing business model while it simultaneously explores for opportunities to adapt the existing business model and develop capabilities required to deal with new circumstances (e.g., Junni et al., 2013). The literature introduces two ambidextrous organizational strands. *Structural* ambidexterity argues that new exploration must be conducted in separate locations from prevailing business operations to eliminate the adverse influence of preexisting norms (e.g., O'Reilly & Tushman, 2013). *Contextual* ambidexterity argues that innovative exploration must be linked to the current insights and capabilities that reside among individuals within the operating entities often in tacit non-generalizable forms to enable effective relevant responses (e.g., Gibson & Birkinshaw, 2004; Raisch et al., 2009). This coincides with views in the strategy field that describe how organizational outcomes derive from top management's intended pre-planned activities and (not least) the emerging responsive actions taken along the way by individuals in the operating entities as opportunities arise in the changing environment (e.g., Burgelman & Grove, 1996, 2007; Mintzberg & Waters, 1985). Organizations that outperform their peers can combine the central intended processes with decentralized autonomous initiatives as they generate superior risk-return profiles over time, that is, they generate higher average returns with lower variation in returns (e.g., Andersen, 2010, 2021; Andersen & Bettis, 2015; Andersen et al., 2007). Central analytics-driven guidance of activities provides an updated understanding of the changing business environment where the decentralized responsive initiatives constitute small exploratory probes that can uncover possible solutions for application across the organization in line with agile innovation adopted to deal with wicked problems (e.g., Rigby et al., 2016). Hence, there are no grand solutions to complex wicked problems, but central analytics based on current insights can provide updated guidance for decentralized or dispersed exploratory responses in the operating units that search for viable solutions to the challenges.

## Solutions from Dispersed Responses

The organization's internal stakeholders, for example, employees and managers, as well as close external stakeholders they interact with as they pursue their daily business activities, for example, customers and suppliers, can be engaged to generate effective solutions in response to unexpected developments honing their deep location-specific insights (e.g., Aaltonen et al., 2010). By managing strong relationships with essential stakeholders, the organization is better positioned to deal with uncertain and unforeseeable conditions through collaborative search processes across diverse relevant experiences (e.g., De Meyer et al., 2002). Access to and consideration for broader knowledge and insights from multiple sources can be facilitated by digital technologies incorporating artificial intelligence and empowered local actors searching for viable solutions.

The ability to adapt toward more sustainable business activities will contribute to organizational resilience as close individual stakeholders are aware of emergent changes in the environment and respond to emergent threats and seize opportunities to generate long-term solutions (e.g., Ortiz-de-Mandojana & Bansal, 2016). This way organizations can observe otherwise ignored threats and opportunities that pass under the central radar of top management and thereby increase the ability to identify and address pending environmental challenges in time with more effective results. It takes a certain set of leadership-driven values to foster these responsive and responsible behaviors that build reputational assets as a trusted and reliable counterpart that in turn can be levered by attracting essential stakeholders into resolutions to complex social issues (e.g., Andersen, 2017). Hence, organizations that confront wicked problems as is the case in contemporary business environments, the ability to generate collaborative collective solutions through open interactive discussions with many internal and external stakeholders are important elements of a successful approach to resolve challenging issues.

## Engaging Public and Private Catalysts

The proper structures for effective organizational adaptation in complex interdependent contexts must involve public institutions as proponents for societal concerns as well as private enterprises that de facto operate and manage the global economic infrastructure. That is, any real change to the current structure of international business conduct must involve the underpinning businesses to develop sustainable operating solutions for the global economic systems that support our societies. This approach builds on a guiding analytics-based sense-making process involving (many) individual stakeholders with sufficient autonomy to take responsive exploratory initiatives that generate new insights where collaborative learning can sketch new solutions. Investing in these collaborative innovation efforts together with important stakeholder institutions can foster more effective adaptation to the global business ecosystem as modifications to the various elements co-evolve in a coherent manner toward sustainable solutions (e.g., Andersen, 2009; Gatti, 2016). Given the complexity of the global economic system that supports our societies, the collaborative structures should engage both public and private stakeholders, possibly including plural sector actors and multilateral institutions, to consider joint development investments in co-evolving economic practices.

Many private and public decision-makers recognize the importance of new approaches to generate sustainable business practices based on a robust and resilient global economic infrastructure, and there are frequent arguments for the need to invest in innovation. However, in truth, only few organizations show an ability to generate innovative strategic renewal while developing core capabilities that are needed to support the transformation from existing toward better adapted operating processes, business models, and economic practices. Investment in innovation is often driven by outdated views giving priority to promising technologies that intend to digitalize existing operations or introduce big data processing to generate economic efficiencies, which fail at transforming current operations. Venture investors typically bet on promising technologies without considering how they can transform existing dominant operating practices in pursuit of an overarching societal strategic rationale. They may invest resources into new ventures, incubators, accelerators, etc., that really constitute a betting game on eventual winners where a lucky home run can ensure that the winner takes it all. However, this approach does not follow a long-term strategy whereby incremental innovative exploratory investments can gain new insights to inform the collaborative development of co-evolving solutions to deal with the collective requirement for resolutions to the complex societal issues.

## Generating Creative Solutions

It is argued that a sustainable performance development relates to how organizations commit resources and the extent to which it is done in a gradual flexible manner leave options to change direction open following an incremental opportunity-driven adaptation of business activities (e.g., Teece, 2007; Teece et al., 1997). This requires strategic response capabilities that can explore for innovative opportunities and modify business activities along the way so that they generate economic value in pursuit of an overarching strategic intent while accommodating responsive initiatives as the business context changes (e.g., Andersen & Bettis, 2015; Burgelman & Grove, 2007). This approach combines high-level forward-looking analytical reasoning with autonomous responses at lower-level operating entities in an interactive strategy-making process (e.g., Andersen, 2013, 2015). This is associated with central and dispersed information processing where insights from decentralized initiatives can update the analytical reasoning at the center to generate an effective dynamic adaptive system. It captures an organizational setting where institutional practices coordinate knowledge, skills, and competencies and authority is delegated to allow that individuals take initiatives and engage in collective problem-solving beyond the formal hierarchical structure (Tsoukas & Chia, 2002).

The strategic thinking around top management should ideally follow an interactive control process that incorporates ongoing discussions with the operating managers to assess performance based on the current experiences they have gained from the responses taken to deal with the emerging environmental changes (Andersen & Torp, 2020). The insights gained from experiences with the evolving business context can make updated information available for the strategic planning purposes that otherwise typically go unnoticed. When strategic decision-makers fail to pay attention to recent insights from within the organization, their understanding of the competitive environment becomes increasingly outdated and skewed, swaying gradually away from reality influenced by cognitive biases and self-reinforced beliefs. These limitations can be reduced by considering current insights and knowledge among many diverse individuals including the organization's own employees that interact with close organizational stakeholders every day (Kirschner et al., 2009).

The information updating view based on dispersed experiential insights depicts a form of retrospective sensemaking where the managerial decision-makers are informed by updated knowledge from current insights when they engage with the surroundings and learn from exploratory experiences. In other words, they think by acting and enacting with the environment observing and interpreting ensuing effects, which give meaning to what they see and experience (Weick, 1988). That is, they observe things in the environment from responses and use the sensed effects to take new actions where "what was noticed forms a basis for what is done next" (Hernes, 2008, p. 131). Hence, sensemaking forms meaning and informs ongoing actions in an "interplay of action and interpretation" (Weick et al., 2005, p. 409). The sensemaking process is also social and presents an organizational phenomenon, as the effects caused by dispersed actions are interpreted based on peoples' reactions and feedback received from individuals (De Jaegher & Di Paolo, 2007; Stewart et al., 2014).

Complexity theory refers to complex adaptive organizations with ongoing interactions and feedback loops among many networked individuals as they continuously change organizational activities in sensemaking processes that discuss emerging changes and the need for adaptive responses (e.g., Grobman, 2005). This requires a flexible operating structure with autonomy that lets individuals take initiatives where they can learn from the observed experiences and create new knowledge by updating current understanding in pursuit of modified ways to conduct business (Nonaka, 1994). Hence, Nonaka (1994) argues that individual doers must be involved to learn from new insights "through direct 'hands-on' experience" (p. 21). In learning organizations, these responsive efforts also require leadership to impose the overarching aims while setting up the supportive structures, norms, and values that can guide and enable individual organizational members. The leaders support engagement of employees to resolve problems in collaboration, and they encourage people rather than develop and impose detailed practices and procedures (Grobman, 2005). So, organizations innovate in complex rapidly changing environments as individual employees learn from adaptive initiatives and collectively while they create new knowledge that can generate better adapted and sustainable solutions (McElroy, 2000).

The ability to communicate openly among individuals across hierarchies and functions can spur learning, knowledge creation, and generate innovative propositions forming a dynamic system to update the common understanding of the business context as it evolves. This combines rational analytical thinking to update the understanding of the changing context with current insights generated from responsive initiatives taken to deal with the impending changes that can thereby form a dynamic adaptive system that applies to social networks like organizations and societies (e.g., Andersen, 2018). A network of connected individuals can form a collective intelligence as their individual insights and expertise is linked together in a digital structure where open exchange of information can foster creativity and generate innovative solutions. The active involvement of individuals throughout different parts of the organization is instrumental for the capacity to develop innovative solutions that can adapt business activities as environmental conditions change. The ability to generate effective responses depends on a capacity for collaborative efforts driven by norms and common values that encourage open discussions sharing information and knowledge to develop joint solutions to emergent problems. That is, the ability to establish interactive information processes can create a basis for developing effective adaptive solutions through collaborative efforts across many individuals.

## A Framework of Adaptive Development

The preceding rationales can support a conceptual model of adaptive strategy-making that integrates rational analytical reasoning initiated by top management as a guide to exploratory responses where current experiences from those responses inform the incremental implementation of innovative solutions (Fig. 1.2). The model integrates the rational environmental analyses around top management with the current insights and experiences of managers and employees in the operating entities. The environmental analysis is conducted to form a common understanding of the business context in which the organization operates pointing to potential challenges that should alert and guide organizational members. It constitutes a causal learning process that can be facilitated and enhanced through open discussions among executives, managers, and employees. The environmental analysis and the specification of the changing business context can guide the responsive initiatives taken in the operating entities as their local task environments face impending changes. The responsive actions taken in the operating entities, in turn, generate new experiences and insights in an experiential learning process that can provide useful updated information to the rational analysis. The updated intelligence gathered from the responsive initiatives can inform the ensuing implementation of concrete adaptive actions taken in incremental steps to avoid overcommitment and use learning along the way. Face-to-face discussions among top management, managers, and employees in the operating entities can identify needed adjustments as the environmental context changes observing what happens in each incremental step. This constitutes an effectual learning process where adaptive actions are introduced incrementally improving things at each step based on outcomes interpreted in open face-to-face discussions.

This conceptual adaptation model combines rational analytical thinking around the top management team with autonomy among operating managers and employees allowing them to take responsive initiatives where the generated experiential insights are used as updated information that reassess the changing business context. It depicts a structured sequential process, or a cyclical process as

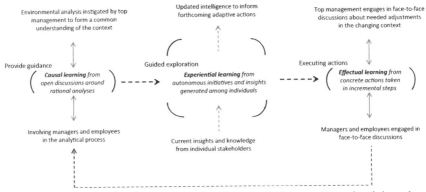

Fig. 1.2.   An Adaptive Strategy-making Process of Causal, Experiential, and Effectual Learning.

it may be repeated periodically over time, of analytically guided exploration with subsequent execution in prudent escalations learning as things evolve.

## Conclusion

We are increasingly faced with complex dynamic contexts where major systemic risks can lead to abrupt events with potentially extreme outcome effects that are difficult to identify, foresee, and quantify where even sophisticated quantitative methodologies fall short in making accurate predictions and risk assessments. This makes all organizations vulnerable to major adverse effects including the societies in which they operate and therefore calls for collaborative co-evolving approaches to develop sustainable solutions for the future. The exposures identified by individual organizations are interlinked and to a significant degree subsumed in systemic risks caused by the way we structure and operate the global economic infrastructure. Hence, future solutions must include private enterprise and public institutions in collaborative efforts that involve private, public, plural, and multilateral organizations in the search for viable solutions that affect all industries, societies, and geographical regions around the world. We must find creative ways to embrace the inherent uncertainties that also hold the possibility to uncover opportunities that may point toward sustainable solutions for societies and the economic agents that create goods, services, and welfare to the people who live in the affected communities. It should engage the collective efforts of many knowledgeable individuals as the better way to resolve complex wicked problems. Furthermore, it must entail analytically guided exploratory processes of causal, experiential, and effectual learning processes as the more effective means to search for viable solutions where the only way to gain insights in complex dynamic contexts is by exploring, experimenting, and learning from acting and doing as things evolve.

It requires leadership to impose supportive decision structures and information systems in an intricate balance between central analytical considerations and autonomy that enables decentralized responsive initiatives to deal with emergent events and experiment with viable solutions. The dispersed responsive initiatives can generate updated experiential insights that inform the ensuing sensemaking and analytical strategic reasoning to identify viable solutions for actions going forward. Rallying many knowledgeable individuals in and around the organizations to work in collaboration with open exchange of information in pursuit of a common goal of creating societal resilience will take leadership skills that hone supportive behavioral norms and core values.

# References

Aaltonen, K., Kujala, J., Lehtonen, P., & Ruuska, I. (2010). A stakeholder network perspective on unexpected events and their management in international projects. *International Journal of Managing Projects in Business, 3*(4), 564–588.

Abdullah, N. A. S., Noor, N. L. M., & Ibrahim, E. N. M. (2013). Resilient organization: Modelling the capacity for resilience. In *International conference on research and innovation in information systems (ICRIIS)* (pp. 319–324). IEEE.

Andersen, T. J. (2009). Effective risk management outcomes: Exploring effects of innovation and capital structure. *Journal of Strategy and Management, 2*(4), 352–379.

Andersen, T. J. (2010). Combining central planning and decentralization to enhance effective risk management outcomes. *Risk Management, 12*, 101–115.

Andersen, T. J. (2013). *Short introduction to strategic management.* Cambridge University Press.

Andersen, T. J. (2015). Interactive strategy-making: Combining central reasoning with ongoing learning from decentralised responses. *Journal of General Management, 40*(4), 69–88.

Andersen, T. J. (2017). Corporate responsible behavior in multinational enterprise. *International Journal of Organizational Analysis, 25*(3), 485–505.

Andersen, T. J. (2018). Responsive dynamics as the source of organizational and societal advantage. Paper presented at the SDM Symposium, MIT Campus, Cambridge, MA. Published in Moser, B. *Characterizing the gap between strategy and implementation* (pp. 182–193). Brightline Initiative.

Andersen, T. J. (2021). Dynamic adaptive strategy-making processes for enhanced strategic responsiveness. In T. J. Andersen (Ed.), *Strategic responsiveness for a sustainable future: New research in international management* (pp. 49–65). Emerald Group Publishing.

Andersen, T. J. (2023). *Responding to uncertain conditions: New research on strategic adaptation.* Emerald Studies in Global Strategic Responsiveness. Emerald Group Publishing.

Andersen, T. J., & Bettis, R. A. (2015). Exploring longitudinal risk-return relationships. *Strategic Management Journal, 36*(8), 1135–1145.

Andersen, T. J., Denrell, J., & Bettis, R. A. (2007). Strategic responsiveness and Bowman's risk-return paradox. *Strategic Management Journal, 28*(4), 407–429.

Andersen, T. J., & Gatti, L. (2022) Generating solutions to systemic risks through on-going experimentation and invested space-forms. Contributing paper: *Global assessment report (GAR) on disaster risk reduction: Our world at risk: Transforming governance for a resilient future.* United Nations Office for Disaster Risk Reduction.

Andersen, T. J., & Torp, S. S. (2020). The influence of autonomous strategy-making and interactive controls on adaptive corporate performance In T. J. Andersen &

S. S. Torp (Eds.), *Adapting to environmental challenges: New research in strategy and international business* (pp. 65–86). Emerald Group Publishing.

Andersen, T. J., & Young, P. C. (2020). *Strategic risk leadership: Engaging a world of risk, uncertainty, and the unknown.* Routledge.

Annarelli, A., & Nonino, F. (2016). Strategic and operational management of organizational resilience: Current state of research and future directions. *Omega, 62,* 1–18.

Burgelman, R. A., & Grove, A. S. (1996). Strategic dissonance. *California Management Review, 38*(2), 8–28.

Burgelman, R. A., & Grove, A. S. (2007). Let chaos reign, then rein in chaos repeatedly: Managing strategic dynamics for corporate longevity. *Strategic Management Journal, 28*(10), 965–979.

Child, J., & McGrath, R. G. (2001). Organizations unfettered: Organizational form in an information-intensive economy. *Academy of Management Journal, 44*(6), 1135–1148.

Datta, P. P., & Christopher, M. G. (2011). Information sharing and coordination mechanisms for managing uncertainty in supply chains: A simulation study. *International Journal of Production Research, 49*(3), 765–803.

De Jaegher, H., & Di Paolo, E. A. (2007). Participatory sense-making: An enactive approach to social cognition. *Phenomenology and the Cognitive Sciences, 6*(4), 485–507.

De Meyer, A., Loch, C. H., & Pich, M. T. (2002). Managing project uncertainty: From variation to chaos. *MIT Sloan Management Review, 43*(2), 60.

EURAM. (2023). Symposium on sustainable strategic solutions to grand challenges: Grand challenges, change and adaptability. In T. J. Andersen (Ed.), *European academy of management 2023 annual conference,* Trinity College, Dublin, Ireland.

Gatti, L. (2016). Innovation: Managing strategic risk. In T. J. Andersen (Ed.), *The Routledge companion to strategic risk management* (pp. 175–198). Routledge.

Gibson, C. B., & Birkinshaw, J. (2004). The antecedents, consequences, and mediating role of organizational ambidexterity. *Academy of management Journal, 47*(2), 209–226.

Grobman, G. M. (2005). Complexity theory: A new way to look at organizational change. *Public Administration Quarterly, 29*(3), 350–382.

Hernes, T. (2008). *Understanding organizations as process.* Routledge.

Junni, P., Sarala, R. M., Taras, V. A. S., & Tarba, S. Y. (2013). Organizational ambidexterity and performance: A meta-analysis. *Academy of Management Perspectives, 27*(4), 299–312.

Kantur, D., & Isery-Say, A. (2012). Organizational resilience: A conceptual integrative framework. *Journal of Management & Organization, 18*(6), 762–773.

Kirschner, F., Paas, F., & Kirschner, P. A. (2009). A cognitive load approach to collaborative learning: United brains for complex tasks. *Educational Psychology Review, 21*(1), 31–42.

McElroy, M. W. (2000). Integrating complexity theory, knowledge management and organizational learning. *Journal of Knowledge Management, 4*(3), 195–203.

Miller, K. D. (2009). Organizational risk after modernism. *Organization Studies, 30*(2–3), 157–180.

Mintzberg, H., & Waters, J. A. (1985). Of strategies, deliberate and emergent. *Strategic Management Journal, 6*(3), 257–272.

Nonaka, I. (1994). A dynamic theory of organizational knowledge creation. *Organization Science, 5*(1), 14–37.

O'Reilly, C. A., III, & Tushman, M. L. (2013). Organizational ambidexterity: Past, present, and future. *Academy of Management Perspectives, 27*(4), 324–338.

Ortiz-de-Mandojana, N., & Bansal, P. (2016). The long-term benefits of organizational resilience through sustainable business practices. *Strategic Management Journal, 37*(8), 1615–1631.

Packard, M. D., Clark, B. B., & Klein, P. G. (2017). Uncertainty types and transitions in the entrepreneurial process. *Organization Science, 28*(5), 840–856.

Raisch, S., Birkinshaw, J., Probst, G., & Tushman, M. L. (2009). Organizational ambidexterity: Balancing exploitation and exploration for sustained performance. *Organization Science, 20*(4), 685–695.

Rigby, D. K., Sutherland, J., & Takeuchi, H. (2016). Master the process that's transforming management: Interaction. *Harvard Business Review, 94*(7), 2.

Smith, D., & Fischbacher, M. (2009). The changing nature of risk and risk management: The challenge of borders, uncertainty and resilience. *Risk Management, 11*, 1–12.

Stewart, J., Gapenne, O., & Di Paolo, E. A. (Eds.). (2014). *Enaction: Toward a new paradigm for cognitive science*. MIT Press.

Taleb, N. N. (2007). *The black swan: The impact of the highly improbable*. Penguin Books.

Taleb, N. N. (2013). *Antifragile: Things that gain from disorder*. Penguin Books.

Taleb, N. N., & Goldstein, D. G. (2012). The problem is beyond psychology: The real world is more random than regression analyses. *International Journal of Forecasting, 28*(3), 715–716. http://doi.org/10.1016/j.ijforecast.2012.02.003

Teece, D. J. (2007). Explicating dynamic capabilities: The nature and microfoundations of (sustainable) enterprise performance. *Strategic Management Journal, 28*(13), 1319–1350.

Teece, D. J., Pisano, G., & Shuen, A. (1997). Dynamic capabilities and strategic management. *Strategic Management Journal, 18*(7), 509–533.

Tsoukas, H., & Chia, R. (2002). On organizational becoming: Rethinking organizational change. *Organization Science, 13*(5), 567–582.

United Nations. (2015). *The sustainable development goals*. https://www.undp.org/united-states/sustainable-development-goals/

Vogus, T. J., & Sutcliffe, K. M. (2007, October). Organizational resilience: Towards a theory and research agenda. In *IEEE international conference on systems, man and cybernetics* (pp. 3418–3422). IEEE.

Weick, K. E. (1988). Enacted sensemaking in crisis situations. *Journal of Management Studies, 25*(4), 305–317.

Weick, K. E., Sutcliffe, K. M., & Obstfeld, D. (2005). Organizing and the process of sensemaking. *Organization Science, 16*(4), 409–421.

World Economic Forum. (2020). *The Global Risk Report 2020*. World Economic Forum, Geneva, Switzerland.

World Economic Forum. (2021). *The Global Risk Report 2021*. World Economic Forum, Geneva, Switzerland.

World Economic Forum. (2022). *The Global Risk Report 2022*. World Economic Forum, Geneva, Switzerland.

Chapter 2

# Adaptation Strategies to Climate Change: Bibliometric Analyses and Emerging Themes

*Giuseppe Danese[a,b]*

[a]*Department of Economics and Management "Marco Fanno," University of Padua, Padua, Italy*
[b]*Center for Social Norms & Behavioral Dynamics, University of Pennsylvania, Philadelphia, PA, USA*

## Abstract

Although adaptation to climate change is a well-researched topic at the individual level and in highly vulnerable industries, its integration into business strategies is poorly researched. In this chapter, we conduct bibliometric analyses on a sample of 368 relevant papers published in business journals to derive descriptive statistics and map the conceptual and intellectual structure of the field. We find an increased interest in adaptation and confirm a strong representation of industry-specific research. We complement the bibliometric analyses with a content analysis focused on emergent themes in the adaptation scholarship. We discuss systemic influences, individual effects, regulations and stakeholders, and exposure as areas likely to attract further scrutiny in future scholarship. For each theme, we derive practical implications for practitioners and policymakers.

*Keywords*: Adaptation; climate change; resilience; sustainability; vulnerability

**Sustainable and Resilient Global Practices:**
**Advances in Responsiveness and Adaptation, 17–36**
Copyright © 2024 by Giuseppe Danese
Published under exclusive licence by Emerald Publishing Limited
doi:10.1108/978-1-83797-611-920241002

## Introduction

Adaptation to climate change (referred to as "adaptation" hereafter) is a topic that is gaining momentum in the discourses of policymakers, practitioners, and scholars. A working definition of adaptation[1] is "... adjustments in ecological, social or economic systems in response to actual or expected climatic stimuli and their effects." After a period of focus on the crafting of a global mitigation compact, when it was common to argue that "adaptation is essential, but it is making the best of a bad job" (Stern, 2009, p. 58), and having ascertained the difficulties of implementing radical measures to contain emissions, countries, individuals, and businesses are increasingly concerned with planning to adapt to the likely consequences of climate change, including global warming, extreme weather events, climate migrations and ensuing geopolitical instability. Unsurprisingly, the IPCC 6th Assessment Report, released in 2023, focuses on adaptation at different levels of analysis.

Our likely inability to remain below the 1.5°C threshold[2] means that the need for adaptation grows, a process that likely entails significant costs (and occasionally benefits)[3] for different agents of adaptation, such as individuals, businesses, cities, and countries. The relationship between adaptation and mitigation strategies is unique and interdependent; failure to achieve the planned emissions reduction targets results in an increased need for adaptation measures (cf., e.g., Colelli et al., 2023) unless adaptation and mitigation are jointly pursued (Beermann, 2011; also Gasbarro & Pinkse, 2016; Rice et al., 2022, discussing "sustainable adaptations").

While discussions of adaptation have a long tradition in sectors such as agriculture (e.g., Mashi et al., 2022) and at the individual level (e.g., Pavanello et al., 2021), the discussion regarding whether and how business organizations adjust to actual or expected climate stimuli appears scattered – as already noticed a while ago by Linnenluecke et al. (2013) and recently by Ponce Oliva et al. (2022). The public and scholarly discourses on the business sector's role in promoting sustainable development are usually focused on decarbonization rather than how business strategies are upgraded to incorporate the likely effects of climate change on core business, profitability, and operations. The discussion about "stranded assets" – organizational resources that reach premature obsolescence because of

---

[1] Available here: https://unfccc.int/topics/adaptation-and-resilience/the-big-picture/what-do-adaptation-to-climate-change-and-climate-resilience-mean (last retrieved: January 15, 2023).

[2] Cf., for example, https://www.scientificamerican.com/article/the-world-will-likely-miss-1-5-degrees-c-why-isnt-anyone-saying-so/#:~:text=World%20leaders%2C%20 activists%20and%20some,over%20the%20next%2010%20years (last retrieved: January 15, 2023).

[3] For example, an *Economist* article in the July 1, 2023, issue titled "The surprising upside of climate migration" claims that some of the migration that climate change will bring about will push people toward urban areas, usually associated with better health and schooling conditions.

the current green transition – constitutes a significant exception (cf., e.g., van der Ploeg & Rezai, 2020).

Views of adaptation are also shifting as policymakers veer away from a "reactive" view of adaptation (cf., e.g., Fankhauser et al., 1999; Tervo-Kankare et al., 2018) toward a "transformational" view[4] that tries to anticipate vulnerabilities associated with climate change (cf., e.g., Bremer & Linnenluecke, 2017) to increase resilience[5] (cf., e.g., Beermann, 2011; Howard-Grenville & Lahneman, 2021; Winn et al., 2011). The desideratum is the early deployment at all levels of decision-making of "resilience capabilities" (Rivera & Clement, 2019). The existence and deployment of these capabilities are likely influenced by specific internal resources and external conditions (Berkhout et al., 2006; Busch, 2011).

The fact that climate change is a "massive discontinuous change" (Winn et al., 2011) in the natural environment into which companies are embedded sets climate change apart from other disturbances routinely monitored by organizations. The lack of internal resources suitable for this grand challenge, or the unique environmental conditions confronting a company that might render climate change "immaterial," might explain the high amount of inaction consistently reported in the adaptation scholarship (Chin et al., 2019; Finke et al., 2016; Hopkins & Maclean, 2014; Su et al., 2013; Wright & Nyberg, 2017; also Linnenluecke & Griffiths, 2010).

The question we ask in this chapter is what might prompt a revision in organizational exploration strategies leading to adaptation to climate change's actual or expected effects. Using bibliometric tools, we provide an overview of the state of the art on adaptation in the business disciplines. We complement the bibliometric analysis with content analysis (Dekkers et al., 2022, p. 336), identifying four emergent themes that scholars might further investigate as conduits to adaptation. The increasingly global and interdependent nature of supply chains means that frictions and disruptions caused by climate change may propagate beyond the original vulnerability points – *systemic effects*. Others argue that a radical shock is needed to trigger incorporating climate-change-related measures into business strategies (Harries et al., 2018) – *exposure*. *Individual features* is the third theme we discuss. Finally, *regulators and other stakeholders* may demand adaptation responses through different institutional mechanisms. We offer practical lessons for policymakers and practitioners deriving from each thematic heading.

---

[4]The French High Council for Climate has recently advocated such shift in its 2023 annual report, available at the website: https://www.hautconseilclimat.fr/wp-content/uploads/2023/06/HCC_RA_2023_.pdf (last retrieved: July 3, 2023).

[5]The United Nations Office for Disaster Risk Reduction (UNDRR) defines resilience as "the ability of a system, community or society exposed to hazards to resist, absorb, accommodate, adapt to, transform and recover from the effects of a hazard in a timely and efficient manner, including through the preservation and restoration of its essential basic structures and functions through risk management." Cf. Linnenluecke (2017) for a systematic review of resilience.

Unlike most existing literature, our discussion of business adaptation strategies to climate change takes a broad and "industry-agnostic" view. Winter tourism, the "canary in the coalmine" (Bicknell & Mcmanus, 2006) of adaptation research, has been the primary focus of attention so far, as we further document below. Discussions of adaptation in tourism are geographically specific, as the impact of climate change on snowfall varies widely across different landscapes (Steiger & Abegg, 2013; Tervo-Kankare et al., 2018). Furthermore, winter tourism has had access for decades to artificial snowmaking (Rice et al., 2022), a technology that has effectively attenuated the problem of "snowless winters" (Scott et al., 2003; Steiger, 2010). As a result of this innovation, the early doom prophecies for this sector have proven largely incorrect (Steiger et al., 2019). The ability of winter tourism businesses to thrive in the face of declining natural snowfall can be seen as a triumph of business ingenuity and adaptability. However, businesses operating in other industries are unlikely to have access to a single and effective adaptation strategy that has not necessitated significant changes since its origins in the 1950s.[6] This is especially true for large multinational enterprises, which must contend with the fact that many of the planet's most exposed countries to the effects of climate change possess low adaptive capacity.[7] A more general discussion of adaptation at the business level is urgently needed.

## Bibliographic Analyses

We query the Scopus database using the following search string:

> TITLE-ABS-KEY(("adapt*") AND ( "climate change*" OR "global warming*" OR "climate cris*" ) AND ( "corporat*" OR "firm*" OR "compan*" OR "business*" OR "enterprise*" OR "organi?ation*")) AND ( LIMIT-TO ( SUBJAREA,"BUSI" ) ) AND ( EXCLUDE ( PUBYEAR, 2023) ) AND ( LIMIT-TO ( LANGUAGE,"English")) AND ( LIMIT-TO ( DOCTYPE,"ar") ) OR LIMIT-TO ( DOCTYPE,"re") ) )

We target articles and reviews featuring in their title, abstract, or keywords: words stemming from the root "adapt," "climate change," or semantically

---

[6]For a brief history of the practice of artificial snowmaking, cf., for example, https://www.foxweather.com/learn/the-panicked-and-accidental-beginnings-of-snowmaking (last retrieved: January 15, 2023). The local nature of many tourism businesses has also made it possible to effectively forecast climate events over the coming decades through tools such as ClimSnow (https://www.climsnow.com/), widely used in the Alpine region.
[7]See, for example, Poor and Vulnerable Countries Need Support to Adapt to Climate Change, by IMF Managing Director Kristalina Georgieva, Vitor Gaspar, and Ceyla Pazarbasioglu, available at the website: https://www.imf.org/en/Blogs/authors?author=Kristalina%20Georgieva (last retrieved: January 15, 2023).

equivalent expressions and "organization" or a synonym. To ensure relevance, we limit the search to the *Business, Management, and Accounting* Subject Area of Scopus. We consider papers published up to and including 2022. We use for our analyses the R-package *bibliometrix* (Aria & Cuccurullo, 2017), which performs a broad variety of bibliometric analyses (Moral-Muñoz et al., 2020). *bibliometrix* is widely used in bibliometric reviews published in business journals (for recent examples, cf. Campobasso & Boscia, 2023; Rao & Shukla, 2023). It performs essential preliminary tasks such as data cleaning, removal of stop words and punctuation, and stemming of the textual corpus. Information scientists and, increasingly, business scholars use bibliometric tools to derive basic statistics and to map the structure of a topic into clusters of authors, journals, documents, countries, or academic institutions (Dekkers et al., 2022, p. 333; Linnenluecke et al., 2020; Zupic & Čater, 2015). This chapter employs bibliometric analyses to derive summary information about the papers we retrieved through our query; pinpoint frequent, emerging, and mature concepts; and uncover conceptual and intellectual links in the adaptation scholarship.

As shown in Table 2.1, we retrieved 368 documents through our query, published since 1994. Considering the entire timespan, which includes a period of stagnation until 2005, the annual growth rate exceeds 10% – a clear sign of burgeoning interest in the topic.

The most relevant sources for our sample of papers are *Journal of Cleaner Production* (50 documents), *Journal of Sustainable Tourism* (22 documents), and *Business Strategy and the Environment* (15 documents). These three journals also have the highest local impact. The most globally cited documents in our sample are Lempert and Groves (2010), a seminal paper about the adaptation strategies of water management agencies in the United States, followed by Linnenluecke et al. (2012), a paper anticipating some currently debated themes such as the need for anticipatory adaptation and the relation between adaptation strategies and organizational resilience building. Looking at the references of our sample of

Table 2.1.　Descriptive Statistics.

| Description | Results |
| --- | --- |
| Timespan | 1994–2022 |
| Sources (journals) | 178 |
| Documents | 368 |
| Annual growth rate, % | 13.05 |
| Average citations per document | 29.09 |
| Authors | 899 |
| Co-authors per document | 2.76 |
| International co-authorships, % | 26.9 |
| Articles | 352 |
| Reviews | 16 |

Table 2.2.    Most Frequent Keywords.

| Terms | Frequency |
|---|---|
| Climate change | 172 |
| Adaptation | 89 |
| Mitigation | 29 |
| Sustainability | 29 |
| Tourism | 19 |
| Resilience | 17 |
| Sustainable development | 14 |
| Vulnerability | 12 |

papers, Berkhout et al. (2006) is the most cited paper and can be considered the seminal contribution to the adaptation literature, inaugurating a line of research focusing on capabilities and different modes of adaptation available to businesses. Curiously, this paper was not published in any of the most relevant sources identified above; it was published in an atmospheric science journal (*Climatic Change*). Table 2.2 shows that two queried terms, "climate change" and "adaptation," are the most frequent author's keywords.[8] The frequency of "mitigation" attests to the frequency with which adaptation and mitigation are jointly addressed in extant scholarship. "Tourism" shows the industry focus of many of the papers in the sample. "Resilience" and "vulnerability," as earlier noticed, are concepts often connected to adaptation (cf., e.g., McLaughlin, 2011; Linnenluecke et al., 2012).

Fig. 2.1 shows trends in adaptation scholarship.[9] Insurance is an early theme that seems to have disappeared. "Climate change adaptation" has appeared consistently since 2014, preceded by references to "organizational adaptation." Some themes appear to have been popular for a certain period, such as "corporate social responsibility" and "stakeholder" – likely attempts to link adaptation to normative concerns; "extreme weather events," "environmental change," and "global warming" – all consequences of climate change of import to tourism and other industries. "Carbon emissions" makes a late appearance – a likely symptom of growing attention to the causes of climate change. Keywords related to tourism appear throughout the consideration period, with an increasing focus on

---

[8]The choice of keywords chosen by the author(s) of each paper as the unit of analysis eliminates the need of having to choose between unigrams, bigrams, and trigrams – a choice that usually carries significant implications for the results of bibliometric analyses. This explains why the authors' keywords are the unit of analysis of choice in this chapter (unless stated otherwise). Authors' keywords are missing in only 7.6% of the sample, which appears prima facie an acceptable level of missing data. On the informational value of authors' keywords, cf. Tripathi et al. (2018).

[9]All figures are produced using bibliometrix. The logo of the package is visible in the bottom-right corner of each figure.

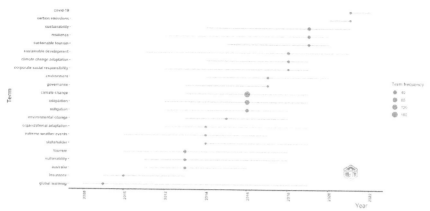

Fig. 2.1.   Trend Topics.

*sustainable* tourism. Keywords related to strategy ("resilience," "vulnerability," "mitigation") also appear consistently.

Fig. 2.2 shows a co-word network, illustrating relationships between co-occurring keywords within our sample. The underlying assumption of co-word analysis is that the frequent appearance of keywords together in documents implies a relationship between the concepts behind these keywords (Callon et al., 1983).

This type of (content) analysis can provide insights into the conceptual structure of the corpus and show how different concepts are interconnected. One conceptual cluster (right-hand side) is concerned with tourism and different tourism destinations. We call this the *tourism cluster*. The cluster in the middle also incorporates some tourism destinations, likely where the link to climate change and adaptive management has been most researched (Australia, United States, and United Kingdom). We call this the *climate change + adaptive management* cluster. Finally, the cluster on the left concerns climate change's causes, its impacts, and the likely facilitators and barriers to adaptive responses. We call this the

Fig. 2.2.   Co-word Network.

*strategy cluster.* It is apparent in Fig. 2.2 that connections between the *strategy* and the *tourism* clusters are rare. Connections exist between the *climate change + adaptative management* cluster and the other two clusters, that is, the middle cluster can be considered, to a certain extent, a conceptual free port for tourism and strategy scholars alike. The lack of connections between the *tourism* and the *strategy* clusters might also be a symptom of the highly specialized nature of the adaptive solutions discussed in the winter tourism scholarship, particularly snowmaking, which lacks counterparts in other industries, as earlier remarked.

Fig. 2.3 shows a thematic map based on network metrics constructed using bigrams (two adjacent words) appearing in the *titles* of the papers in the sample.

The unit of analysis we have used so far appears highly sensitive to recent phenomena, such as COVID-19. The map is divided into four areas: niche themes, motor themes, emerging or declining themes, and basic themes. We simplify visualization by grouping together closely related terms. Motor and basic themes relate to the queried terms. The tourism industry can also be considered a basic theme. Niche themes relate to recent events such as COVID-19, circularity concerns and life cycle assessments, and agri-food. Water management is likely a declining theme linked to the highly cited paper by Lempert and Groves (2010). Emergent themes include discussions of supply chains, a topic we return to below, and sustainable tourism.

Multiple correspondence analysis (Fig. 2.4) plots keywords along two thematic dimensions, providing insights into the level of proximity among various concepts and constructs. The first (horizontal) dimension is concerned with climate change and tourism. The second (vertical) dimension is concerned with the causes and effects of climate change. The proximity of the "tourism" and "climate change adaptation" keywords along the horizontal dimension indicates the maturity of the juxtaposition of the adaptation and tourism lexicons.

We now move to the intellectual structure of our sample of papers. Fig. 2.5 shows a co-citation network using the papers as the unit of analysis. Co-citation analysis quantifies the frequency with which a specific pair of documents

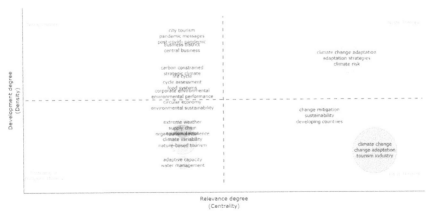

Fig. 2.3.   Thematic Map.

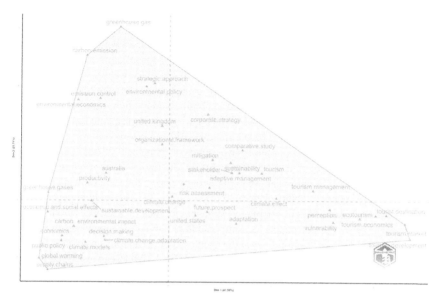

Fig. 2.4.   Factorial Analysis.

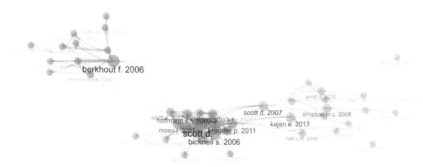

Fig. 2.5.   Co-citation Network.

is cited together, indicating similarity in their content (Linnenluecke et al., 2020, pp. 181–183). The map is divided into three clusters. The first (in the middle) is related to winter tourism. A highly recognizable paper in this cluster is Bicknell and Mcmanus (2006), a representative of the "first generation" of adaptation scholarship in winter tourism. The second cluster (on the right) is also related to winter tourism, showing many of the same first authors appearing in the central cluster. The third cluster (on the left) takes a broader perspective on adaptation, exemplified by the seminal paper by Berkhout et al. (2006). We confirm the limited interaction between the stream of scholarship concerned with winter tourism and the other papers.

## Emerging Themes

We conduct a content-based analysis to engage at a deeper level with emerging insights from the adaptation scholarship. The systematic method for selecting papers is outlined in greater detail in Danese and De Marchi (2023). In summary, we read the abstract and titles of the 368 records used for the bibliometric analyses presented in the previous section, excluding papers unrelated to our focus on business adaptation strategies. The papers were then imported into the software MAXQDA, where we implemented an open coding process (Corbin & Strauss, 2015) based on keywords that emerged in the abstract and title vetting stages. We engaged in successive rounds of refinement of our coding system. For this chapter, we present a selective overview of the results of this exercise, focusing on emergent themes. In particular, we exclude many papers focusing on winter tourism for their lack of generalizability elaborated upon earlier. We also exclude papers focusing on different taxonomies of adaptation strategies for lack of relevance to our present inquiry. Finally, we exclude papers focusing on different dynamic capabilities that extant literature has suggested might influence the likelihood of an adaptive response. This line of research, pioneered by Berkhout et al. (2006) and Busch (2011), can also be considered mature. We are left with four emergent themes in the adaptation scholarship: regulations and stakeholders, systemic influences, exposure, and individual effects.

### *Regulations and Stakeholders*

At least in principle, companies might increase their reputation by undertaking environmental commitments and communicating them to their stakeholders (Kouloukoui et al., 2019). In this way, they avoid public backlash (Furlan Alves et al., 2019). Kouloukoui et al. (2019) find that the forces of inaction often prevent companies from following this path, leading to a call for enacting regulations followed by mandatory audits (cf. also de Jongh & Möllmann, 2014; Wissman-Weber & Levy, 2018). However, companies often adopt a defensive stance when threatened with new regulations (Martin & Rice, 2010).

Stakeholders have been consistently found to hold the power to facilitate or hinder adaptation practices (Csete & Szécsi, 2015; Jopp et al., 2010; Lopes de Sousa Jabbour et al., 2020).

### *Lessons*

A holistic approach might break the impasse of climate inaction (Loehr, 2020; Martin & Rice, 2010). In this approach, product and process innovation are accompanied by decarbonization and adaptation measures, engaging stakeholders such as the local community, industry organizations, government authorities, and nongovernmental organizations (NGOs) in the process. Bolder moves might also be required to promote sustainable business models, such as amplifying climate change risks and the urgency of adaptation (Shakeela & Becken, 2015) and removing attenuators (Shakeela & Becken, 2015), such as climate denialism and fatalism (cf. also Bicknell & Mcmanus, 2006). Tax credits or subsidies to companies adopting adaptation measures might also help (Galbreath, 2014).

### Systemic Influences

Learning dynamics within vertical chains and horizontally among competitors might be powerful drivers for adopting adaptation practices (Galbreath, 2015; Galbreath et al., 2016). Adaptation partnerships are rarer than mitigation partnerships (Pinkse & Kolk, 2012). Such partnerships might take the form of joint investments in physical and institutional infrastructure, insurance schemes, research and development, or information-sharing arrangements in the most common case (Pinkse & Kolk, 2012). The literature has also documented communities of practice (Nicolletti et al., 2019; Orsato et al., 2019). The uniformity in characteristics among community members leads to the perception that their discussions are highly pertinent. The participants then disseminate their experience within their organizations. This process of "reframing" the experience of others into an actionable internal plan can be decomposed into three parts: "the realization of the materiality of the climate change agenda to the company; the potential to work on adaptation through concrete measures connected to current projects; and the climate change criteria inserted in investment decision-making" (Nicolletti et al., 2019, p. 755, boldface in the original omitted). Daddi et al. (2020) stress the importance of mimetic pressures in adaptation choices, that is, imitating successful competitors.

Several others discuss the need to coordinate with other actors adaptation measures, a "spatiotemporal approach" (DiBella, 2020). "Entrainment" (Schmitt & Klarner, 2015) often happens tacitly and may result in a more equitable division of adaptation burdens between the company and the stakeholders.

Climate change might affect global value chains (Lei et al., 2017) and supply chains in general (Lintukangas et al., 2022) at many potential levels. Certain industries, such as agri-food (Dvigun et al., 2022), appear particularly sensitive to the chain-wide adoption of adaptation strategies (Mukhovi et al., 2020; Touboulic et al., 2018).[10] In general, one might conjecture that the higher the degree of interdependence among chain links, the stronger the collective component of adaptation (Canevari-Luzardo et al., 2020). In those cases, one segment cannot decrease climate sensitivity unless others do the same.

Power dynamics will likely determine the likelihood of adaptation measures and the division of burdens in global value chains (Touboulic et al., 2018). The degree of trust among actors, the like-mindedness on environmental issues (Touboulic et al., 2018), and the type of resource flows within the value chain might predict the extent to which climate change risks are allowed to penetrate the chain (Canevari-Luzardo et al., 2020). As a result, the strategy implemented will be different from "the formulated strategy, as the focal firm and its suppliers negotiate its meaning, manage tensions between their interests and respond to unanticipated events" (Touboulic et al., 2018, p. 316).

---

[10]The automotive, chemical, mining, and electronics sectors are in a similar situation of value-chain susceptibility (Pinkse & Kolk, 2012).

*Lessons*

Multi-stakeholder initiatives and other forms of partnerships and consortia might hold the power of "inaugurating the complex learning dynamic required for adaptive capacity building to face climate change" (Nicolletti et al., 2019, p. 753; cf. also Boyer & Touzard, 2021; Daddi et al., 2020; Orsato et al., 2019; Tisch & Galbreath, 2018; Touboulic et al., 2018). Knowledge sharing is easier when information leakage concerns are kept at bay (Galbreath et al., 2016). In some industries, adaptation strategies might lead to competitive advantage, decreasing thus the probability that partnership initiatives might lead to the effective sharing of best practices. Local conditions and regulations must also be considered when addressing adaptation in global value chains (Lei et al., 2017).

***Exposure***

In a highly cited early contribution, Hoffmann et al. (2009) do *not* find a statistically significant (at the conventional threshold) relationship between awareness of possible climate change effects and the scope of corporate adaptation using a sample of Swiss ski lift operators. Vulnerability to climate change is also not significantly related to the scope of adaptation. Although the findings of this paper are often misreported, this paper has inaugurated a rich stream of literature exploring the relationship between awareness, vulnerability, and climate agency on one side and adaptation to the other.

At the core of this thematic concentration lies the question of why climate-related information might go undetected by the "organizational radar" (e.g., Galbreath, 2014; Lei et al., 2017). The answer provided by Pinkse and Gasbarro (2019) is that attention is "selective, situated, and structured" (p. 340). Factors influencing awareness (the condition of noticing, p. 357) of climate change are "risk perceptions of climate stimuli," "perceived uncertainty of climate stimuli," and "knowledge of local ecosystem" (p. 346). Factors influencing the perceived vulnerability (the interpretation of climate stimuli) are "perceived impact of climate stimuli," "past experience with climate stimuli,"[11] and "controllability of climate stimuli" (p. 349). The combination of low awareness and low vulnerability likely results in inaction.

Rivera and Clement (2019) discuss the notion of "nature adversity intensity" ("the magnitude of unfavorable chronic conditions generated by the natural environment," p. 1286) to predict the likelihood of a protective adaptive response ("organizational adjustment efforts aimed at reducing the vulnerability of firms' core features to adverse operating conditions," p. 1286). They propose and empirically validate "an inverted U-shaped relationship between nature adversity intensity and protective adaptation, such that firms facing lower or higher than medium levels of nature adversity intensity tend to adopt lower levels of protective adaptation" (p. 1286). Those facing high-intensity levels might

---

[11]Winn et al. (2011) point out that overreliance on prior experiences of climate change might be detrimental, given the non-stationarity of climate change.

be unable to safeguard their core business through protective adaptation and will be less incentivized to do so. Inertia will work against protective adaptation in the case of low-intensity signals or rapid environmental change because of internal forces favoring the status quo or lack of sensemaking[12] capabilities for low-intensity events.

Climate signals might not be interpreted as such. For example, tourism entrepreneurs might construe declining snowfall as the result of (physiological) weather variability rather than the result of epochal shifts in climate (Steiger et al., 2019). Indeed, geographically, socially, or temporally proximate signals are most likely to prompt adaptive responses because they are construed as concrete risks (Craig, 2019). Several authors notice that entrepreneurs might doubt the effectiveness of any adaptation measure they undertake (Bicknell & Mcmanus, 2006; Ng et al., 2018). In contrast, others might feel empowered to pursue opportunities related to climate change (Wissman-Weber & Levy, 2018).

Harries et al. (2018) argue that low levels of adaptation can be traced back to affirming existing "sensemaking structures and associated identities" (p. 712). Revisions in these structures are prompted by ontological shocks, that is, large-scale events that prompt a crisis in existing sensemaking structures. Helgenberger (2011, p. 80) gives some practical examples of sensemaking attitudes among tourism entrepreneurs: the confused, who experiences dissonance between personal denialism and mounting evidence; the optimist, who experiences no dissonance but believes climate change lacks impact on their business (the most common attitude, cf. also Chin et al., 2019; Shakeela & Becken, 2015, p. 69, speak of "exceptionalism"); the pessimist, whose personal concern about climate change is borne out by experience; the differentiator, who monitors weather swings for a period before making causal attributions to climate change. Another further profile of entrepreneurs is "proactive" rather than sensemaking, as captured by the attitude "climate changes and so do I" (p. 81).

*Lessons*

Tisch and Galbreath (2018) remark that dairy farmers exhibit different sensemaking frames for weather and climate resilience, and as a result, they seem to pay close attention to the weather and little to the climate (p. 6). Similarly, Roman et al. (2010, p. 249) caution against an excessive emphasis on (temporally distant) climate change, claiming instead that "issues pertaining to climatic change are best regarded as opportunities for transformative action that bring broader sustainability goals in a less abstract and more tangible perspective" (cf. also Craig, 2019).

Harries et al. (2018, p. 727) wonder whether "an external shock such as a flood creates sufficient emotional impact on the owner." Using the sensemaking lens,

---

[12]Sensemaking is defined by Tisch and Galbreath (2018, p. 2, and references cited therein) as "a process whereby organizational actors attach meaning to external events to resolve the uncertainty surrounding them."

one would be led to predict that increasing the frequency and intensity (within a certain range, per the inverted U hypothesis) of extreme events would be beneficial, as "sensemaking is altered by the stimulus of increasingly intense weather events" (Tisch & Galbreath, 2018, p. 3). However, the ethical pitfalls of pushing this agenda are apparent (cf. also Chen et al., 2022). It also seems reasonable to predict that the response to a large-scale extreme event will not be forward-looking, an instance of "maladaptation."

### Individual Effects

Various individual features and situational conditions may influence the adaptation decisions of organizational decision-makers. Brouder and Lundmark (2011) point out that tourism-venue entrepreneurs are worried about climate change because of the irrecoverable nature of venue investments. Those already affected, coastland entrepreneurs, tend to be more "accepting" (p. 931) of the effects of climate change. Tervo-Kankare (2019) discusses the role of winter tourism entrepreneurs' "lifestyle factors" and personal features to explain whether they view themselves as "change agents" (p. 9). For example, entrepreneurs who stress the need to be flexible in responding to rapidly changing customer needs might be less interested in investing in adaptation measures (p. 9). Wongnaa and Babu (2020) find that the age of farmers negatively correlates with adaptation choices, while farming experience, farm size, access to climate information via local officials, capital availability, farm income, and land productivity positively correlate. Bremer and Linnenluecke (2017) find that age negatively correlates with risk perceptions related to climate change.

Lessons are currently difficult to derive from this thematic concentration. The microfoundation of adaptation choices remains a research program deserving further elaboration. For example, awareness might be determined by the idiosyncratic features of the entrepreneurs (Mashi et al., 2022).

## Conclusion

Although adaptation is extensively studied in industries such as winter tourism and at the individual level, research into the determinants and consequences of organizational adaptation choices remains scattered. The topic shows many signs of increasing interest, as we have documented. Many questions remain, including the desirability of a proactive and forward-looking approach to adaptation rather than reactive and merely fixing urgent vulnerabilities. An open question is how companies budget resources across different headings of the European Union (EU) Taxonomy of sustainable activities: adaptation, mitigation, circularity, air pollution reduction, stewardship of water and marine resources, and biodiversity; the ability to finance such strategies (Gajanayake & Iyer-Raniga, 2022); and the provenance of the required resources (public vs private). As companies face mounting calls for climate action, tough decisions await companies as they decide how to budget their resources across manifestations versus the root causes of climate change. Some companies have been accused of "pushing" the adaptation agenda to the detriment of the mitigation agenda, leveraging the necessity of local, rapid, and "win-win" action on climate change (Nyberg & Wright, 2022).

An open issue we have not addressed here is the ability of adaptation policies not to worsen the strategic menu of options available to businesses over time – the issue of maladaptation extensively discussed in the winter tourism literature (cf., e.g., Rice et al., 2022).

Climate change might have profound marketing and operational implications that are starting to be explored (cf., e.g., Ponce Oliva et al., 2022). The mitigation objective seems more straightforward in its messaging to decarbonize operations and divest from fossil assets. Incorporating adaptation concerns into business strategies involves many local nuances, some of which have been discussed in this chapter (cf. also Berkhout, 2005). The COVID-19 pandemic might be a useful benchmark. It has implied a profound rethinking of long-established strategies and operations under the weight of its urgency and vividness.[13] As we have seen in our discussion of the role of exposure in adaptation choices, as climate change manifestations intensify, the materiality of adaptation might be established for a larger and larger arena of organizations.

# References

Aria, M., & Cuccurullo, C. (2017). Bibliometrix: An R-tool for comprehensive science mapping analysis. *Journal of Informetrics, 11*(4), 959–975. https://doi.org/10.1016/J.JOI.2017.08.007

Beermann, M. (2011). Linking corporate climate adaptation strategies with resilience thinking. *Journal of Cleaner Production, 19*(8), 836–842. https://doi.org/10.1016/J.JCLEPRO.2010.10.017

Berkhout, F. (2005). Rationales for adaptation in EU climate change policies. *Climate Policy, 5*(3), 377–391. https://doi.org/10.1080/14693062.2005.9685564

Berkhout, F., Hertin, J., & Gann, D. M. (2006). Learning to adapt: Organisational adaptation to climate change impacts. *Climatic Change, 78*(1), 135–156. https://doi.org/10.1007/s10584-006-9089-3

Bicknell, S., & Mcmanus, P. (2006). The canary in the coalmine: Australian ski resorts and their response to climate change. *Geographical Research, 44*(4), 386–400. https://doi.org/10.1111/j.1745-5871.2006.00409.x

Boyer, J., & Touzard, J. M. (2021). To what extent do an innovation system and cleaner technological regime affect the decision-making process of climate change adaptation? Evidence from wine producers in three wine clusters in France. *Journal of Cleaner Production, 315*, 128218. https://doi.org/10.1016/J.JCLEPRO.2021.128218

Bremer, J., & Linnenluecke, M. K. (2017). Determinants of the perceived importance of organisational adaptation to climate change in the Australian energy industry.

---

[13]This emerges from a series of interviews conducted by the French National Archives of Labor. Cf. https://www.lemonde.fr/idees/article/2023/06/09/l-histoire-des-entreprises-enseigne-que-rien-n-est-plus-faux-qu-un-suppose-processus-de-selection-darwinienne_6176875_3232.html (last retrieved: September 1, 2023).

*Australian Journal of Management, 42*(3), 502–521. https://doi.org/10.1177/0312896216672273/ASSET/IMAGES/LARGE/10.1177_0312896216672273-FIG1.JPEG

Brouder, P., & Lundmark, L. (2011). Climate change in Northern Sweden: Intra-regional perceptions of vulnerability among winter-oriented tourism businesses. *Journal of Sustainable Tourism, 19*(8), 919–933. https://doi.org/10.1080/09669582.2011.573073

Busch, T. (2011). Organizational adaptation to disruptions in the natural environment: The case of climate change. *Scandinavian Journal of Management, 27*(4), 389–404. https://doi.org/10.1016/j.scaman.2010.12.010

Callon, M., Courtial, J. P., Turner, W. A., & Bauin, S. (1983). From translations to problematic networks: An introduction to co-word analysis. *Social Science Information, 22*(2), 191–235. https://doi.org/10.1177/053901883022002003/ASSET/053901883022002003.FP.PNG_V03

Campobasso, F., & Boscia, V. (2023). Sustainability frontiers of strategic risk management and firm survival: The Altman score effectiveness. A bibliometric analysis. *Business Strategy and the Environment, 32*(6), 3783–3791. https://doi.org/10.1002/BSE.3336

Canevari-Luzardo, L. M., Berkhout, F., & Pelling, M. (2020). A relational view of climate adaptation in the private sector: How do value chain interactions shape business perceptions of climate risk and adaptive behaviours? *Business Strategy and the Environment, 29*(2), 432–444. https://doi.org/10.1002/BSE.2375

Chen, J. S., Wang, W., Kim, H., & Liu, W.-Y. (2022). Climate resilience model on Arctic tourism: Perspectives from tourism professionals. *Tourism Recreation Research, 1*–12. https://doi.org/10.1080/02508281.2022.2122341

Chin, N., Day, J., Sydnor, S., Prokopy, L. S., & Cherkauer, K. A. (2019). Exploring tourism businesses' adaptive response to climate change in two Great Lakes destination communities. *Journal of Destination Marketing & Management, 12*, 125–129. https://doi.org/10.1016/J.JDMM.2018.12.009

Colelli, F. P., Wing, I. S., & De Cian, E. (2023). Air-conditioning adoption and electricity demand highlight climate change mitigation-adaptation tradeoffs. *Scientific Reports, 13.* https://doi.org/10.1038/s41598-023-31469-z

Corbin, J., & Strauss, A. (2015). *Basics of qualitative research: Techniques and procedures for developing grounded theory* (4th ed.). Sage.

Craig, C. A. (2019). The weather-proximity-cognition (WPC) framework: A camping, weather, and climate change case. *Tourism Management, 75*, 340–352. https://doi.org/10.1016/J.TOURMAN.2019.06.005

Csete, M., & Szécsi, N. (2015). The role of tourism management in adaptation to climate change – A study of a European inland area with a diversified tourism supply. *Journal of Sustainable Tourism, 23*(3), 477–496. https://doi.org/10.1080/09669582.2014.969735

Daddi, T., Bleischwitz, R., Todaro, N. M., Gusmerotti, N. M., & de Giacomo, M. R. (2020). The influence of institutional pressures on climate mitigation and adaptation strategies. *Journal of Cleaner Production, 244*, 118879. https://doi.org/10.1016/J.JCLEPRO.2019.118879

Danese, G., & De Marchi, V. (2023). *Business adaptation strategies to climate change: A systematic review.* mimeo.

de Jongh, D., & Möllmann, C. M. (2014). Market barriers for voluntary climate change mitigation in the South African private sector. *South African Journal of Economic and Management Sciences, 17*(5), 639–652.

Dekkers, R., Carey, L., & Langhorne, P. (2022). *Making literature reviews work: A multidisciplinary guide to systematic approaches.* Springer International Publishing. https://doi.org/10.1007/978-3-030-90025-0

DiBella, J. (2020). The spatial representation of business models for climate adaptation: An approach for business model innovation and adaptation strategies in the private sector. *Business Strategy & Development, 3*(2), 245–260. https://doi.org/10.1002/BSD2.92

Dvigun, A., Datsii, O., Levchenko, N., Shyshkanova, G., & Dmytrenko, R. (2022). Rational use of fresh water as a guarantee of agribusiness development in the context of the exacerbated climate crisis. *Science and Innovation, 18*(2), 85–99. https://doi.org/10.15407/scine18.02.085

Fankhauser, S., Smith, J. B., & Tol, R. S. J. (1999). Weathering climate change: Some simple rules to guide adaptation decisions. *Ecological Economics, 30*(1), 67–78. https://doi.org/10.1016/S0921-8009(98)00117-7

Finke, T., Gilchrist, A., & Mouzas, S. (2016). Why companies fail to respond to climate change: Collective inaction as an outcome of barriers to interaction. *Industrial Marketing Management, 58*, 94–101. https://doi.org/10.1016/j.indmarman.2016.05.018

Furlan Alves, M. B., Lopes de Sousa Jabbour, A. B., & Barberio Mariano, E. (2019). How can we solve the puzzle of strategic climate management and appreciate its long-term effects? *Journal of Organizational Change Management, 32*(7), 687–708. https://doi.org/10.1108/JOCM-01-2018-0013

Gajanayake, A., & Iyer-Raniga, U. (2022). Infrastructure financing for climate change adaptation in Australia: Practitioners' perspectives. *Construction Economics and Building, 22*(4), 1–16.

Galbreath, J. (2014). Climate change response: Evidence from the Margaret River Wine Region of Australia. *Business Strategy and the Environment, 23*(2), 89–104. https://doi.org/10.1002/BSE.1762

Galbreath, J. (2015). To cooperate or compete? Looking at the climate change issue in the wine industry. *International Journal of Wine Business Research, 27*(3), 220–230. https://doi.org/10.1108/IJWBR-10-2014-0049

Galbreath, J., Charles, D., & Oczkowski, E. (2016). The drivers of climate change innovations: Evidence from the Australian wine industry. *Journal of Business Ethics, 135*(2), 217–231. https://doi.org/10.1007/s10551-014-2461-8

Gasbarro, F., & Pinkse, J. (2016). Corporate adaptation behaviour to deal with climate change: The influence of firm-specific interpretations of physical climate impacts. *Corporate Social Responsibility and Environmental Management, 23*(3), 179–192. https://doi.org/10.1002/csr.1374

Harries, T., McEwen, L., & Wragg, A. (2018). Why it takes an 'ontological shock' to prompt increases in small firm resilience: Sensemaking, emotions and flood risk. *International Small Business Journal: Researching Entrepreneurship, 36*(6), 712–733. https://doi.org/10.1177/0266242618765231/ASSET/IMAGES/LARGE/10.1177_0266242618765231-FIG2.JPEG

Helgenberger, S. (2011). The capacity of locally bound tourism firms to respond to climate variability and long-term change: Qualitative case studies on organizational learning in the Austrian winter tourism sector. *Tourism Planning and Development, 8*(1), 69–86. https://doi.org/10.1080/21568316.2011.554042

Hoffmann, V. H., Sprengel, D. C., Ziegler, A., Kolb, M., & Abegg, B. (2009). Determinants of corporate adaptation to climate change in winter tourism: An econometric analysis. *Global Environmental Change, 19*(2), 256–264. https://doi.org/10.1016/j.gloenvcha.2008.12.002

Hopkins, D., & Maclean, K. (2014). Climate change perceptions and responses in Scotland's ski industry. *Tourism Geographies, 16*(3), 400–414. https://doi.org/10.1080/14616688.2013.823457

Howard-Grenville, J., & Lahneman, B. (2021). Bringing the biophysical to the fore: Re-envisioning organizational adaptation in the era of planetary shifts. *Strategic Organization, 19*(3), 478–493. https://doi.org/10.1177/1476127021989980

Jopp, R., Delacy, T., & Mair, J. (2010). Developing a framework for regional destination adaptation to climate change. *Current Issues in Tourism, 13*(6), 591–605. https://doi.org/10.1080/13683501003653379

Kouloukoui, D., Marinho, M. M. d. O., Gomes, S. M. d. S., Kiperstok, A., & Torres, E. A. (2019). Corporate climate risk management and the implementation of climate projects by the world's largest emitters. *Journal of Cleaner Production, 238*, 117935. https://doi.org/10.1016/J.JCLEPRO.2019.117935

Lei, L., Voss, H., Clegg, L. J., & Wu, X. (2017). Climate change strategies of multinational enterprises in China. *Journal of Cleaner Production, 160*, 98–108. https://doi.org/10.1016/J.JCLEPRO.2017.03.150

Lempert, R. J., & Groves, D. G. (2010). Identifying and evaluating robust adaptive policy responses to climate change for water management agencies in the American west. *Technological Forecasting and Social Change, 77*(6), 960–974. https://doi.org/10.1016/j.techfore.2010.04.007

Linnenluecke, M. K. (2017). Resilience in business and management research: A review of influential publications and a research agenda. *International Journal of Management Reviews, 19*(1), 4–30. https://doi.org/10.1111/ijmr.12076

Linnenluecke, M. K., & Griffiths, A. (2010). Beyond adaptation: Resilience for business in light of climate change and weather extremes. *Business and Society, 49*(3), 477–511. https://doi.org/10.1177/0007650310368814

Linnenluecke, M. K., Griffiths, A., & Winn, M. (2012). Extreme weather events and the critical importance of anticipatory adaptation and organizational resilience in responding to impacts. *Business Strategy and the Environment, 21*(1), 17–32. https://doi.org/10.1002/BSE.708

Linnenluecke, M. K., Griffiths, A., & Winn, M. I. (2013). Firm and industry adaptation to climate change: A review of climate adaptation studies in the business and management field. *Wiley Interdisciplinary Reviews: Climate Change, 4*(5), 397–416. https://doi.org/10.1002/wcc.214

Linnenluecke, M. K., Marrone, M., & Singh, A. K. (2020). Conducting systematic literature reviews and bibliometric analyses. *Australian Journal of Management, 45*(2), 175–194. https://doi.org/10.1177/0312896219877678/ASSET/IMAGES/LARGE/10.1177_0312896219877678-FIG7.JPEG

Lintukangas, K., Arminen, H., Kähkönen, A. K., & Karttunen, E. (2022). Determinants of supply chain engagement in carbon management. *Journal of Business Ethics, 186*(1), 87–104. https://doi.org/10.1007/S10551-022-05199-7/TABLES/5

Loehr, J. (2020). The Vanuatu Tourism Adaptation System: A holistic approach to reducing climate risk. *Journal of Sustainable Tourism, 28*(4), 515–534. https://doi.org/10.1080/09669582.2019.1683185

Lopes de Sousa Jabbour, A. B., Vazquez-Brust, D., Chiappetta Jabbour, C. J., & Andriani Ribeiro, D. (2020). The interplay between stakeholders, resources and capabilities in climate change strategy: Converting barriers into cooperation. *Business Strategy and the Environment, 29*(3), 1362–1386. https://doi.org/10.1002/BSE.2438

Martin, N., & Rice, J. (2010). Analysing emission intensive firms as regulatory stakeholders: A role for adaptable business strategy. *Business Strategy and the Environment, 19*(1), 64–75. https://doi.org/10.1002/BSE.661

Mashi, S. A., Inkani, A. I., & Oghenejabor, O. D. (2022). Determinants of awareness levels of climate smart agricultural technologies and practices of urban farmers in Kuje, Abuja, Nigeria. *Technology in Society, 70*, 102030. https://doi.org/10.1016/j.techsoc.2022.102030

McLaughlin, P. (2011). Climate change, adaptation, and vulnerability: Reconceptualizing societal-environment interaction within a socially constructed adaptive landscape. *Organization and Environment, 24*(3), 269–291. https://doi.org/10.1177/1086026611419862

Moral-Muñoz, J. A., Herrera-Viedma, E., Santisteban-Espejo, A., & Cobo, M. J. (2020). Software tools for conducting bibliometric analysis in science: An up-to-date review. *El Profesional de La Información, 29*(1), 1–20. https://doi.org/10.3145/epi.2020.ene.03

Mukhovi, S., Jacobi, J., Speranza, C. I., Rist, S., & Kiteme, B. (2020). Learning and adaptation in food systems: Insights from four case studies in the global south. *International*

*Journal on Food System Dynamics, 11*(4), 313–328. https://doi.org/10.18461/ijfsd. v11i4.57

Ng, A. K. Y., Wang, T., Yang, Z., Li, K. X., & Jiang, C. (2018). How is business adapting to climate change impacts appropriately? Insight from the commercial port sector. *Journal of Business Ethics, 150*(4), 1029–1047. https://doi.org/10.1007/s10551-016-3179-6

Nicolletti, M., Lutti, N., Souza, R., & Pagotto, L. (2019). Social and organizational learning in the adaptation to the process of climate change: The case of a Brazilian thermoplastic resins and petrochemical company. *Journal of Cleaner Production, 226*, 748–758. https://doi.org/10.1016/J.JCLEPRO.2019.04.058

Nyberg, D., & Wright, C. (2022). Defending hegemony: From climate change mitigation to adaptation on the Great Barrier Reef. *Organization, 31*(2), 247–268. https://doi.org/10.1177/13505084221115836

Orsato, R. J., Ferraz de Campos, J. G., & Barakat, S. R. (2019). social learning for anticipatory adaptation to climate change: Evidence from a community of practice. *Organization and Environment, 32*(4), 416–440. https://doi.org/10.1177/1086026618775325/ ASSET/IMAGES/LARGE/10.1177_1086026618775325-FIG2.JPEG

Pavanello, F., De Cian, E., Davide, M., Mistry, M., Cruz, T., Bezerra, P., Jagu, D., Renner, S., Schaeffer, R., & Lucena, A. F. P. (2021). Air-conditioning and the adaptation cooling deficit in emerging economies. *Nature Communications, 12*(1), 1–11. https://doi.org/10.1038/s41467-021-26592-2

Pinkse, J., & Gasbarro, F. (2019). Managing physical impacts of climate change: An attentional perspective on corporate adaptation. *Business and Society, 58*(2), 333–368. https://doi.org/10.1177/0007650316648688/ASSET/IMAGES/LARGE/ 10.1177_0007650316648688-FIG2.JPEG

Pinkse, J., & Kolk, A. (2012). Addressing the climate change-sustainable development nexus: The role of multistakeholder partnerships. *Business and Society, 51*(1), 176–210. https://doi.org/10.1177/0007650311427426

Ponce Oliva, R. D., Huaman, J., Vásquez-Lavin, F., Barrientos, M., & Gelcich, S. (2022). Firms adaptation to climate change through product innovation. *Journal of Cleaner Production, 350*, 131436. https://doi.org/10.1016/j.jclepro.2022.131436

Rao, P. K., & Shukla, A. (2023). Sustainable strategic management: A bibliometric analysis. *Business Strategy and the Environment, 32*(6), 3902–3914. https://doi.org/10.1002/ bse.3344

Rice, H., Cohen, S. A., & Scott, D. (2022). Perceptions of climate change risk and sustainable adaptations in the Swedish ski industry. *Journal of Sustainable Tourism, 32*(2), 1–17. https://doi.org/10.1080/09669582.2022.2151858

Rivera, J., & Clement, V. (2019). Business adaptation to climate change: American ski resorts and warmer temperatures. *Business Strategy and the Environment, 28*(7), 1285–1301. https://doi.org/10.1002/BSE.2316

Roman, C. E., Lynch, A. H., & Dominey-Howes, D. (2010). Uncovering the essence of the climate change adaptation problem-a case study of the tourism sector at Alpine Shire, Victoria, Australia. *Tourism and Hospitality, Planning and Development, 7*(3), 237–252. https://doi.org/10.1080/1479053X.2010.503049

Schmitt, A., & Klarner, P. (2015). From snapshot to continuity: A dynamic model of organizational adaptation to environmental changes. *Scandinavian Journal of Management, 31*(1), 3–13. https://doi.org/10.1016/J.SCAMAN.2014.06.003

Scott, D., McBoyle, G., & Mills, B. (2003). Climate change and the skiing industry in southern Ontario (Canada): Exploring the importance of snowmaking as a technical adaptation. *Climate Research, 23*, 171–181.

Shakeela, A., & Becken, S. (2015). Understanding tourism leaders' perceptions of risks from climate change: An assessment of policy-making processes in the Maldives using the social amplification of risk framework (SARF). *Journal of Sustainable Tourism, 23*(1), 65–84. https://doi.org/10.1080/09669582.2014.918135

Steiger, R. (2010). The impact of climate change on ski season length and snowmaking requirements in Tyrol, Austria. *Climate Research, 43*(3), 251–262. https://doi.org/10.3354/cr00941

Steiger, R., & Abegg, B. (2013). The sensitivity of Austrian ski areas to climate change. *Tourism Planning and Development, 10*(4), 480–493. https://doi.org/10.1080/21568316.2013.804431

Steiger, R., Scott, D., Abegg, B., Pons, M., & Aall, C. (2019). A critical review of climate change risk for ski tourism. *Current Issues in Tourism, 22*(11), 1343–1379. https://doi.org/10.1080/13683500.2017.1410110

Stern, N. (2009). *The global deal: Climate change and the creation of a new era of progress and prosperity.* Public Affairs.

Su, Y. P., Hall, C. M., & Ozanne, L. (2013). Hospitality industry responses to climate change: A benchmark study of Taiwanese tourist hotels. *Asia Pacific Journal of Tourism Research, 18*(1–2), 92–107. https://doi.org/10.1080/10941665.2012.688513

Tervo-Kankare, K. (2019). Entrepreneurship in nature-based tourism under a changing climate. *Current Issues in Tourism, 22*(11), 1380–1392. https://doi.org/10.1080/13683500.2018.1439457

Tervo-Kankare, K., Kaján, E., & Saarinen, J. (2018). Costs and benefits of environmental change: Tourism industry's responses in Arctic Finland. *Tourism Geographies, 20*(2), 202–223. https://doi.org/10.1080/14616688.2017.1375973

Tisch, D., & Galbreath, J. (2018). Building organizational resilience through sensemaking: The case of climate change and extreme weather events. *Business Strategy and the Environment, 27*(8), 1197–1208. https://doi.org/10.1002/BSE.2062

Touboulic, A., Matthews, L., & Marques, L. (2018). On the road to carbon reduction in a food supply network: A complex adaptive systems perspective. *Supply Chain Management, 23*(4), 313–335. https://doi.org/10.1108/SCM-06-2017-0214/FULL/PDF

Tripathi, M., Kumar, S., Sonker, S. K., & Babbar, P. (2018). Occurrence of author keywords and keywords plus in social sciences and humanities research : A preliminary study. *COLLNET Journal of Scientometrics and Information Management, 12*(2), 215–232. https://doi.org/10.1080/09737766.2018.1436951

van der Ploeg, F., & Rezai, A. (2020). Stranded assets in the transition to a carbon-free economy. *Annual Review of Resource Economics, 12*, 281–298. https://doi.org/10.1146/ANNUREV-RESOURCE-110519-040938

Winn, M., Kirchgeorg, M., Griffiths, A., Linnenluecke, M. K., & Gunther, E. (2011). Impacts from climate change on organizations: A conceptual foundation. *Business Strategy and the Environment, 20*(3), 157–173. https://doi.org/10.1002/BSE.679

Wissman-Weber, N. K., & Levy, D. L. (2018). Climate adaptation in the anthropocene: Constructing and contesting urban risk regimes. *Organization, 25*(4), 491–516. https://doi.org/10.1177/1350508418775812

Wongnaa, C. A., & Babu, S. (2020). Building resilience to shocks of climate change in Ghana's cocoa production and its effect on productivity and incomes. *Technology in Society, 62*, 101288. https://doi.org/10.1016/J.TECHSOC.2020.101288

Wright, C., & Nyberg, D. (2017). An inconvenient truth: How organizations translate climate change into business as usual. *Academy of Management Journal, 60*(5), 1633–1661. https://doi.org/10.5465/amj.2015.0718

Zupic, I., & Čater, T. (2015). Bibliometric methods in management and organization. *Organizational Research Methods, 18*(3), 429–472. https://doi.org/10.1177/1094428114562629

# Chapter 3

# Assessing Long-term Performance in Manufacturing Companies Hit by a Natural Disaster: The Role of Organizational Resilience and Human Capital*

*Elisa Martinelli, Elena Sarti and Giulia Tagliazucchi*

*University of Modena and Reggio Emilia, Italy*

## Abstract

Natural disasters represent an increasing threat to businesses, putting at risk their continuity in light of sustainable performance conditions. The present chapter explores the role of organizational resilience and of human capital in manufacturing companies hit by a natural disaster, an earthquake in the current study, by considering performance in the long run. In doing so, a survey has been performed on a sample of 131 manufacturing companies hit by the Emilia earthquake (Italy) in 2012, considering both perceptual data and balance sheet data. This represents a key contribution of this chapter, as extant literature on the impact of resilience on business performance has mainly used perceptual data; conversely, our study, considering balance sheet data, enables a more comprehensive and realistic view of the phenomenon. The sample was selected from

*This research has been supported by Comune di Mirandola and Centro Documentazione Sisma. Authors' contributions: Elisa Martinelli mainly focused on the introduction, conclusions and managerial implications of the study. Elena Sarti mainly focused on empirical analysis, results and discussion. Giulia Tagliazucchi mainly focused on background and hypothesis development of the study. All the authors wrote, read and approved the final manuscript.

**Sustainable and Resilient Global Practices:**
**Advances in Responsiveness and Adaptation, 37–54**
**doi:10.1108/978-1-83797-611-920241003**

the AIDA database, as it includes revenue data that we could add to the perceptual measures obtained by administering a structured questionnaire. Partial least squares structural equation modeling (PLS-SEM) was then employed. The results show the importance of developing adaptive processes that leverage on the organization's human capital and resilience to respond to adverse exogenous events. More specifically, it has been found that human capital and organizational resilience are profitable to post-disaster economic performance in the long run, supporting the economic sustainability of affected businesses. The implications are related to reinforcing new business solutions and adaptive strategies, looking at both organizational resilience and human capital investment to reach a stable economic business performance in the long-run after a detrimental event.

*Keywords*: Earthquake; human capital; organizational resilience; post-disaster performance; PLS-SEM

## Introduction

Exogenous and unexpected shocks are constantly increasing, negatively affecting businesses' activities and economic sustainability (Fiksel et al., 2015; Linnenluecke, 2017). Direct damages and loss of revenues caused by the disruptive event (Cochrane, 2004) are accompanied by indirect losses related to issues arising at both the supply and the demand sides (Kachali et al., 2012). Among external shocks, disruptive natural events are constantly increasing in frequency and magnitude, requiring companies to engage in dynamic adaptive strategies to realign their activities and to find opportunities of renewal. Indeed, companies may be renewed in response to disruptive and unexpected events, through dynamic adaptive strategies that can align business activities with the changing structural internal conditions, the emerging needs of customers and stakeholders and also to reshape interactions between the organization and all the people involved in it.

Previous studies and the observation of past shocking events clearly show that some businesses are able to face unfavorable and exogenous events better than others (Fiksel et al., 2015; Gittell et al., 2006). Why does this happen? What are the determinants of a business capacity to face a natural disaster? Extant literature has identified organizational resilience (OR) as the ability to not only survive but to be able to thrive through times of adversity (McManus et al., 2008). Resilient businesses can even prosper after a natural disaster (Corey & Deitch, 2011; Martinelli et al., 2018; Sharma & Chrisman, 1999; Tagliazucchi et al., 2023). In addition, on the one hand, if OR has assumed a growing importance according to academics and practitioners in the recovery after unexpected and disruptive events of a business, on the other hand, one cannot fail to also consider the central role of the human capital (HC) that operates and is part of the business itself (Makkonen et al., 2014; Pal et al., 2014). However, empirical studies on this topic are mainly based on economic series or perceptual data, ignoring the "businesses' perspective" together with their balance sheet data.

In this chapter, we try to fill this gap by analyzing the factors impacting business performance in terms of revenues of a sample of manufacturing companies impacted by an earthquake. We refer to what happened in May 2012 in the northern part of the Province of Modena (in the Emilia-Romagna Region), one of the most industrialized areas of Italy, not classified as subject to strong seismic events at that time. The use of balance sheet data jointly with the entrepreneur/manager's voice enable us to get a more comprehensive and realistic view of the phenomenon, strongly contributing to the academic knowledge on the determinants of business performance after a natural disaster as well as to the business resilience literature. In doing so, we were able to avoid the "dead business walking" effect[1] (Tierney, 1997), usually present when data are collected just after or only a few years after the natural disaster took place. Our work is also interesting as it shows the effect of a natural disaster in a territory rich of economic activities and important companies, key part of global supply chains (such as the biomedical cluster located in Mirandola or the knitting and fashion cluster in Carpi); seldom the work on natural disasters consider areas so industrialized. Specifically, the analysis tests a model in which OR and HC impact business revenues in the long term (i.e., after six years from the earthquake, in 2018). To our knowledge, this represents one of the few empirical studies verifying the impact of an external shock on business performance, using both perceptual data together with balance sheet data.

The results shed light on the role of OR and HC in impacting objective measures of business economic performance sustainability in terms of increasing revenues, sales and marginality. This contributes to the existing literature by looking at business resilience not only in a *bouncing back* perspective but also in a proper *bouncing forward* view, along with the role of the HC, in converting a detrimental event in growing capabilities and new opportunities. Managerial and policymaking implications are relevant too.

The chapter first presents the background of the study and then supports and formulates the proposed hypotheses to be verified. Then, the empirical analysis performed is described, highlighting the way in which the sample has been selected and its features, the measurements employed and the empirical model. The results description and discussion follow. This chapter ends with some final remarks aimed at highlighting the main managerial and policymaking implications deriving from the study, together with some limitations and avenues for future research.

---

[1]This effect is defined as a situation in which "business owners continually put money into a failing business by draining their personal assets after the business assets are gone. The business shrinks in a slow death until nothing is left but a hollow shell" (Alesch et al., 2001, p. 92). Not only individual resources but also public funds can be used to support businesses hit by natural disasters (Martinelli et al., 2018), generating a negative effect.

## Background

Resilience has become a very popular topic after the economic crises since 2007 (Dallago & Guglielmetti, 2012; Sabatino, 2016) – and it regained interest with the COVID-19 pandemic so that both academics and practitioners have increased efforts in studying this concept. However, there is still no real consensus on how resilience can be defined,[2] and authors stressed that the notion of resilience is particularly dependent on the context analyzed (Linnenluecke, 2017). However, two main and consolidated approaches can be highlighted in the academic literature in assessing resilience. The first one considers resilience as the capacity of a system to return to the same state before the external event, thus in a *bouncing back* approach, as defined by Pimm (1984) and Tilman and Downing (1994). From this perspective, resilience therefore allows the overcoming of a critical event and the restoration to preexisting conditions. This perspective opens up to potential vulnerability, as the return to the previous state can be interpreted as a return to the conditions in which the negative and critical event manifested itself (Glantz & Jamieson, 2000; Kelman et al., 2016; Tobin, 1999). Conversely, the second approach considers resilience as the ability to recover and improve the conditions preexisting the detrimental event, in a *bouncing forward* perspective (Manyena et al., 2011). This approach in some way overcomes the limit of the first approach and configures the critical event almost as an opportunity for improvement or adaptation to be seized (Martinelli et al., 2018). From this perspective, resilience manifests itself only when it is necessary and activated, and Boin et al. (2010) conclude that it can be seen as a result of a critical event or as a process which leads to "negotiate flux without succumbing to it" (p. 8).

Several scholars have indeed questioned whether resilience manifests itself before or after the exogenous and unpredictable event (e.g., Boin & McConnell, 2007). Most agree that resilience is an organizational characteristic that can be developed and nurtured over time (Lengnick-Hall & Beck, 2005; Sutcliffe & Vogus, 2003; Wildavsky, 1988). For example, Gittell et al. (2006, p. 303) define resilience as a "dynamic capacity of organizational adaptability that grows and develops over time," thus representing a positive response toward adverse events (Bhamra et al., 2011). However, it has to be noted that OR and its effect can be studied only when the negative event occurs, even though resilience could be already present in the organization, and it could be seen as a potential intrinsic characteristic of the organization itself. In fact, the capacities and competencies of companies are evolving over time and consequently also their resilience capacity: this is in line with a dynamic capability perspective of business resilience, as highlighted by the qualitative study of Martinelli et al. (2018). Recently, Conz and Magnani (2020) conducted a systematic literature review and performed an inductive content analysis in order to offer a specific definition of resilience as "a dynamic attribute of the firm characterised by (a) a proactive phase at time $(t-1)$;

---

[2]For an overview of the main definitions of resilience in the literature, see Martinelli and Tagliazucchi (2018, p. 19).

an absorptive or adaptive phase at time *t*, and (b) a reactive phase at time (t+1), where *t* is the time when an unexpected event occurs and alters the equilibrium of the firm" (p. 408). This definition reinforces the temporal nature of resilience as viewed as a dynamic process in time.

As external critical events increase in number and frequencies (Fiksel et al., 2015; Linnenluecke, 2017), having an extreme impact on the continuity and sustainability of businesses, scholars underline the need of new procedures and cooperation paths in order to quickly face and cope with unexpected and critical events and ultimately adapt to them (Van der Vegt et al., 2015). In this context, the *adaptive capacity* becomes a key point in organizational studies (McManus et al., 2008) and can be defined as "the ability [of an organization] to continuously design and develop solutions" (Lee et al., 2013, p. 32). Studies on OR are therefore closely linked to dynamic adaptive strategies. Folke (2006, p. 259) looks at the adaptive capacity issue and interprets it as "not only about being persistent or robust to disturbance. It is also about the opportunities that disturbance opens up in terms of recombination of evolved structures and processes, renewal of the system and emergence of new trajectories." Thus, these systems have both a passive role and an active role by continuously evolving themselves and increasing their capacity to prepare for turbulence (Carpenter et al., 2001). By integrating these two concepts, Limnios et al. (2014) assume that OR is a combination of *adaptive capacity* and *resistance to change* and does not only look at the organization *recovery* but also at the opportunities of *renewal* (Kantur & İşeri-Say, 2012) – in a *bouncing forward* perspective.

More recently, studies on OR have also begun to analyze the impact on and role of corporate resources. For example, Battisti and Deakins (2017) analyze the role of dynamic capabilities on the performance after earthquakes and find a positive effect of a firm's proactive posture on its capability to integrate resources from external sources. This, in turn, positively affects the extent to which the resource base is affected by natural disasters, and in addition, they find that those firms with resource base negatively affected reported significant decrease in performance. Among the possible resources that a firm can leverage on, recent studies have also focused on the HC and its role in resilience studies (e.g., Portuguez Castro & Gómez Zermeño, 2021). In this vein, Do et al. (2022) stress how the resource-based management initiatives as organizational capability can foster OR and innovation. In addition, with respect to HC, Hartmann et al. (2020) evidence the significant role of employee-level and team-level resilience, so those firms displaying a better performance in a dynamic and changing environment are those able to combine organizational-level resilience and employees-level resources.

To date, however, the role of HC alongside OR in overcoming – from a *bouncing forward* perspective – a critical event requires further in-depth analysis and empirical studies. In particular, HC, which is part of and constitutes one of the main resources of the organization itself, may assume a central role also in facing critical event, just as its effect on organizational performance in times of quiet has been demonstrated (e.g., Felício et al., 2014; Wang & Zatzick, 2019).

## Hypotheses Development

Most studies on resilience are of theoretical (Bhamra et al., 2011) or qualitative (among others Lee et al., 2013; Martinelli et al., 2018; Pal et al., 2014) nature and only recently, in particular with the advent of the COVID-19 pandemic, a growing body of studies start to apply empirical methods to gain a deeper knowledge of this phenomenon (Conz & Magnani, 2020). In order to obtain an even more comprehensive understanding of the elements impacting on the recovering process in the aftermath of a natural disaster, in the present study, we both consider the OR and the role of HC in shaping a positive economic response to natural disasters in the long term, by considering the fluctuation in business performance and revenues. In fact, as previously explained, former contributions are lacking in integrating both perceptual and objective data in assessing business performance, while we rely on both.

As previous scholars focus on the importance of fostering OR (e.g., Guillén Mondragón et al., 2022), we investigated this construct as it is, in fact, positively associated with learning opportunity and helps in handling crises and overcoming them but also in transforming disruptive events in a real opportunity for transformation. Therefore, we expect that those firms who displayed higher levels of OR also report a better economic business performance after the earthquake. This point is in line with the studies on the development of resilience over time and the definition of resilience as the ability to adapt, which extends the analysis toward a dichotomy between adaptation and adaptability (Martin & Sunley, 2015; Pike et al., 2010): the first is about the capacity to move toward a preconceived development paths in order to reproduce existing structures, and the second is on the capacity to *bounce forward* by creating new trajectories of development. It implies the existence of a trade-off between the short-term capacity to reinforce existing structures and the long-term ability to explore new trajectories (Grabher, 1993). Therefore, resilience becomes a real organizational characteristic that develops and grows over time (Lengnick-Hall & Beck, 2005; Sutcliffe & Vogus, 2003; Wildavsky, 1988), representing a positive response toward adverse events (Bhamra et al., 2011).

Thus, we test the impact of OR on the post-disaster economic performance (PDEP) in the long run (six years after the earthquake):

*H1.* OR has a positive impact on the PDEP – $\gamma_{31}$.

In order to design a comprehensive picture and to push forward our understanding of the elements that impact the overcoming of an adverse event, we also examine the HC role, by considering employees' involvement in the business and in achieving common goals. The role of human resources has been also underlined by Lengnick-Hall et al. (2011) that focus on employees' competencies as a means to respond in a resilient manner to severe shock when aggregated at the organizational level. Garavan (1991, 2007) focuses on integrating human resource development activities with organizational goals and values to develop core capabilities and enhance business competitive advantage. Similarly, Hillyard (2000) interprets the strategic human resource development as a way to accumulate wisdom by "learning together from an event to prevent, less the severity of, or

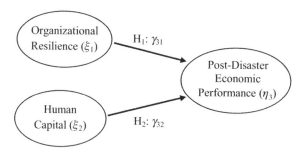

Fig. 3.1.   Graphical Representation of the Empirical Model.
*Source*: Authors' elaboration.

improve on responses to future crises" (p. 9). Thus, in our model, HC becomes a predictor of business economic performance, and we hypothesizes that:

*H2*. HC has a positive impact on the PDEP – $\gamma_{32}$.

The hypotheses and the interactions put into play among the variables of interest are summarized in Fig. 3.1.

## Empirical Analysis

### Sample Selection

The present study explores the role of OR and HC for 131 businesses located in the Province of Modena, in the Emilia-Romagna Region (Italy), that survived an exogenous and unexpected disruptive event. In particular, this area has indeed been hit by a disruptive earthquake in May 2012, which caused many damages to man-made infrastructures and had a huge negative impact on economic activities. The area, home to several industrial manufacturing districts, was not considered to be at high seismic risk, making such an event even more impactful and unexpected.

Overall, the purpose of the present study is to assess the constituent elements of OR and the role of HC, in a sample of manufacturing businesses that cope with such an adverse event and its consequences.

The population of interest has been extracted from the AIDA – Bureau Van Dijk database that collects balance sheet data and information regarding the activities of over 1 million companies in Italy. Balance sheet data were employed. The database was queried to extrapolate the sample of interest, that is, formed by all the companies that had the following characteristics:

- They were located within the earthquake area (2012).[3]
- They had an ATECO code corresponding to that of "manufacturer."

[3]This area of the Emilia-Romagna Region includes the following municipalities: Bastiglia, Bomporto, Campogalliano, Camposanto, Carpi, Cavezzo, Concordia sulla Secchia, Finale Emilia, Medolla, Mirandola, Nonantola, Novi di Modena, Ravarino, San Felice sul Panaro, San Possidonio, San Prospero and Soliera.

- They were founded at least before 2012.
- Their financial ratios present at least a continuity of 10 years, therefore since 2009.

After this, the number of companies that corresponded to the requirements was just over 1,000. Subsequently, all companies in liquidation or definitively closed were eliminated from the sample. Finally, only those companies whose last available financial statements were attributable to the years 2016, 2017 and 2018 were considered.

Once the sample cleaning was completed, the companies identified were 546.

At this point, all the identified companies were contacted by phone and/or email to enquire about their possible cooperation to the survey, consisting in their willingness to be administered with a quantitative questionnaire by a research team's member. At the same time, the structured questionnaire designed to minimize biases was prepared. The businesses had to have directly experienced the earthquake in May 2012 and to be still in activity at the time of the survey.

The questionnaire was administered in Spring 2020, and a final sample of 131 businesses was collected; three interviewers made appointments and administered the questionnaire in a face-to-face mode. Subsequently, a database was built adding the revenues data extracted from AIDA to the perceptual measures obtained by administering the structured questionnaire. Finally, partial least squares structural equation modeling (PLS-SEM) was employed to test the model.

### Measurements

The three latent concepts – named **OR, HC** and **PDEP** – were constructed starting from the reference literature and integrating secondary data from balance sheets with perceptive measures collected through surveys.

As for our dependent variables, we partially make use of the measurement tools for **OR** proposed by Kantur and İşeri-Say (2015) and, in particular, we include in our model two of the three dimensions suggested by the authors, in particular the robustness and the agility dimensions of resilience. The robustness dimension is defined as the ability of the organization to act boldly and captures the elements of solidity and soundness of the mission and vision of the company, and the stability of those resources and competences employed in the business. Ultimately, it summarizes the organization's ability to pursue its development and growth path and to adapt it in the face of adversity. The agility dimension is defined as the adaptation capacity and flexibility of the organization in analyzing the context, so that in taking decisions quickly to implement the actions necessary to stay on course. The choice of including these key dimensions is in line with the perspective and approaches of different authors, such as Comfort (1994) that stresses the importance of being able to properly answer to unfavorable events through reorganization strategies. In particular, the two dimensions of robustness and agility highlight the capacity to convert challenges into opportunities, in a *bounce-forward* perspective (Martinelli & Tagliazucchi, 2018).

It has to be noted that we did not consider the integrity dimension proposed by Kantur and İşeri-Say (2015), as it measures the cohesion of the organization and its capacity to achieve a common and shared goal. This indicator is limited to aspects of employees' cohesion, and – in our opinion – may not capture nuances related to the contribution in terms of HC in the face of adversities. This is why we have considered HC as a construct per se, including it in the model as a latent variable to better catch these dynamics. This concept slightly recalls the one on social capital as developed by Makkonen et al. (2014), Pal et al. (2014) and Lengnick-Hall and Beck (2005), but it is specific as focused on human resources and employees' commitment, rather than the network of stakeholder.

Finally, as for the independent variable, it has been assessed by using both objective and perceptive data. The questionnaire administered included a specific section on the post-disaster economic sustainability in a long-term perspective (six years after the earthquake) with objective indicators measuring margins, revenues and sales volume, so as some perceptive data.

All variables and items included in the questionnaire and employed in the empirical model are listed in Table 3.1.

Table 3.1.    Indicators of the Latent Constructs.

| *Items for OR* | |
| --- | --- |
| OR1 | My organization stands straight and preserves its position |
| OR2 | My organization is successful in generating diverse solutions to problems |
| OR3 | My organization shows resistance to the end |
| OR4 | My organization is agile in taking required action when needed |
| Seven-point Likert scale ranging from 1 (fully disagree) to 7 (fully agree). | |
| *Items for HC* | |
| HC1 | My organization values the working experience of its employees and collaborators |
| HC2 | People working in the organization can try new working modalities that are in line with the normal economic activity |
| HC3 | People working in the organization is stimulated to propose new visions of the business, as well as new goals and ideas |
| Seven-point Likert scale ranging from 1 (fully disagree) to 7 (fully agree). | |
| *Items for PDEP with respect to the direct competitor* | |
| PDEP1 | Marginality |
| PDEP2 | Revenues |
| PDEP3 | Capacity to increase sales volumes from one year to the other |
| Seven-point Likert scale ranging from 1 (very much lower) to 7 (very much higher). | |

*Source*: Authors' elaboration.

Table 3.2 reports the summary statistics of all variables included in the final model and also described in Table 3.1.

### Empirical Model

The empirical model analyzes the impact of OR and HC separately on the post-disaster performance in terms of constant increasing in sales volume, margins and revenues and in a long-term perspective.

The model assumes that the three variables are latent constructs (i.e., not directly observable) and a PLS-SEM is employed as it allows for a limited sample size and explores the predictive relationships between the different constructs (Hair, Hult, et al., 2017; Hair, Matthews, et al., 2017).

The model is composed of two parts: the measurement (or *outer*) one and the structural (or *inner*) one. The first displays the relations between the latent variables and their indicators (i.e., observed variables), and the indicators are associated with their latent construct through their *loadings*, whereas the second part shows the relations between the latent variables themselves (two exogenous latent variables, named OR ($\xi_1$) and HC ($\xi_2$), and one endogenous latent variable named PDEP ($\eta_3$)).

This empirical strategy can be interpreted as an advanced multivariate technique performing two analyses at one go: the structural one similar to a regression model and a measurement one in line with a factor or a principal component analysis (Venturini & Mehmetoglu, 2019). As PLS-SEM is a distribution-free method, we rely on the nonparametric bootstrap (Davison & Hinkley, 1997; Venturini & Mehmetoglu, 2019).

Table 3.2.    Model Constructs and Items: Summary Statistics.

| Variable | Observation | Mean | Standard Deviation | Minimum | Maximum |
|---|---|---|---|---|---|
| *OR* | | | | | |
| OR1 | 131 | 5.18 | 1.58 | 1 | 7 |
| OR2 | 131 | 6.02 | 1.03 | 3 | 7 |
| OR3 | 131 | 5.52 | 1.35 | 1 | 7 |
| OR4 | 131 | 5.84 | 1.13 | 2 | 7 |
| *HC* | | | | | |
| HC1 | 131 | 5.77 | 1.08 | 2 | 7 |
| HC2 | 131 | 5.17 | 1.55 | 1 | 7 |
| HC3 | 131 | 5.25 | 1.46 | 1 | 7 |
| *PDEP* | | | | | |
| PDEP1 | 131 | 4.35 | 1.26 | 1 | 7 |
| PDEP2 | 130 | 4.19 | 1.64 | 1 | 7 |
| PDEP3 | 130 | 4.62 | 1.31 | 1 | 7 |

*Source*: Authors' elaboration.

## Results and Discussion

Most of the individual items included in the model showed acceptable reliability with loadings around or higher the recommended threshold. According to Hair, Hult, et al. (2017), this means that the latent construct explains more than 50% of the indicator's variance, hence the indicator itself exhibits a satisfactory degree of reliability. Looking at the OR factor, it has to be noted that highest loading is the one on the agility dimension, while for HC is on the third indicator on the stimuli to propose new goals and ideas by people working in the organization.

Moreover, the Cronbach's alpha values for internal consistency reliability of the indicators exceed the threshold of 0.6. In addition, composite reliability ($\rho_c$) is above 0.7 and below 0.95[4] confirming "satisfactory to good" reliability levels (Hair, Hult, et al., 2017). For what concerns the reliability coefficient ($\rho_A$), it also displays expected values (Hair et al., 2021). These values are reported in Table 3.3.

Switching to the structural part, for all the latent constructs, the convergence validity is assessed by the average variance extracted (AVE) that measures the level of variance captured by a construct versus the level due to measurement error. The AVE is computed across all items associated with a latent construct, and it is higher than the recommendation threshold of 0.5 (Table 3.4), meaning

Table 3.3.    Measurement Model – Standardized Loadings.

| Factor Loadings | OR | HC | PDEP |
|---|---|---|---|
| OR1 | 0.707 | | |
| OR2 | 0.740 | | |
| OR3 | 0.697 | | |
| OR4 | 0.876 | | |
| HC1 | | 0.682 | |
| HC2 | | 0.816 | |
| HC3 | | 0.893 | |
| PDEP1 | | | 0.800 |
| PDEP2 | | | 0.713 |
| PDEP3 | | | 0.827 |
| Cronbach's alpha ($\alpha$) | 0.766 | 0.727 | 0.712 |
| Composite reliability – Dillon–Goldstein's coefficient ($\rho_c$) | 0.843 | 0.842 | 0.824 |
| Reliability coefficient ($\rho_A$) | 0.899 | 0.806 | 0.718 |

*Source*: Authors' elaboration.

---

[4]According to Hair et al. (2017a), values above 0.95 suggest that the items are almost identical and redundant (see also Diamantopoulos et al., 2012).

Table 3.4.  Discriminant Validity.

|  | OR | HC | PDEP |
|---|---|---|---|
| OR | 1.000 | 0.159 | 0.060 |
| HC | 0.159 | 1.000 | 0.054 |
| PDEP | 0.060 | 0.054 | 1.000 |
| AVE | 0.575 | 0.643 | 0.611 |

*Source*: Authors' elaboration.

that the constructs explain more than 50% of the variance of their items (Hair, Hult, et al., 2017; Hair, Matthews, et al., 2017).

In addition, the discriminant validity is verified, thus the AVE is larger than the squared correlations among the latent variables as reported in Table 3.4.

Table 3.5 shows the structural model, evidencing that both the postulated hypotheses *H1* and *H2* are verified. Thus, the higher is the OR, as measured by the robustness and the agility dimensions, the higher the level reached by PDEP, in terms of stable marginality, constantly increasing sales volume and revenues.

The positive role of resilience is in line with previous studies by Tagliazucchi et al. (2023), Yang and Hsieh (2013) and Comfort (1994). The choice of focusing on the long-run revenues and performance lies in the belief that long-term value creation is a targeted construct. This result also corroborates the approach to resilience as a factor "to leverage [organization] resources and capabilities not only to resolve current dilemmas but to exploit opportunities and build a successful future" (Lengnick-Hall et al., 2011, p. 244).

Similarly, HC is positively associated with PDEP, meaning that the more the company values the employees' work and their new ideas and goals (the variable is mainly focused on internal human resources), the higher would be the final post-disaster revenues (*H2*).

Table 3.5.  Structural Model (Standardized Path Coefficients) and Path Model Results.

|  | PDEP |
|---|---|
| OR | *H1*: 0.181** |
|  | (0.029) |
|  | OR → PDEP |
|  | (supported) |
| HC | *H2*: 0.159* |
|  | (0.60) |
|  | OR → PDEP |
|  | (supported) |

**$p < 0.05$, *$p < 0.1$. *Source*: Authors' elaboration.

This result strengthens the contribution of recent empirical studies (Do et al., 2022; Portuguez Castro & Gómez Zermeño, 2021) that evidenced a central role of HC, alongside OR, in post-disaster recovery, appearing as key resources. Overall, we can conclude that a sustainable economic recovery after a disruptive natural event, such as the Emilia earthquake in Italy, can be thus interpreted as a real adaptive process in which both OR and HC play a key role for achieving a long-term economic stability.

The goal of reaching a positive, sustainable and durable economic condition in terms of revenues and increasing sales volume (PDEP) implies to invest in different adaptive strategies related to key dimensions, such as OR and HC. This result is ultimately in line with the approach of Kantur and İşeri-Say (2012) about the opportunity to change toward the better after a negative event.

## Conclusions and Managerial Implications

The need for further studies on the impact of natural disasters on the activities of businesses (Battisti & Deakins, 2017; Liu et al., 2013) calls for in-depth analyses on the actions and approaches that may help in facing unpredictable and extreme outcomes. To contribute to the academic debate, this analysis focuses on a sample of 131 Italian manufacturing companies that have been exposed to a disruptive earthquake in May 2012 in the North Province of Modena (Emilia-Romagna Region). In particular, this study focuses on their responsive actions based on OR and HC, in order to assess if companies' responses are positively associated with a long-term (six years after the event) performance.

Empirical results confirm our hypotheses. More specifically, PDEP – in terms of objective measure such as margins, volume sales and revenues – benefits from the implementation of actions for resilience – assessed as robustness and agility (OR) and acting as the main determinant of long-term post-disaster performance in our model – and of the contribution and the involvement of HC.

These results are in line with a *bouncing forward* approach to OR (Manyena et al., 2011; Tagliazucchi et al., 2023), confirming that resilience is not only about persistency and going back to the pre-disaster situation. Beside this, being resilient and investing in HC as a real organizational characteristic and approach leads to foster economic business performance and achieve a long-term stability and, in doing so, a real economic sustainability. Thus, our study contributes to the academic literature on the determinants of business performance after a natural disaster as well as to the business resilience literature and its outcomes. Having proved the positive contribution of OR and HC to long-term economic performance on the basis of realistic balance sheet data joint with perceptual measures, our work fosters and boosts the current knowledge on the topic.

From a practical point of view, this study aims at developing guidance for companies and for policymakers concerned with reducing the negative consequences of natural disasters for businesses too, helping in understanding how to enhance the resilience of businesses in the face of critical events.

Regarding managerial implications, our results provide further support to managers and entrepreneurs operating in the manufacturing sector on the importance of enhancing a resilience approach both at the organizational and human resource levels in order to face the negative effects of any natural disasters and gaining economic sustainability in the long run. Actually, investigating and assessing the antecedents of long-term performance in the aftermath of critical events become of primary importance in order to convince manufacturers and managers that investing in resilience and human resources is valuable and able to bring to a superior capacity to better perform in the long run when a critical event hit. Moreover, our findings constitute practical evidence that facing natural disasters is not only a matter of technical preparedness and business continuity, but it is also a question of arranging a robust and agile organization where human resources are key determinants to economic success. Business unions and public authorities responsible for local and national economic development may be critical in supporting businesses hit by natural disasters too: the former should use our results to help manufacturing companies in understanding the economic value of being resilient and have an involved and supportive employees' base, while the latter should promote entrepreneurial and managerial awareness of the importance of developing a solid company structure and strategical project in order to positively perform even in adverse conditions; this is possible also thanks to operational agility and the involvement of the human resources of the company.

Finally, some limitations of the analysis may be mentioned. First, the limited sample of reference does not allow an analysis for the economic sector, and it is mainly due to the availability of the managers and owners to answer specific questions about the companies prior and after the earthquake. Second, the need of interviewing those businesses still in activity at the time of the survey, as they can be considered as resilient, may induce a selection bias of the sample itself. Third, the questionnaire has been addressed to the managers and the owners, so we are not able to capture the perspective of employees, suppliers, stakeholders and clients. Future research could then deeper investigate the role of resources and competencies, in particular slack resources, and compare the results obtained with effects and recovery paths in other national contexts and on other types of natural disasters.

Nevertheless, this contribution represents one of the few empirical studies verifying the impact of an external negative shock on business performance using both perceptual data together with balance sheet data and in a longitudinal view. In addition, it sheds light on new dynamic processes and adaptation strategies in response to unpredictable and adverse shocks, which are more and more frequent in our society.

# References

Alesch, D. J., Holly J. N., Mittler E., & Nagy, R. (2001). Organizations at risk: What happens when small businesses and not-for-profits encounter natural disasters. Public Entity Risk Institute.

Battisti, M., & Deakins, D. (2017). The relationship between dynamic capabilities, the firm's resource base and performance in a post-disaster environment. *International Small Business Journal*, 35(1), 78–98.

Bhamra, R., Dani, S., & Burnard, K. (2011). Resilience: The concept, a literature review and future directions. *International Journal of Production Research, 49*(18), 5375–5393.

Boin, A., Comfort, L. K., & Demchak, C. C. (2010). *The rise of resilience*. In L. K. Comfort, A. Boin, & C. C. Demchak (Eds.), *Designing resilience: Preparing for extreme events* (pp. 1–12). University of Pittsburgh Press.

Boin, A., & McConnell, A. (2007). Preparing for critical infrastructure breakdowns: The limits of crisis management and the need for resilience. *Journal of Contingencies and Crisis Management, 15*(1), 50–59.

Carpenter, S., Walker, B., Anderies, J. M., & Abel, N. (2001). From metaphor to measurement: Resilience of what to what? *Ecosystems, 4*(8), 765–781.

Cochrane, H. (2004). Economic loss: Myth and measurement. *Disaster Prevention and Management, 13*, 290–296.

Comfort, L. K. (1994). Risk and resilience: Inter-organizational learning following the Northridge earthquake of 17 January 1994. *Journal of Contingencies and Crisis Management, 2*(3),157–170.

Conz, E., & Magnani, G. (2020). A dynamic perspective on resilience of firms: A systematic literature review and a framework for future research. *European Management Journal, 38*, 400–412.

Corey, C. M., & Deitch, E. A. (2011). Factors affecting business recovery immediately after Hurricane Katrina, *Journal of Contingencies and Crisis Management, 19*(3), 169–181.

Dallago, B., & Guglielmetti, C. (Eds.). (2012). *The consequences of international crisis for European SMEs: Vulnerability and resilience*. Routledge.

Davison, A. C., & Hinkley, D. V. (1997). *Bootstrap methods and their applications.* Cambridge University Press.

Diamantopoulos, A., Sarstedt, M., Fuchs, C., Wilczynski, P., & Kaiser, S. (2012). Guidelines for choosing between multi-item and single-item scales for construct measurement: A predictive validity perspective. *Journal of the Academy of Marketing Science, 40*, 434–449.

Do, H., Budhwar, P., Shipton, H., Nguyen, H.-D., & Nguyen, B. (2022). Building organizational resilience, innovation through resource-based management initiatives, organizational learning and environmental dynamism. *Journal of Business Research, 141*, 808–821.

Felício, J. A., Couto, E., & Caiado, J. (2014). Human capital, social capital and organizational performance. *Management Decision, 52*(2), 350–364.

Fiksel, J., Polyviou, M., Croxton, K. L., & Pettit, T. J. (2015). From risk to resilience: Learning to deal with disruption. *MIT Sloan Management Review, 56*(2), 79–86.

Folke, C. (2006). Resilience: The emergence of a perspective for social-ecological systems analyses. *Global Environmental Change, 16*(3), 253–267.

Garavan, T. N. (1991). Strategic human resource development. *Journal of European Industrial Training, 15*(1), 17–30.

Garavan, T. N. (2007). A strategic perspective on human resource development. *Advances in Developing Human Resources, 9*, 11–30.

Gittell, J. H., Cameron, K., Lim, S., & Rivas, V. (2006). Relationships, layoffs, and organizational resilience: Airline industry responses to September 11. *Journal of Applied Behavioral Science, 42*(3), 300–329.

Glantz, M. H., & Jamieson, D. (2000). Societal response to hurricane mitch and intra-versus intergenerational equity issues: Whose norms should apply? *Risk Analysis, 20*(6), 869–882.

Grabher, G. (1993). *The embedded firm: On the socioeconomics of industrial networks.* Routledge.

Guillén Mondragón, I. J., Rendón Trejo, A., & Morales Alquicira, A. (2022). Is organizational resilience a competitive advantage? *Mercados y Negocios, 46*, 57–82.

Hair, J. F., Hult, G. T. M., Ringle, C. M., & Sarstedt, M. (2017). *A primer on partial least squares structural equation modeling ( PLS-SEM)* (2nd ed.). Sage Publications Inc.

Hair, J. F., Hult, G. T. M., Ringle, C. R., Sarstedt, M., Danks, N. P., & Ray, S. (2021). *Evaluation of reflective measurement models.* In *Partial least squares structural equation modeling (PLS-SEM) using R: A workbook* (Classroom Companion Business, pp. 75–90). Springer.

Hair, J. F., Matthews, L. M., Matthews, R. L., & Sarstedt, M. (2017). PLS-SEM or CB-SEM: Updated guidelines on which method to use. *International Journal of Multivariate Data Analysis, 1*(2), 107–123.

Hartmann, S., Weiss, M., Newman, A., & Hoegl, M. (2020). Resilience in the workplace: A multilevel review and synthesis. *Applied Psychology, 69*(3), 913–959.

Hillyard, M. T. (2000). *Public crisis management, how and why organisations work together to solve society's most threatening problems.* Writers Press Club.

Kachali, H., Stevenson, J. R., Whitman, Z., Seville, E., Vargo, J., & Wilson, T. (2012). Organisational resilience and recovery for canterbury organisations after the 4 September 2010 earthquake. *Australian Journal of Disaster and Trauma Studies, 1*, 11–19.

Kantur, D., & İşeri-Say, A. (2012). Organizational resilience: A conceptual integrative framework. *Journal of Management & Organization, 18*(6), 762–773.

Kantur, D., & İşeri-Say, A. (2015). Measuring organizational resilience: A scale development. *Journal of Business Economic and Finance, 4*(3), 456–472.

Kelman, I., Gaillard, J. C., Lewis, J., & Mercer, J. (2016). Learning from the history of disaster vulnerability and resilience research and practise for climate change. *Natural Hazards, 82*(1), 129–143.

Lee, A. V., Vargo, J., & Seville, E. (2013). Developing a tool to measure and compare organizations' resilience. *Natural Hazards Review, 14*(1), 29–41.

Lengnick-Hall, C. A., & Beck, T. E. (2005). Adaptive fit versus robust transformation: How organizations respond to environmental change. *Journal of Management, 31*(5), 738–757.

Lengnick-Hall, C. A., Beck, T. E., & Lengnick-Hall, M. L. (2011). Developing a capacity for organizational resilience through strategic human resource management. *Human Resource Management Review, 21*(3), 243–255.

Limnios, E. A. M., Mazzarol, T., Ghadouani, A., & Schilizzi, S. G. (2014). The resilience architecture framework: Four organizational archetypes. *European Management Journal, 32*(1), 104–116.

Linnenluecke, M. K. (2017). Resilience in business and management research: A review of Influential publications and research agenda. *International Journal of Management Reviews, 19*(1), 4–30.

Liu, Z., Xu, J., & Han, B. T. (2013). Small- and medium-sized enterprise post-disaster reconstruction management patterns and application. *Natural Hazards, 68*(2), 809–835.

Makkonen, H., Pohjola, M., Olkkonen, R., & Koponen, A. (2014). Dynamic capabilities and firm performance in a financial crisis. *Journal of Business Research, 67*(1), 2707–2719.

Manyena, B., O'Brien, G., O'Keefe, P., & Rose, J. (2011). Disaster resilience: A bounce back or bounce forward ability? *Local Environment: The international Journal of Justice and Sustainability, 16*(5), 417–424.

Martin, R., & Sunley, P. (2015). On the notion of regional economic resilience: Conceptualization and explanation. *Journal of Economic Geography, 15*, 1–42.

Martinelli, E., & Tagliazucchi, G. (2018). *Resilienza e Impresa. L'impatto dei disastri naturali sulle piccole imprese commerciali al dettaglio.* Franco Angeli.

Martinelli, E., Tagliazucchi, G., & Marchi, G. (2018). The resilient retail entrepreneur: Dynamic capabilities for facing natural disasters. *International Journal of Entrepreneurial Behavior & Research, 24*(7), 1222–1243.

McManus, S., Seville, E., Vargo, J., & Brunsdon, D. (2008). Facilitated process for improving organizational resilience. *Natural Hazards Review*, *9*(2), 81–90.

Pal, R., Torstensson, H., & Mattila, H. (2014). Antecedents of organizational resilience in economic crises – An empirical study of Swedish textile and clothing SMEs. *International Journal of Productive Economics*, *147*, 410–428.

Pike, A., Dawley, S., & Tomaney, J. (2010). Resilience, adaptation and adaptability. *Cambridge Journal of Regions, Economy and Society*, *3*, 59–70.

Pimm, S. L. (1984). The complexity and stability of ecosystems. *Nature*, *307*, 321–326.

Portuguez Castro, M., & Gómez Zermeño, M. G. (2021). Being an entrepreneur post-COVID-19 – Resilience in terms of crisis: A systematic literature review. *Journal of Entrepreneurship in Emerging Economies*, *13*(4), 721–746.

Sabatino, M. (2016). Economic crisis and resilience: Resilient capacity and competitiveness of the enterprises. *Journal of Business Research*, *69*(5), 1924–1927.

Sharma, P., & Chrisman, S. J. J. (1999). Toward a reconciliation of the definitional issues in the field of corporate entrepreneurship. *Entrepreneurship Theory & Practice*, *23*(3), 11–27.

Sutcliffe, K. M., & Vogus, T. J. (2003). Organizing for resilience. In K. S. Cameron, J. E. Dutton, & R. E. Quinn (Eds.), *Positive organizational scholarship: Foundations of a new discipline* (pp. 94–110). Berrett-Koehler.

Tagliazucchi, G., De Canio, F., & Martinelli, E. (2023). Exploring perceived post-disaster performance in micro-businesses: How does entrepreneur psychological resilience matter? *Entrepreneurship & Regional Development*, *35*(5–6), 445–459.

Tierney, K. J. (1997). Business impacts of the Northridge earthquake. *Journal of Contingencies and Crisis Management*, *5*(2), 87–97.

Tilman, D., & Downing, J. A. (1994). Biodiversity and stability in grasslands. *Nature*, *367*, 363–365.

Tobin, G. A. (1999). Sustainability and community resilience: The holy grail of hazards planning? *Global Environmental Change Part B: Environmental Hazards*, *1*(1), 13–25.

Van der Vegt, G. S., Essens, P., Wahlström, M., & George, G. (2015). Managing risk and resilience. *Academy of Management Journal*, *58*(4), 971–980.

Venturini, S., & Mehmetoglu, M. (2019). plssem: A stata package for structural equation modeling with partial least squares. *Journal of Statistical Software*, *88*(8), 1–35.

Wang, T., & Zatzick, C. D. (2019). Human capital acquisition and organizational innovation: A temporal perspective. *Academy of Management Journal*, *62*(1), 99–116.

Wildavsky, A. (1988). *Searching for safety*. Transition Books.

Yang, T. K., & Hsieh, M. H. (2013). Case analysis of capability development in crisis prevention and response. *International Journal of Information Management*, *33*(2), 408–412.

Chapter 4

# Environmental Sustainability Orientation, Dynamic Capability, Entrepreneurial Orientation, and Green Innovation in Small- and Medium-sized Enterprise

*Kwadwo Asante, Petr Novak and Michael Adu Kwarteng*

*Tomas Bata University, Czech Republic*

## Abstract

Environmental sustainability orientation has emerged to drive firms into eco-friendly production. Yet, the consequence of this new strategic thinking on firms' green innovations, especially small- and medium-scale enterprises (SMEs), remains unresolved. Recognizing that the connection between environmental sustainability orientation and green innovation may not always be direct, the study theorizes that dynamic capability and entrepreneurial orientation may form part of the boundary conditions that strengthen its effect on small enterprises' green innovation. The study adjoins the dynamic capability theory with the entrepreneurial orientation theory to test this relationship among small businesses within a developing economy. Results from the partial least squares–structural equation modeling (PLS-SEM) suggest that environmental sustainability orientation will result in green innovation when the SME's dynamic capability can develop a creative reconfiguration of knowledge and new distinctive resources to support this new strategic direction. Similarly, findings from the study suggest that environmental sustainability orientation will translate into better green innovation outcomes when the SME entrepreneurial orientation has a solid attraction to protect the ecosystem and does not perceive green innovation as a risky enterprise.

*Keywords*: Environmental sustainability orientation; dynamic capability; entrepreneurial orientation; SMEs; PLS-SEM

Sustainable and Resilient Global Practices:
Advances in Responsiveness and Adaptation, 55–79
Copyright © 2024 by Kwadwo Asante, Petr Novak and Michael Adu Kwarteng
Published under exclusive licence by Emerald Publishing Limited
doi:10.1108/978-1-83797-611-920241004

## Introduction

The growing interest in a better world (United Nations Environment Programme, 2015) has increased the calls for business enterprises to modify their operations and product offerings (Arora et al., 2020). Presently, sustainability is no longer seen as a cost but as a primary driver for innovation and competitive advantage (Porter & Kramer, 2011). Integrating environmental sustainability orientation (ESO) into a firm strategy is seen as indispensable *"for co-creating value and achieving competitiveness in the network of a complex service system"* (Enquist et al., 2015, p. 182). ESO is viewed as a new strategic orientation which seeks to help a firm create a new production value to meet the United Nations' sustainable development goals (SDGs) (Arora et al., 2020).

ESO predominantly comprises deep-rooted ideals and principles that provide behavioral norms to guide an enterprise's sustainability activity (Varadarajan, 2017). Enterprises with ESO ensure that their new product and service innovations are always guided by ecological principles and features (Adams et al., 2016). Earlier proponents of ESO identified this new strategic direction as a primary driver of green innovation (GINN) (Claudy et al., 2016; Fraj-Andrés et al., 2009). The increasing hype surrounding ESO seems to have enticed many firms to integrate ESO into their production process (Govindan et al., 2020). While some studies have reported a significant relationship between ESO and GINN (e.g., Cheng, 2020; Genc & Benedetto, 2019), other strands of the literature have failed to confirm such a relationship (e.g., Adams et al., 2016; Klewitz & Hansen, 2014).

The ambivalent results in this context suggest that the expected relationship between ESO and GINN may not be direct but be contingent on other boundary conditions which the extant literature has failed to overlook (Cheng, 2020). For instance, as the request or demand for green products is usually induced externally through new regulatory requirements, customer and supplier requests, or market entry requirements (Khan et al., 2021; Zhao et al., 2018), firms that can sense these market changes much earlier are most likely to use this insight to shape their innovation process (Wilhelm et al., 2016). From the dynamic capability (DC) theory, an enterprise with the right capabilities can build a creative reconfiguration of knowledge and consequently identify the new distinctive resources to support a new market need (Sheng, 2017). This suggests that a firm's DC becomes paramount in strengthening its response to market needs.

Additionally, a firm's proclivity to chart a new path depends on its entrepreneurial orientation (EO) (Rauch & Frese, 2007; Wiklund et al., 2009). This suggests that ESO will not certainly result in GINN but will be influenced by the owner-manager EO, which emerges from their degree of proactiveness, innovativeness, and risk-taking. Notwithstanding the potential impact of EO and DC on GINN, there is a lack of clarity as to how these antecedents collectively influence firms' GINN outcomes (Liu et al., 2017; Tuan, 2022) as often the effects have been studied in isolation (Monferrer et al., 2021). Considering that the variable effects of EO and DC are measured at different levels, exploring the interplay these capabilities have on a firm's GINN outcomes, it is crucial to understand the interaction these firm-level capabilities have on their GINN (Sarwar et al., 2021). Not having an in-depth understanding of these variables' interactive effect on firm outcomes limits us in identifying which firm-level attributes lead to better GINN outcomes.

The study, therefore, has three main contributions. First, there is a lack of clarity on how DC and EO collectively influence firms' GINN outcomes (Liu et al., 2017), as the effects have been investigated in isolation (Monferrer et al., 2021). Accordingly, by considering these antecedents in a single study, the study provides a deeper perspective into the interactive effect of these variables on small- and medium-sized enterprise (SME) outcomes and consequently enables us to identify the ideal firm-level factors that result in better GINN among SMEs. Second, the study findings address the lack of clarity in ESO and GINN studies by identifying the other latent variables that improve ESO and GINN outcomes. For instance, as the variable effects of EO and DC are usually measured at different levels, we cannot understand the possible interaction between ESO, DC, and GINN. Accordingly, as this study combines ESO, GINN, and EO in a single study, it provides a more nuanced understanding of how and why DC and EO are critical to strengthening ESO and GINN relationship. Lastly, although studies on ESO and GINN have increased significantly in the last decade, most of these studies have predominantly focused on larger firms in developed economies (Guo & Wang, 2022; Roxas et al., 2017). However, as SMEs are usually faced with several constraints, such as limited capital, owner-manager influence, non-formalized operating processes, and tighter span of control, using SMEs as the study context provides a strong theoretical contribution to understanding how these contextual issues influence SMEs' ESO and GINN relationship (Scuotto et al., 2020).

## Theory and Hypothesis Development

The capability theory provides the theoretical lens for this study. The proponents of the capability theory (Eisenhardt & Martin, 2000; Teece et al., 1997) posit that firm performance outcomes center on suitable combinations of resources and capabilities. According to Helfat and Winter (2011), firms without the necessary resources and abilities may be unable to convert their internal and external resources to support superior innovation outcomes. Since the demand for green products is usually induced externally by either a new regulatory requirement, customer and supplier request or market entry requirements, firms that accept ESO cannot develop their innovations in isolation but are required to take account of this external insight into their strategy development (Claudy et al., 2016; Gimenez & Tachizawa, 2012). Firms with the necessary capabilities can sense, build, and reconfigure their internal and external resources to respond to the changing market needs. Likewise, a DC allows a firm to take early notice of the changes within its market space and increases its adaptiveness to new market changes by inducing innovation. According to Lee and Yoo (2019), this becomes a central capability to improve firm innovation outcomes. Again, as the insight acquired from the external environment has a vital role in enterprise innovation, it becomes crucial for a firm to have in place the right capabilities that can facilitate its access to this information and the sharing of this new information within its organizational setup (Lee et al., 2016). Another position of the capability theory is that a new capability that can transform this insight into new knowledge by integrating it with existing knowledge to improve the evolutionary fitness of the new business model is critical to firm innovation performance (Pavlou & Sawy, 2011). From the DC theory argument, GINN success can be attained through the organic recipe of three capabilities: identification of market-changing activities (sensing capability), seizing identified opportunities, selecting a business model which is responsive to the seized opportunity, develop/channel the necessary resources, and commercialize the product (seizing capability) and reorganizing of resources to accomplish these activities (transforming capability) (Helfat & Martin, 2015). Accordingly, for businesses' ESO to translate into better GINN outcomes, they must have these capabilities at their disposal (Helfat & Martin, 2015; Zhou et al., 2018).

### *ESO and GINN*

ESO is made up of innate ideals and values that provide behavioral norms to guide an enterprise's sustainability agenda (Varadarajan, 2017). Roxas and Coetzer (2012) described ESO "as the general proactive strategic position of a firm towards the incorporation of environmental and social issues and practices into their strategic and operational activities" (p. 464). Enterprises with ESO ensure that all the processes supporting their product development, design, and features guarantee the complete protection of the environment (Adams et al., 2016).

Strong strategic support for lower emissions motivates businesses to integrate sustainable practices into their business processes (Arora et al., 2020; Cheng, 2020; Govindan et al., 2020). For instance, a strategic orientation that firmly commits to social responsibility and environmental stewardship results in implementing green production practices (Brockhaus et al., 2019; Hong et al., 2019). This suggests that ESO demonstrating a firm's support and preference for green practices could sufficiently determine its innovation success (Jagani & Hong, 2022). Firms with ESO are more likely to integrate sustainable principles into their operational activities, from their product and process design to the distribution of their final product (Brockhaus et al., 2019; Hong et al., 2019). Accordingly, a strategic orientation reflecting sustainable principles is more crucial to GINN's success than a strategic orientation that abhors green principles (Jo et al., 2014; Klassen & Vereecke, 2012). As GINN becomes an output of ESO (Jagani & Hong, 2022), business innovations are most likely to be guided by environmental sustainability when the existing strategic orientation of the firm supports the same (Papagiannakis et al., 2014). It is anticipated that businesses with ESO are more likely to improve their GINN outcomes than firms whose strategy orientation has lower support or preference for environmental sustainability (Chang, 2011). On this basis, we make the following hypothesis.

*H1*. ESO has a significant relationship with GINN.

### The Mediating Role of DC

Since Teece et al. (1997) presented the concept of DC, it has become one of the most discussed and researched areas in business strategy, marketing, and management (Jiang et al., 2019). Teece et al. (1997) described DC as a firm's ability to sense, build, and reconfigure its internal and external capabilities to respond to changing business needs. As Zhou et al. (2018) suggested, for businesses to function effectively in these changing times, they must have DCs. According to De Marchi (2012), since GINN is more complex and demanding than traditional innovations, merely adopting an ESO without introducing the right capability will not automatically translate into superior GINN. For instance, most GINNs are multifaceted, have various stakeholder perspectives, and demand a certain level of serious relationship and out and inside processes (Du et al., 2016; Halme & Korpela, 2014). Therefore, merely instigating a new strategic orientation may not be sufficient to induce the necessary impact across the various divisions of the organization (Juntunen et al., 2019).

Also, because of the complexity of ecological sustainability issues, enterprises seeking to implement this new strategic direction must build an effective relationship with a wide range of external actors (i.e., suppliers, customers, state agencies, and manufacturers) (Dangelico et al., 2017). However, the ability of an enterprise to build an effective relationship with these external actors will largely depend on its sensing capabilities (Buccieri et al., 2021). As ESO and GINN may have difficulties, a firm must create new knowledge and competencies and reconfigure its existing resources to address them (Dangelico et al., 2017). This will include developing/acquiring new resources by engaging new employees with specific environmental know-how, training team members, investing in environmental research and development (R&D), and reconfiguring existing resources by creating a new green division (Dangelico et al., 2017).

Again, the success of a firm's GINN outcomes will depend on how it effortlessly carries out its cross-disciplinary coordination and integration (Shrivastava, 1995). Integrating environmental principles into strategic decisions brings additional complexity to organizational processes (Hart, 1995), demanding that all functions (e.g., design, marketing, and R&D) are involved and integrated into the development of green products (Dangelico et al., 2017). Since this new environmental principle requires a new set of thinking and collaboration, failing to transform the existing resources and working arrangements to accommodate this new thinking will ultimately limit GINN outcomes. Such transformation is required because obtaining and exploiting external knowledge will be challenging without changing the existing resources to accommodate this new outside knowledge (Becker & Dietz, 2004). This suggests that by possessing the relevant dynamic capabilities, a firm can anticipate the environmental changes in their industry and respond by using that new insight to produce, extend, and modify their organizational resources (Helfat & Martin, 2015). This leads to the following hypotheses:

*H2.* DC mediates the relationship between ESO and GINN.

*H3.* DC has a significant positive relationship to GINN.

### The Mediating Role of EO

EO, which emerged from the strategic management literature (Child, 1972), comprises the firm-level strategies and practices that allow an enterprise to take full advantage of its market opportunities (Lumpkin & Dess, 1996). EO, therefore, depicts managerial techniques, methods, and decision-making styles that encompass a strategic posture to revitalize market offerings; take risks to try out new products, services, and markets; and become more proactive than competitors toward new spotted market opportunities (Wales et al., 2013). EO is a multifaceted construct depicted in proactiveness, innovativeness, and risk-taking. Generally, a firm with a high EO is most likely to be proactive, exhibit a higher tendency to look for opportunities, and consequently seize the opportunities spotted in the market (Cui et al., 2018; Moreno-Menéndez et al., 2022). Innovativeness reflects a firm's propensity to spearhead new ideas and experiments, resulting in the development of a new product or service (Lumpkin & Dess, 1996). Proactiveness is a forward-looking outlook to spot future needs and to leverage the market needs more swiftly (Zahra & Covin, 1995). Risk-taking is a propensity to channel substantial resources to ventures characterized by high uncertainty yet potentially resulting in a considerable outcome (Covin & Wales, 2012). As EO portrays a firm's propensity to be proactive and innovative and shows their high tendency to follow unfamiliar territory or try new things, a firm characterized with low EO is less likely to explore a risky venture such as GINN (Alshanty & Emeagwali, 2019). Accordingly, an enterprise EO can induce the capability of innovation activities via learning, the creation of new ideas, routines and practices, the flow of information, upgrading processes, and product design (Martín-de Castro et al., 2011).

Again, as a business owner's personality is best reflected in their organization EO (Rauch & Frese, 2007; Wiklund et al., 2009), it suggests that ESO will not certainly result in GINN. For instance, a business owner who regards GINN as capital-intensive and risky will not invest in such an uncertain enterprise (Alshanty & Emeagwali, 2019; Ferreira et al., 2020). However, this may not be true for a business owner whose personality reflects intense environmental care (Adomako et al., 2021). Papagiannakis et al. (2014) and Chen and Hsu (2013) came to a similar conclusion: they posit that business owners and managers with a strong attraction toward environmental sustainability tend to put more attention, time, or effort into developing GINNs. Therefore, we make the following hypotheses (Fig. 4.1):

*H4.* EO mediates the relationship between ESO and GINN.

*H5.* EO has a significant positive relationship to GINN.

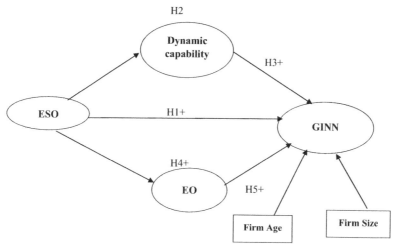

Fig. 4.1. Proposed Research Model.

## Methodology

### *Research Design and Sampling*

Ghana SMEs were chosen as the study context based on the following reasons. First, many developing countries have begun institutionalizing GINN among SMEs to encourage sustainable production and consumption (Adomako et al., 2021; Lindley et al., 2018). Such policies have been substantially boosted with the creation of the "Science, Technology, and Innovation Strategy for Africa 2024" (STISA-2024), spearheaded by the African Union. The strategic purpose of this policy is to encourage and support GINN among small African businesses (Lee & Butler, 2016). Though these policies and regulations can drive GINN, their implementation has overlooked the peculiar characteristics of SMEs, particularly those operating in highly non-formalized sectors like Ghana (Avenyo, 2018). As most Ghanaian SMEs are non-formalized and have limited access to finances, using Ghanaian SMEs as the study context provides a solid theoretical contribution to understanding how these attributes of developing economy SMEs influence their ESO and GINN outcomes (Arzubiaga et al., 2018; Mu et al., 2017). Second, as Ghanaian SMEs exhibit the same characteristics as their counterparts in sub-Saharan Africa (Aidoo et al., 2021), using Ghana SMEs as the study context will improve the generalization of the study results to SMEs operating in sub-Saharan Africa. Ghana is one of the first countries in the sub-Saharan to host the project, "Boosting Green Employment and Enterprise Opportunities in Ghana (GrEEn) Innovation Challenge." This is a four-year joint project of the European Union, the Embassy of the Kingdom of the Netherlands in Ghana, the United Nations Capital Development Fund (UNCDF), and SNV. This not-for-profit international organization seeks to promote a green and circular economy and encourage green product/service innovation among SMEs (Climateaction. africa, 2022). Accordingly, using Ghanaian SMEs as the study will provide additional perspective to the existing literature by responding to calls for assessing the impact of ESO, DC, and EO on SMEs' GINN outcomes (Alshanty & Emeagwali, 2019).

In this study, data were collected from SMEs located in the Greater Kumasi Metropolis and Western Region of Ghana because these regions were the primary beneficiaries of the GrEEn project. Only SMEs who have commenced or introduced a green product or services were targeted. Accordingly, SMEs that have not introduced GINN into the market were excluded from the study. According to the Association of Ghana Industries (2021), Kumasi and Takoradi are two major cities in Ghana with a significant share of SMEs spread in the areas of agro-processing (food and beverages), pharmaceuticals, mining, information technology, utilities, service industries, transport, construction, textiles, and garments and leather (Association of Ghana Industries, 2021).

Following the recommendations of earlier scholars, the owners and managers of the SMEs who have introduced or are about to introduce green products or services within the last year were first contacted to identify their readiness and preparedness to participate in the study (Murnieks et al., 2020). After this initial interaction, SMEs who showed enthusiasm and willingness to participate in the study formed the target population. Specifically, 460 SMEs fall within this category, making the final target population 460. However, out of this number, 60% (276) constituted SMEs within the Greater Kumasi Metropolis, and the remaining 40% (184) operated their business within the Western region. Since a convenience sampling technique has shown to be very effective in generating a higher response rate, especially in studies of this nature (Lee, 2013), a convenience sampling method was used. However, to determine the sample size needed to generate a relevant effect size, an a priori power analysis was performed to establish the suitable sample required to produce a medium effect size of 0.15, a power of 0.90, and an alpha value of 0.05 (Memon et al., 2020; Uttley, 2019). As the study model comprised six predictors, a sample size of 116 was needed to obtain the medium effect size of 0.15. This is way below our sampled firms, as our study received 352 valid questionnaires representing an effective response rate of 76.5%. On the profile of the surveyed SMEs, the majority of the respondents, 84.5%, performed as either a manager or owner. The mean age of the SMEs surveyed was 3.5 years. On the specific industries their operations fall within, 28.9% (102) operated as manufacturing entities, 27.5% (97) worked as service companies, 15.1% (53) were engaged in the business of exporting, and the remaining 28.4% (100) were involved in the business of importing.

### *Variables and Measures*

The measuring items were adapted from validated scales. Except for the firm's characteristics scale, all the other items were measured by a 7-point Likert scale

(1 = strongly disagree to 7 = strongly agree). Specifically, ESO was assessed by a three-dimensional scale comprising knowledge of the environment, environmental practices, and commitment to environmental sustainability (Roxas et al., 2017). Five items measured ecological knowledge, while sustainable practices were assessed with eight items. The last dimension under ESO, environmental sustainability, was measured by four items.

EO is operationalized as three constructs: innovativeness, proactiveness, innovation, and risk-taking, with three items each. A firm must adopt or use these three dimensions simultaneously before an entity can be seen to espouse the tenets of EO (Cui et al., 2018). The validated scale of Covin and Slevin (1989) was used to measure the SMEs' EO. All three dimensions of EO had eight items assessed by a 7-point Likert scale. With GINN, earlier studies have measured the construct either by the number of patents (Aldieri et al., 2019; Li et al., 2017), ISO14001 certification (Li et al., 2018), or survey items (Cai & Li, 2018). Following the studies of Chang (2011), De Marchi (2012), and Guo et al. (2020), survey items were used to measure the GINN construct. It comprised five items and was measured by a 7-point item scale (1 = strongly disagree to 7 = strongly agree).

Moreover, with DC, it is a first-order reflective construct (sensing, seizing, and reconfiguring) adapted from the studies of Mikalef and Pateli (2016), Protogerou et al. (2012), and Ilmudeen et al. (2021). It comprised 11 items in all and was measured by a 7-point scale. Finally, firm age and size were used as the control variables. Given that firm size could induce how an SME builds its DC (Drnevich & Kriauciunas, 2011), enterprise size was controlled using the natural logarithm of the total number of employees (Zhang et al., 2022). Likewise, an SME age, computed as the number of years since the firm was established, is anticipated to negatively affect SME DC because matured firms are subject to organizational inertia, which limits their desire to build their DC (Sapienza et al., 2006). Since these firm characteristics can affect the model's predictability, they were included to restrict the occurrence of alternative explanations (Huiying et al., 2016; Riquelme & Alqallaf, 2020).

## *Data Analysis*

The partial least squares–structural equation modeling (PLS-SEM) was first used to test the proposed model. PLS-SEM has been established to optimize the difference in the dependent variable rather than the factor-based approach used in covariance-based SEM (CB-SEM) (Hair et al., 2019). As the model is complex (i.e., characterized by more constructs and relationships), using PLS-SEM is very effective because of its ability to consider the entire model during the parameter's estimation simultaneously (Benitez et al., 2020; Hair et al., 2019). Again, as the study sample size is yet representative of SMEs in Ghana, PLS-SEM has proven to be more beneficial to a sample of such characteristics than other SEM-based approaches and is very robust in estimating latent variable scores explicitly (Hair et al., 2019). This study used the SMartPLS 3.0 application to assess the study model.

### Common Method Bias

Common method bias (CMB) becomes a fundamental issue in survey-based studies, especially when both endogenous and exogenous data are collected from the same respondent simultaneously (Krause et al., 2020; Podsakoff et al., 2012). Since CMB could improve the strength of the relationship among a measured construct because of the measurement procedure (Conway & Lance, 2010), stringent measures must be taken to minimize its occurrence. Admittedly, using a single respondent, especially in survey studies (Montabon et al., 2018), has been viewed to be challenging because of its increase in systematic error (Kaufmann & Saw, 2013). Nevertheless, unlike larger firms, many SMEs' business decisions are monadic and usually taken solely by the owner or manager with no participation of other members or parties. In such a case, using multiple sources of respondents in SMEs could limit a study from having an accurate picture of the issues at stake. Accordingly, using Type 1 design (i.e., single respondent for all items) has been deemed very suitable mainly when dealing with SMEs (Kull et al., 2018). Notwithstanding the recognition of the occurrence of this Type 1 design in SME survey studies, other procedural and statistical measures were utilized to minimize the incidence of CMB.

Particularly on the procedural method, the study used several approaches (i.e., ensuring respondents' anonymity, describing the study purpose to the respondent, and including a different measuring scale between the dependent and dependent variables) (Podsakoff et al., 2012). However, a widely recommended statistical method, the Harman single-factor test (Podsakoff et al., 2003), was used in the statistical procedure. In this procedure, the unrotated solution from the exploratory factor analysis (EFA) showed that the first factor explained 21.56% of the variance in the data, which is far below the recommended threshold of 50% (Malhotra et al., 2017). Subsequently, a more robust test for CMB in PLS-SEM was performed using the measured latent marker variable. In this study, the five-item scale of the social desirability scale of Crowne and Marlowe (1960) was adopted as the measured latent market variable (MLMV) since its inclusion in the survey has shown to be a very effective statistical procedure to spot and control CMB in PLS models (Chin et al., 2013). It formed part of the measuring items, and the respondents were asked to rate them with the main measuring items. Results from the model revealed that the addition of the MLMV did not result in any significant difference in the $R^2$ values for DC, EO, and GINN. Specifically, the $R^2$ value for DC, entrepreneur orientation, and GINN changed from 0.386 to 0.393, from 0.684 to 0.697, respectively, and that of GINN remained unchanged at 0.915. The $R^2$ change on these variables was far below the recommended threshold of 10% (Chin et al., 2013), confirming that CMB is not a significant issue in this study.

## Results

### Measurement and Model Assessment

The conventional measurement indicators, convergent, discriminant, and construct validity, were used to assess the model (Bandalos, 2018; Hair et al., 2019).

Average variance extract (AVE) and factor loadings were used to measure convergent validity (Bandalos, 2018; Fornell & Cha, 1994). Generally, an AVE value of 0.5 or higher has been suggested to give robust empirical support for convergent validity (Fornell & Larcker, 1981). Additionally, an indicator factor loading of 0.6 or higher has been acknowledged to be adequate, implying that more than 50% of the variation in a single indicator can be explained by the equivalent latent variable (Benitez et al., 2020). In this study, all the AVE scores were higher than the suggested threshold of 0.6, with the lowest AVE value being 0.785 (Table 4.1). Also, with the factor loadings, all items were above the recommended value range of 0.70 (Hair et al., 2019). Moreover, the Fornell–Larcker (Table 4.2) and heterotrait–monotrait (HTMT) (Table 4.3) ratio was used to establish empirical support for discriminant validity. HTMT has been recognized to be more robust than the often-favored convention procedures, Fornell–Lacrcker criterion and cross-loadings (Henseler et al., 2015). As reported in the literature, to obtain a stricter or more lenient threshold, HTMT should be lower than 0.85 or 0.95, respectively (Franke & Sarstedt, 2019). In this study, except for GINN, whose value was slightly higher than 0.90, all the other constructs HTMT were lower than 0.90, confirming that the HTMT values are within the stricter recommended threshold (see Table 4.3).

### *Analyzing the Structural Equation Model*

The standardized root mean square residual (SRMR) was used to determine the model's overall fit (Henseler et al., 2015). An SRMR value smaller than 0.080 suggests an acceptable model fit (Hu & Bentler, 1999). In this study, SRMR obtained a value of 0.062, indicating that the model is suitable for producing empirical evidence for the proposed theory (Hayduk, 2014). Next, we continued assessing the structural model (Fig. 4.2), the effect size, the coefficient of determination, variance inflation factor (VIF) and the predictive relevance of the model. Following the suggestions of Streukens and Leroi-Werelds (2016), 10,000 resamples (bootstrapping approach) were used to produce $t$-statistics to calculate the statistical significance of the various path coefficients. The result of the structural model assessment is presented in Table 4.4. The $R^2$ value of our model ranged from 0.385 to 0.915; per these values, it can be argued that our model's predictive power is significant. Also, the path coefficient estimates for our hypothesized relationships ranged from 0.091 to 0.827 and are all significant at a 5% level. Again, none of the control variables were statistically significant. The effect size of the study model ($f^2$) ranged from 0.052 to 1.572, signifying a weak to large effect size (Cohen, 1988). Again, on the predictive relevance of the model, the $Q^2$ were all greater than the required threshold of $>0$, confirming that the endogenous variables were all within the acceptable point.

### *Hypothesis Testing*

Table 4.5 presents the results of the study hypotheses. Results in Table 4.5 reveal that all the study hypotheses were statistically significant. Specifically, the relationship between ESO → GINN ($\beta = 0.840$), DC → GINN ($\beta = 0.142$), EO →

Table 4.1. Construct Indicators and Measures.

| Constructs | Alpha | Rho_A | AVE | CR | Factor Loading |
|---|---|---|---|---|---|
| **ESO** | **0.988** | **0.973** | **0.904** | **0.989** | |
| *Environmental knowledge* | | | | | |
| Knowledge about climate change | | | | | 0.953 |
| Waste management issues in the city | | | | | 0.956 |
| Issues about sources of drinking water | | | | | 0.952 |
| Issues concerning the source of electricity | | | | | 0.951 |
| *Sustainable practices* | | | | | |
| Practice recycling wastes | | | | | 0.969 |
| Water and electricity conservation | | | | | 0.949 |
| Training on environmental awareness | | | | | 0.933 |
| *Commitment to environmental sustainability* | | | | | |
| Environmental protection is part of the business | | | | | 0.933 |
| Practices are good for my business | | | | | 0.950 |
| Gain more customers | | | | | 0.967 |
| **EO** | **0.971** | **0.972** | **0.897** | **0.978** | |
| *Proactiveness* | | | | | |
| Relative to our competitors, we act in anticipation of future environmental market needs and wants | | | | | 0.931 |
| The organization has an intensive drive toward its environmental goals | | | | | 0.926 |
| We act in the recognition of clear environmental needs | | | | | |

| | | | | |
|---|---|---|---|---|
| *Innovativeness* | | | | |
| Relative to our competitors, we have the propensity to engage in and support new environmental ideas, experimentation, and creative processes | 0.965 | | | |
| Changes in this company's green products or service lines are quite high | 0.978 | | | |
| We encourage employees to think and behave in original and distinctive ways, particularly when it comes to environmental innovation | | | | |
| *Risk-taking* | | | | |
| We have a strong and aggressive attitude toward taking decisions to achieve our environmental goals | 0.936 | | | |
| Our company always invests in untested green products and technologies | | | | |
| **DC** | **0.968** | **0.973** | **0.886** | **0.975** |
| *Sensing* | | | | |
| Our company is up-to-date on the current environmental market situation | 0.939 | | | |
| In our organization, we systematically look for information on the current market situation | | | | |
| Our company always has an eye on our competitors' environmental activities | 0.938 | | | |
| *Seizing* | | | | |
| We identify what new environmental information can be used in our company | | | | |

*(Continued)*

Table 4.1. (*Continued*)

| Constructs | Alpha | Rho_A | AVE | CR | Factor Loading |
|---|---|---|---|---|---|
| Our company is capable of turning new environmental knowledge into process and product innovation | | | | | 0.919 |
| We recognize what new information can be utilized in our company | | | | | |
| Current environmental information leads to the development of new products or services | | | | | |
| *Reconfiguration* | | | | | 0.960 |
| Reconfiguring organizational structure to focus on environmental sustainability (e.g., creating a new division, and reconfiguring product lines) | | | | | |
| Reconfiguring product development teams to include environmental specialists | | | | | 0.950 |
| Reconfiguring relationships with suppliers (e.g., supplier environmental audit and changing suppliers) to reduce the environmental impact of products | | | | | |
| Training (e.g., through attendance at conferences, workshops, and courses) product development team members to upgrade their environmental knowledge and competencies | | | | | |
| *GINN* | 0.931 | 0.936 | 0.785 | 0.948 | |
| The final product uses recycled materials | | | | | 0.870 |
| Uses waste materials for new product development | | | | | 0.845 |
| The manufacturing process uses renewable energy sources | | | | | 0.915 |
| The final product is reusable | | | | | 0.883 |
| The manufacturing process has a competitive record on energy consumption (e.g., gas and electricity) | | | | | 0.916 |

Table 4.2.  Testing the Fornell–Larcker Criterion.

|      | **Fag** | **DC** | **EO** | **ESO** | **GINN** | **Sz** |
|------|---------|--------|--------|---------|----------|--------|
| **Fag** | 1.000 | | | | | |
| DC   | 0.131 | 0.941 | | | | |
| EO   | 0.008 | 0.647 | 0.947 | | | |
| ESO  | −0.046 | 0.621 | 0.827 | 0.951 | | |
| GINN | 0.032 | 0.685 | 0.942 | 0.861 | 0.886 | |
| Sz   | 0.014 | 0.065 | 0.094 | 0.100 | 0.085 | 1.000 |

Table 4.3.  Calculating the HTMT Ratio.

|      | **Fag** | **DC** | **EO** | **ESO** | **GINN** | **Sz** |
|------|---------|--------|--------|---------|----------|--------|
| Fag  | | | | | | |
| DC   | 0.134 | | | | | |
| EO   | 0.025 | 0.661 | | | | |
| ESO  | 0.048 | 0.630 | 0.841 | | | |
| GINN | 0.041 | 0.716 | 0.986 | 0.896 | | |
| Sz   | 0.014 | 0.066 | 0.095 | 0.100 | 0.088 | |

Table 4.4.  Coefficient of Determination and Predictive Relevance of PLS-SEM.

| Constructs | $R^2$ | Adjusted $R^2$ | $F^2$ | $Q^2$ | VIF |
|------------|-------|----------------|-------|-------|-----|
| DC   | 0.385 | 0.379 | 0.052 | 0.289 | 1.202 |
| EO   | 0.684 | 0.681 | 1.572 | 0.545 | 1.611 |
| GINN | 0.915 | 0.909 | 0.200 | 0.667 | 1.397 |

GINN ($\beta = 0.638$) were statistically significant at $p = 0.001$. This suggests that *H1*, *H3*, and *H5* are supported.

### Mediation Analysis

The indirect effect was studied to establish EO and DC's mediating role in the relationship between ESO and GINN. The procedure suggested by Cepeda et al. (2017) was followed when estimating the mediating effect of EO and DC in the relationship analysis. The indirect effect results in Table 4.6; ESO → DC → GINN was statistically significant ($\beta = 0.088$, $t = 2.632$, 95% confidence interval

Table 4.5.   Path Coefficients (Direct Effect).

| Structural Path | Coefficient ($\beta$) | Standard Deviation | t-Values | p Values | 95% BCa CI | Conclusion |
|---|---|---|---|---|---|---|
| Fag → GINN (control variable) | 0.026 | 0.044 | 0.595 | 0.552 | –0.051, 0.120 | |
| FSz → GINN (control variable) | –0.014 | 0.034 | 0.404 | 0.687 | –0.000, 0.186 | |
| EO → GINN | 0.638 | 0.071 | 8.984 | 0.000 | 0.469, 0.736 | *H5* supported |
| ESO → EO | 0.814 | 0.045 | 18.160 | 0.000 | 0.722, 0.891 | |
| ESO → DC | 0.622 | 0.062 | 10.078 | 0.000 | 0.504, 0.737 | |
| ESO → GINN | 0.840 | 0.033 | 25.283 | 0.000 | 0.773, 0.899 | *H1* supported |
| DC → GINN | 0.142 | 0.051 | 2.785 | 0.006 | 0.052, 0.243 | *H3* supported |

Table 4.6.   Relationship Between Variables (Indirect Effect).

| Structural Path | Coefficient ($\beta$) | SD | t-Statistics | p Values | 95% BCa CI | Conclusion |
|---|---|---|---|---|---|---|
| ESO → DC → GINN | 0.088 | 0.034 | 2.632 | 0.009 | 0.029, 0.164 | *H2* supported |
| ESO → EO→ GINN | 0.520 | 0.046 | 11.348 | 0.000 | 0.402, 0.587 | *H4* supported |

(CI) = 0.029–0.164). Also, the indirect effect of ESO → EO → GINN was statistically significant ($\beta$ = 0.520, $t$ = 11.348, 95% CI = 0.402–0.587) (see Table 4.6). The results suggest that EO and DC mediated the relationship between ESO and GINN, supporting *H2* and *H4*, respectively.

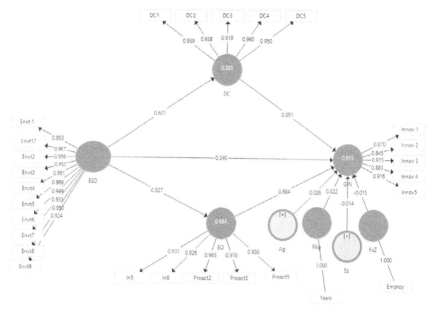

Fig. 4.2.   Evaluation of Measures and Structural Equation Model.

## Discussion

Earlier proponents of ESO identified it as the primary driver of GINN (Adams et al., 2016; Claudy et al., 2016; Fraj-Andrés et al., 2009). However, the ambivalent results in this area (Adams et al., 2016; Klewitz & Hansen, 2014) suggest that the expected relationship between ESO and GINN will rely on other important firm-level factors (Cheng, 2020; Du et al., 2016). Results from the study established that firm-level factors, particularly DC and EO, significantly mediated the relationship between ESO and GINN. Looking at the multifaceted nature of GINN, firms that have the right capability in place, especially sensing capability, can spot this new demand for ecological products on time via their sensing capability and subsequently use this new insight to reconfigure their existing resources to modify their product innovation to reflect the needs of the market (Wilhelm et al., 2016). Also, because ESO and GINN may be faced with some implementation challenges, a firm must create new knowledge and competencies which can allow the firm to anticipate the potential challenges likely to impede this new strategic direction (Dangelico et al., 2017). This will take the form of developing/acquiring new resources through engaging new employees with specific environmental know-how, training team members, and reconfiguring existing resources by creating a new green division (e.g., undertaking suppliers' ecological audits) (Dangelico et al., 2017). The study results suggest that an SME GINN performance lies in the suitable combination of resources and capabilities (Teece, 2007).

Additionally, as EO depicts a firm tendency to be proactive and innovative and shows a high tendency to follow unfamiliar territory or try new things, a firm characterized with high EO is most likely to explore a risky venture such as GINN (Alshanty & Emeagwali, 2019). Results from the study suggest that the right combinations of DC and EO become quintessential in strengthening the ESO and GINN relationship. The result implies that for SMEs to improve their GINN, they ought to have the suitable capabilities to sense, seize, learn, and reconfigure their internal and external resources and knowledge to support their new ESO (Wilhelm et al., 2015). Similarly, for SMEs to ensure that their ESO results in better GINN, they ought to have an EO that regards GINN as less risky and consequently have the zeal to follow unfamiliar territory or try new things (Alshanty & Emeagwali, 2019; Ferreira et al., 2020). Accordingly, as the personality of a business owner is best reflected in the firm's EO (Rauch & Frese, 2007; Wiklund et al., 2009), it suggests that a business owner or manager who attaches a high value or importance to the protection of the environment will put more attention, time, or effort into developing GINNs (Chen & Hsu 2013; Papagiannakis et al., 2014).

Second, there was a lack of clarity on how DC and EO collectively influence SMEs' GINN outcomes (Liu et al., 2017), as the effects were often investigated in isolation (Monferrer et al., 2021). However, by considering these antecedents in a single study, results from the survey have brought to bear the interactive effect DC and EO tend to have on the ESO and GINN relationship. Results from the study have demonstrated that ESO will result in GINN when the organization's DC can build creative combinations of knowledge and new distinctive resources to support new product development (Sheng, 2017). Similarly, ESO will result in GINN when the SME EO has a strong affinity to safeguard the environment and does not regard GINN as risky (Adomako et al., 2021; Alshanty & Emeagwali, 2019).

### *Implication for Practice*

In addition to the study's theoretical contributions, its result provides practical implications for how SMEs can enhance their GINN outcomes. Results from the study suggest that GINN is more complex and uncertain than conventional innovation (Spence et al., 2011). Accordingly, firms' GINN success will depend on establishing a new strategic orientation and value integration processes (Slevin & Terjesen, 2011), strongly supporting GINN (Xavier et al., 2017). Therefore, SMEs' GINN outcomes depend on the suitable combinations of resources and capabilities. For instance, firms without the necessary resources and capabilities may not be able to sense these market changes earlier, seize this opportunity, and consequently reconfigure their existing resources to support this innovation agenda.

Second, the demand for green products is frequently persuaded from an external source by either a new regulatory requirement, customer, and supplier request or market entry requirements. Therefore, firms that accept ESO cannot develop their innovations in seclusion but should consider these external issues in their strategy development (Claudy et al., 2016; Gimenez & Tachizawa, 2012). Accordingly, building a solid DC to improve a firm's sensing of these market changes and reconfiguring its internal and external will be critical to its GINN success.

*Limitations and Future Research*

Although the study result has brought several implications for theory and practice, it still has some limitations. First, because of the one-point data collection characteristics of the research design used (survey design), it is likely to restrict the study from making a more reliable causal inference about the relationship between ESO and GINN outcomes. Accordingly, to improve the strength of the causality between ESO and GINN, future studies should use longitudinal design, enabling the analysis to collect its data on several data points. Again, even though prior, and posterior actions were taken to limit CMB, we still acknowledge that collecting both endogenous and exogenous data from the same respondent at the same time may affect the study conclusion. Future studies could adopt a more robust way by collecting these data from different sources to improve the validity of the study conclusion.

## Conclusion

The study finds that SMEs in Ghana with dynamic capabilities to sense, seize, and reconfigure their resources, and where their business owners have an EO, are more prone to adapt and uphold their ESO and ensure GINN outcomes. Hence, the presence of dynamic capabilities interacts with managerial emphasis on environmental protection to enhance the development of GINN.

## References

Adams, R., Jeanrenaud, S., Bessant, J., Denyer, D., & Overy, P. (2016). Sustainability-oriented innovation: A systematic review. *International Journal of Management Reviews, 18*(2), 180–205.

Adomako, S., Amankwah-Amoah, J., Danso, A., & Dankwah, G. (2021). Chief executive officers' sustainability orientation and firm environmental performance: Networking and resource contingencies. *Business Strategy and the Environment, 30,* 2184–2193.

Aidoo, S., Agyapong, A., Acquaah, M., & Akomea, S. (2021). The performance implications of strategic responses of SMEs to the COVID-19 pandemic: Evidence from an African economy. *African Journal of Management, 7,* 74–103.

Aldieri, L., Carlucci, F., Cirà, A., Ioppolo, G., & Vinci, C. P. (2019). Is green innovation an opportunity or a threat to employment? An empirical analysis of three main industrialised areas: The USA, Japan and Europe. *Journal of Cleaner Production, 214,* 758–766.

Alshanty, A., & Emeagwali, O. (2019). Market-sensing capability, knowledge creation and innovation: The moderating role of entrepreneurial-orientation. *Journal of Innovation & Knowledge, 4,* 171–178.

Arora, A., Arora, A., Sivakumar, K., & Burke, G. (2020). Strategic sustainable purchasing, environmental collaboration, and organisational sustainability performance: The moderating role of supply base size. *Supply Chain Management, 25,* 709–728.

Arzubiaga, U., Kotlar, J., De Massis, A., Maseda, A., & Iturralde, T. (2018). Entrepreneurial orientation and innovation in family SMEs: Unveiling the (actual) impact of the board of directors. *Journal of Business Venturing, 33,* 455–469.

Association of Ghana Industries. (2021). https://www.agighana.org/barometer.php

Avenyo, E. (2018). *Informal sector innovation in Ghana: Data set and descriptive analysis* (p. 30). Maastricht Economic and Social Research Institute on Innovation and Technology (UNU-MERIT).

Bandalos, D. L. (2018). *Measurement theory and applications for the social sciences.* Guilford Press.

Becker, W., & Dietz, J. (2004). R&D cooperation and innovation activities of firms – Evidence for the German manufacturing industry. *Research Policy, 33,* 209–223.

Benitez, J., Henseler, J., Castillo, A., & Schuberth, F. (2020). How to perform and report an impactful analysis using partial least squares: Guidelines for confirmatory and explanatory IS research. *Information & Management, 57,* 1–15.

Brockhaus, S., Petersen, M., & Knemeyer, A. (2019). The fallacy of "trickle-down" product sustainability: Translating strategic sustainability targets into product development effort. *International Journal of Operations & Product Management, 39,* 1166–1190.

Buccieri, D., Javalgi, R. G., & Jancenelle, V. E. (2021). Dynamic capabilities and performance of emerging market international new ventures: Does international entrepreneurial culture matter? *International Small Business Journal, 39*(5), 474–499.

Cai, W., & Li, G. (2018). The drivers of eco-innovation and its impact on performance: Evidence from China. *Journal of Cleaner Production, 176,* 110–118.

Cepeda, G., Nitzl, C., & Roldán, J. L. (2017). Mediation analyses in partial least squares structural equation modeling: Guidelines and empirical examples. *Partial least squares path modeling: Basic concepts, methodological issues and applications* (pp. 173–195) Springer International.

Chang, C. (2011). The influence of corporate environmental ethics on competitive advantage: The mediation role of green innovation. *Journal of Business Ethics, 104*(3), 361–370.

Chen, H. L., & Hsu, C. H. (2013). Entrepreneurial orientation and firm performance in non-profit service organizations: contingent effect of market orientation. *The Service Industries Journal, 33*(5), 445–466.

Cheng, C. (2020). Sustainability orientation, green supplier involvement, and green innovation performance: Evidence from diversifying green entrants. *Journal of Business Ethics, 161*(2), 393–414.

Child, J. (1972). Organisation structure and strategies of control: A replication of the Aston study. *Administrative Science Quarterly, 17*(2), 163–177.

Chin, W., Thatcher, J., Wright, R., & Steel, D. (2013). Controlling for common method variance in PLS analysis: The measured latent marker variable approach. In H. Abdi, W. W. Chin, V. E. Vinzi, G. Russolillo, & L. Trinchera (Eds.), *New perspectives in partial least squares and related methods* (pp. 231–239). Springer.

Claudy, M., Peterson, M., & Pagell, M. (2016). The roles of sustainability orientation and market knowledge competence in new product development success. *Journal of Product Innovation Management, 33*(S1), 72–85.

Climateaction.africa. (2022). 2021 GrEEn Innovation Challenge for Ghana-based SMEs. https://climateaction.africa/green-innovation-challenge-for-ghana-based-smes/

Cohen, J. (1988). *Statistical power analysis for behavioral sciences* (2nd ed.). Erlbaum.

Covin, J., & Slevin, D. (1989). Strategic management of small firms in Hostile and benign environments. *Strategic Management Journal, 10*(1), 75–87.

Covin, J., & Wales, W. (2012). The measurement of entrepreneurial orientation. *Entrepreneurship Theory and Practice, 36*(4), 677–702.

Crowne, D. P., & Marlowe, D. (1960). Marlowe-Crowne Social Desirability Scale (M-C SDS) [Database record]. APA PsycTests. *Journal of Consulting Psychology, 24,* 349–354. https://doi.org/10.1037/t05257-000

Cui, L., Fan, D., Guo, F., & Fan, Y. (2018). Explicating the relationship of entrepreneurial orientation and firm performance: Underlying mechanisms in the context of an emerging market. *Industrial Marketing Management, 71,* 27–40.

Dangelico, R., Pujari, D., & Pontrandolfo, P. (2017). Green product innovation in manufacturing firms: A sustainability-oriented dynamic capability perspective. *Business Strategy and the Environment, 26*(4), 490–506.

De Marchi, V. (2012). Environmental innovation and R&D cooperation: Empirical evidence from Spanish manufacturing firms. *Research Policy, 41,* 614–623.

Drnevich, P., & Kriauciunas, A. P. (2011). Clarifying the conditions and limits of the contributions of ordinary and dynamic capabilities to relative firm performance. *Strategic Management Journal, 32*(3), 254–279.

Du, S., Yalcinkaya, G., & Bstieler, L. (2016). Sustainability, social media-driven open innovation, and new product development performance. *Journal of Product Innovation Management, 33*(S1), 55–71.

Eisenhardt, K., & Martin, J. (2000). Dynamic capabilities: What are they? *Strategic Management Journal, 21*(10–11), 1105–1121.

Enquist, B., Petros Sebhatu, S., & Johnson, M. (2015). Transcendence for business logic in value networks for sustainable service business. *Journal of Service Theory and Practice, 25*(2), 181–197.

Ferreira, J., Coelho, A., & Moutinho, L. (2020). Dynamic capabilities, creativity and innovation capability and their impact on competitive advantage and firm performance: The moderating role of entrepreneurial orientation. *Technovation, 92–93*, 1–18.

Fornell, C. and Cha, J. (1994) Partial Least Squares. *Advanced Methods of Marketing Research, 407*, 52–78.

Fornell, C., & Larcker, D. (1981). Evaluating structural equation models with unobservable variables and measurement error. *Journal of Marketing Research, 18(1)*, 39–50.

Fraj-Andrés, E., Martinez-Salinas, E., & Matute-Vallejo, J. (2009). A multidimensional approach to the influence of environmental marketing and orientation on the firm's organisational performance. *Journal of Business Ethics, 88*(2), 263–286.

Franke, G., & Sarstedt, M. (2019). Heuristics versus statistics in discriminant validity testing: A comparison of four procedures. *Internet Research, 29*(3), 430–447.

Genc, E., & Benedetto, C. A. D. (2019). A comparison of proactive and reactive environmental strategies in green product innovation. *International Journal of Innovation and Sustainable Development, 13*(3–4), 431–451.

Gimenez, C., & Tachizawa, E. (2012). Extending sustainability to suppliers: A systematic literature review. *Supply Chain Management: An International Journal, 17*(5), 531–543.

Govindan, K., Rajeev, A., Padhi, S., & Pati, R. (2020). Supply chain sustainability and performance of firms: A meta-analysis of the literature. *Transportation Research Part E: Logistics and Transportation Review, 137*, 101923. https://doi.org/10.1016/J.TRE.2020.101923

Guo, Y., & Wang, L. (2022). Environmental entrepreneurial orientation and firm performance: The role of environmental innovation and stakeholder pressure. *SAGE Open, January-March*, 1–13.

Guo, Y., Wang, L., & Yang, Q. (2020). Do corporate environmental ethics influence firms' green practices? The mediating role of green innovation and the moderating role of personal ties. *Journal of Cleaner Production, 266*, 122054.

Hair, J., Risher, J., Sarstedt, M., & Ringle, C. (2019). When to use and how to report the results of PLS-SEM. *European Business Review, 31*(1), 2–24.

Halme, M., & Korpela, M. (2014). Responsible innovation toward sustainable development in small and medium-sized enterprises: A resource perspective: Resources behind responsible innovation in SMEs. *Business Strategy and the Environment, 23*(8), 547–66.

Hart, S. (1995). A natural-resource-based view of the firm. *Academy of Management Review, 20*, 986–1014.

Hayduk, L. (2014). Shame for disrespecting evidence: The personal consequences of insufficient respect for structural equation model testing. *BMC Medical Research Methodology, 14*(124), 1–10.

Helfat, C. E., & Winter, S. G. (2011). Untangling dynamic and operational capabilities: Strategy for the (N) ever‐changing world. *Strategic management journal, 32*(11), 1243–1250.

Helfat, C. E., & Martin, J. A. (2015). Dynamic managerial capabilities: Review and assessment of managerial impact on strategic change. *Journal of Management, 41*(5), 1281–1312.

Henseler, J., Ringle, C., & Sarstedt, M. (2015). A new criterion for assessing discriminant validity in variance-based structural equation modeling. *Journal of the Academy of Marketing Science*, *43*, 115–135.

Hong, P., Jagani, S., Kim, J., & Youn, S. (2019). Managing sustainability orientation: An empirical investigation of manufacturing firms. *International Journal of Production Economics*, *211*, 71–81.

Hu, L., & Bentler, P. (1999). Cutoff criteria for fit indexes in covariance structure analysis: Conventional criteria versus new alternatives. *Structural Equation Modeling: A Multidisciplinary Journal*, *6*(1), 1–55.

Huiying, M., Xiangyang, Z., & Haitao, W. (2016). A novel dual-channel matching method based on time reversal and its performance for sound source localization in enclosed space. *Acoustics Australia*, *44*, 417–428.

Ilmudeen, A., Bao, Y., Alharbi, I., & Zubair, N. (2021). Revisiting dynamic capability for organisations' innovation types: Does it matter for organisational performance in China? *European Journal of Innovation Management*, *24*(2), 507–532.

Jagani, S., & Hong, P. (2022). Sustainability orientation, by product management and business performance: An empirical investigation. *Journal of Cleaner Production*, *357*(131707), 1–11.

Jiang, W., Mavondo, M., & Zhao, W. (2019). The impact of business networks on dynamic capabilities and product innovation: The moderating role of strategic orientation. *Asia Pacific Journal of Management*, *37*(4), 1239–1266.

Jo, H., Kim, H., & Park, K. (2014). Corporate environmental responsibility and firm performance in the financial services sector. *Journal of Business Ethics*, *131*, 257–284.

Juntunen, J., Halme, M., Korsunova, A., & Rajala, R. (2019). Strategies for integrating stakeholders into sustainability innovation: A configurational perspective. *Journal of Product Innovation Management*, *36*(3), 331–355.

Kaufmann, L. & Saw, A. (2014). Using a multiple-informant approach in SCM research. *International Journal of Physical Distribution & Logistics Management*, *44*(6), 511–527

Kull, T. J., Kotlar, J., & Spring, M. (2018). Small and medium enterprise research in supply chain management: The case for single respondent research designs. *Journal of Supply Chain Management*, *54*(1), 23–34.

Khan, P., Johl, S., & Johl, S. K. (2021). Does the adoption of ISO 56002-2019 and green innovation reporting enhance the firm sustainable development goal performance? An emerging paradigm. *Business Strategy and the Environment*, *30*, 2922–2936.

Klassen, R., & Vereecke, A. (2012). Social issues in supply chains: Capabilities link responsibility, risk (opportunity), and performance. *International Journal of Production Economics*, *140*, 103–115.

Klewitz, J., & Hansen, E. (2014). Sustainability-oriented innovation of SMEs: A systematic review. *Journal of Cleaner Production*, *65*, 57–75.

Krause, N., Freiling, I., Beets, B., & Brossard, D. (2020). Fact-checking as risk communication: The multi-layered risk of misinformation in times of COVID-19. *Journal of Risk Research*, *23*(7–8), 1052–1059.

Lee, J., & Butler, A. (2016). *The impact of entrepreneurs' characteristics on the performance of venture businesses.* Martin School of Public Policy and Administration Graduate Capstone. Retrieved May 22, 2022, from https://uknowledge.uky.edu/mpampp_etds/301/

Lee, K., & Yoo, J. (2019). How does open innovation lead to competitive advantage? A dynamic capability view perspective. *PLoS One*, *14*(11), 1–18.

Lee, K., Yoo, J., Choi, M., Zo, H., & Ciganek, A. P. (2016). Does external knowledge sourcing enhance market performance? Evidence from the Korean manufacturing industry. *PLoS One*, *11*(12), 1–17.

Li, D., Huang, M., Ren, S., Chen, X., & Ning, L. (2018). Environmental legitimacy, green innovation, and corporate carbon disclosure: Evidence from CDP China 100. *Journal of Business Ethics, 150*(4), 1089–1104.

Li, D., Zheng, M., Cao, C., Chen, X., Ren, S., & Huang, M. (2017). The impact of legitimacy pressure and corporate profitability on green innovation: Evidence from China's top 100. *Journal of Cleaner Production, 141*, 41–49.

Lindley, S., Pauleit, S., Yeshitela, K., Cilliers, S., & Shackleton, C. (2018). Rethinking urban green infrastructure and ecosystem services from the perspective of sub-Saharan African cities. *Landscape and Urban Planning, 180*, 328–338.

Liu, X., Shen, M., Ding, W., & Zhao, X. (2017). Tie strength, absorptive capacity and innovation performance in Chinese manufacturing industries. *Nankai Business Review International, 8*(4), 475–494.

Lumpkin, G. T., & Dess, G. G. (1996). Clarifying the entrepreneurial orientation construct and linking it to performance. *Academy of Management Review, 21*, 135–172.

Malhotra, G., Leslie, D., Ludwig, C., & Rafal, B. (2017). Overcoming indecision by changing the decision boundary. *Journal of Experimental Psychology, 146*(6), 776–805.

Martín-de Castro, G., López-Sáez, P., & Delgado-Verde, M. (2011). Linking organisational learning with technical innovation and organisational culture. *Journal of Knowledge Management, 15*, 997–1015.

Memon, M., Ting, H., Cheah, J., Thurasamy, R., Chuah, F., & Cham, T. (2020). Sample Size for Survey Research: Review and Recommendations. *Journal of Applied Structural Equation Modeling, 4(2)*, 1–10.

Mikalef, P., & Pateli. (2016). *Developing and validating a measurement instrument of it-enabled dynamic capabilities: Serving society in the advancement of knowledge and excellence in the study and profession of information systems.* Research Paper 39. Association for Information Systems.

Monferrer, D., Moliner, M. A., Irún, B., & Estrada, M. (2021). Network market and entrepreneurial orientations as facilitators of international performance in born globals: The mediating role of ambidextrous dynamic capabilities. *Journal of Business Research, 137*, 430–443.

Montabon, F., Daugherty, P. J., & Chen, H. (2018). Setting standards for single respondent survey design. *Journal of Supply Chain Management, 54*(1), 35–41.

Moreno-Menéndez, A. M., Arzubiaga, U., Díaz-Moriana, V., & Casillas, J. C. (2022). The impact of a crisis on entrepreneurial orientation of family firms: The role of organisational decline and generational change. *International Small Business Journal, 40*(4), 425–452.

Mu, J., Thomas, E., Peng, G., & Di Benedetto, A. (2017). Strategic orientation and new product development performance: The role of networking capability and networking ability. *Industrial Marketing Management, 64*, 187–201.

Murnieks, C., Klotz, A. C., & Shepherd, D. A. (2020). Entrepreneurial motivation: A review of the literature and an agenda for future research. *Journal of Organizational Behavior, 41*(2), 115–143.

Papagiannakis, G., Voudouris, I., & Lioukas, S. (2014). The road to sustainability: Exploring the process of corporate environmental strategy over time. *Business, Strategy and the Environment, 23*(4), 254–271.

Pavlou, P., & Sawy, O. (2011). Understanding the elusive black box of dynamic capabilities. *Decision Sciences, 42*(1), 239–273.

Podsakoff, P., MacKenzie, S. B., Lee, J.-Y., & Podsakoff, N. P. (2003). Common method biases in behavioural research: A critical review of the literature and recommended remedies. *Journal of Applied Psychology, 88*(5)*, 879–903.

Podsakoff, P., MacKenzie, S. B., & Podsakoff, N. P. (2012). Sources of method bias in social science research and recommendations on how to control it. *Annual Review of Psychology, 63*, 539–569.

Porter, M., & Kramer, M. (2011). The big idea: Creating shared value. *Harvard Business Review, 89*(1/2), 62–77.

Protogerou, A., Caloghirou, Y., & Lioukas, S. (2012). Dynamic capabilities and their indirect impact on firm performance. *Industrial and Corporate Change, 21*(3), 615–647.

Rauch, A., & Frese, M. (2007). Let's put the person back into entrepreneurship research: A meta-analysis of the relationship between business owners' personality traits, business creation, and success. *European Journal of Work and Organizational Psychology, 16*, 353–385.

Riquelme, H., & Alqallaf, A. (2020). Anticipated emotions and their effects on risk and opportunity evaluations. *Journal of International Entrepreneurship, 18*(3), 312–335.

Roxas, B., Ashill, N., & Chadee, D. (2017). Effects of entrepreneurial and environmental sustainability orientations on firm performance: A study of small businesses in the Philippines. *Journal of Small Business Management, 55*, 163–178.

Roxas, B., & Coetzer, A. (2012). Institutional environment, managerial attitudes and environmental sustainability orientation of small firms. *Journal of Business Ethics, 111*, 461–476.

Sapienza, H., Autio, E., George, G., & Zahra, S. A. (2006). A capabilities perspective on the effects of early internationalisation on firm survival and growth. *Academy of Management Review, 31*(4), 914–933.

Sarwar, Z., Asif Khan, M., Yang, Z., Khan, A., Haseeb, M., & Sarwar, A. (2021). An investigation of entrepreneurial SMEs' network capability and social capital to accomplish innovativeness: A dynamic capability perspective. *SAGE Open*, July–September, 1–14.

Scuotto, V., Alexeis, G., Valentina, C., & Elisa, G. (2020). Do stakeholder capabilities promote sustainable business innovation in small and medium-sized enterprises? Evidence from Italy. *Journal of Business Research, 119*, 131–141.

Sheng, M. (2017). A dynamic capabilities-based framework of organisational sensemaking through combinative capabilities towards exploratory and exploitative product innovation in turbulent environments. *Industrial Marketing Management, 65*(2), 28–38.

Shrivastava, P. (1995). Environmental technologies and competitive advantage. *Strategic Management Journal, 16*, 183–200.

Slevin, D. P., & Terjesen, S. A. (2011). Entrepreneurial orientation: Reviewing three papers and implications for further theoretical and methodological development. *Entrepreneurship Theory and Practice, 35*, 973–987.

Spence, M., Gherib, J., & Biwolé, V. (2011). Sustainable entrepreneurship: Is entrepreneurial will enough? A north–south comparison. *Journal of Business Ethics, 99*, 335–367.

Streukens, S., & Leroi-Werelds, S. (2016). Bootstrapping and PLS-SEM: A step-by-step guide to getting more out of your bootstrap results. *European Management Journal, 34*, 618–632.

Teece, D. J., Pisano, G., & Shuen, A. (1997). Dynamic capabilities and strategic management. *Strategic management journal, 18*(7), 509–533.

Teece, D. (2007). Explicating dynamic capabilities: The nature and micro-foundations of (sustainable) enterprise performance. *Strategic Management Journal, 28*, 1319–1350.

Tuan, L. T. (2022). Fostering green product innovation through green entrepreneurial orientation: The roles of employee green creativity, green role identity, and organisational transactive memory system. *Business Strategy and the Environment, 32*(1), 639–653.

United Nations Environment Programme. (2015). *UNEP 2014 annual report*. Retrieved July 10, 2016, from http://www.unep.org/annualreport/2015/en/index.html

Uttley, J. (2019). Power Analysis, Sample Size, and Assessment of Statistical Assumptions—Improving the Evidential Value of Lighting Research. *LEUKOS, 15*(2-3), 143–162, DOI: 10.1080/15502724.2018.1533851

Varadarajan, R. (2017). Innovating for sustainability: A framework for sustainable innovations and a model of sustainable innovations orientation. *Journal of the Academy of Marketing Science, 45*(1), 14–36.

Wales, W., Gupta, V., & Mousa, F. (2013). Empirical research on entrepreneurial orientation: An assessment and suggestions for future research. *International Small Business Journal, 31*(4), 357–383.

Wiklund, J., Patzelt, H., & Shepherd, D. (2009). Building an integrative model of small business growth. *Small Business Economics, 32*, 351–374.

Wilhelm, H., Schlomer, M., & Maurer, I. (2015). How dynamic capabilities affect the effectiveness and efficiency of operating routines under high and low levels of environmental dynamism. *British Journal of Management, 26*(2), 327–345.

Wilhelm, M., Blome, C., Bhakoo, V., & Paulraj, A. (2016). Sustainability in multi-tier supply chains: Understanding the double agency role of the first-tier supplier. *Journal of Operations Management, 41*, 42–60.

Xavier, A., Naveiro, R., Aoussat, A., & Reyes, T. (2017). Systematic literature review of eco-innovation models: Opportunities and recommendations for future research. *Journal of Cleaner Production, 149*, 1278–1302.

Zahra, S. A., & Covin, J. G. (1995). Contextual influences on the corporate entrepreneurship-performance relationship: A longitudinal analysis. *Journal of business venturing, 10*(1), 43–58.

Zhang, X., Xie, L., Jiatao Li, J., & Cheng, L. (2022). Outside in: Global demand heterogeneity and dynamic capabilities of multinational enterprises. *Journal of International Business Studies, 53*, 709–722.

Zhao, Y., Feng, T., & Shi, H. (2018). External involvement and green product innovation: The moderating role of environmental uncertainty. *Business Strategy and the Environment, 27*(8), 1167–1180.

Zhou, Y., Hong, J., Zhu, K., Yang, Y., & Zhao D. (2018). Dynamic capability matters: Uncovering its fundamental role in decision-making of environmental innovation. *Journal of Cleaner Production, 177*, 516–526.

Chapter 5

# Supporting Green Business Growth: Towards a Transformative Approach[*]

*Polina Baranova*

*University of Derby, UK*

## Abstract

The study analyzes a survey of 372 businesses operating in the East Midlands and reveals the trends of engagement with green growth, demand for green skills development and pro-environmental business support. The findings confirm major differences in how large and small businesses engage with green growth and the challenges they face. Sectorial characteristics are of significance in growth trends and confirm manufacturing companies derive more turnover from the green products when compared to services. Manufacturing companies are also more proactive than services in integrating the green growth ambitions with the business strategy. Green skills and information gaps are major obstacles to business engagement with green growth. Business support agencies are urged to broaden the scope and availability of the pro-environmental enterprise support. Policy community is advised to develop support mechanisms that reduce skills and information gaps. A *transformative approach* to enterprise support is advocated in order to catalyze the contribution of the business community to sustainable regional development.

*Keywords*: Business strategy; business support; policy; green skills; transformation; regional development

---

[*]This chapter presents the study undertaken by the University of Derby and East Midlands Chamber as part of a long-standing strategic and collaborative initiative to gather the evidence-based data on green growth trends in the East Midlands since 2015.

---

**Sustainable and Resilient Global Practices:**
**Advances in Responsiveness and Adaptation, 81–98**
Copyright © 2024 by Polina Baranova
**Published under exclusive licence by Emerald Publishing Limited**
**doi:10.1108/978-1-83797-611-920241005**

## Introduction

Green growth is seen as an alternative to the conventional view of the economic growth and means "fostering economic growth and development while ensuring that natural assets continue to provide the resources and environmental services on which our well-being relies" (OECD, 2011). According to the World Bank, "green growth is growth that is efficient in its use of natural resources, clean in that it minimizes pollution and environmental impacts, and resilient in that it accounts for natural hazards" (World Bank, 2012, p. 2).

The academic literature on green growth is gaining the momentum with scholars paying attention to the green growth trends (Bassetti et al., 2021) and indicators (Alrasheedi et al., 2021), technology and innovation for green growth (Fernandes et al., 2021). There are advances to understand policy and support for green growth (De Angelis et al., 2019) and contribution toward sustainable development (Gupta & Vegelin, 2016). Despite these advances, the studies of green growth are rare due to a lack of empirical data on how firms of different sizes and sectoral characteristics engage with green growth. As part of this picture, there are gaps in understanding of how businesses respond to policy and business support mechanisms targeting pro-environmental businesses.

This is not surprising as the configuration of enterprise support either through local enterprise partnership (LEP) mechanisms, for example, growth hubs, or through various national and European Union (EU)-funded programmers paid little attention to provision of support programs where contribution to the economic growth and care for the natural environmental are balanced. There is a distinct lack of support programs for businesses operating in the emerging pro-environmental market niches and with a focus on stimulating supply of green goods and service (GGS). At the same time, business support programs aimed at strengthening business engagement with green growth require a re-imagining of enterprise support ethos.

This study aims to address these gaps by addressing the following research questions: *What is the level of business engagement with green growth? What are the engagement strategies used across the regional businesses? And what are the characteristics for business support toward green growth?* This chapter proceeds with a review of the literature on green growth, pro-environmental business support and environmental sustainability policy agenda. It moves onto outlining the study design and methods followed by the analytical developments and discussions. This chapter culminates in identifying characteristics of business support toward green growth. Further, this chapter concludes with the recommendations for theory and practice.

## Green Growth – Scope, Direction and Challenges

Literature on green growth is emerging with the main scholarly debates centered on the nature of the green growth (Dinda, 2014; Stoknes & Rockström, 2018), indicators (Reilly, 2012) and policy (Bowen & Hepburn, 2014; Rodrik,

2014). Many authors agree with a view of green growth where economic growth is achievable at the same time as the reduction of the ecological footprint. This so-called decoupling effect started to emerge already as reported in the *Economist* article stating that "over the past decade a growing number of countries – 33, home to over 1 billion people – have managed to increase their GDP while reducing their emissions" (*Economist*, 2022). The article claims two reasons for the decoupling trend. One is the changing structure of economies; as countries became richer, they expanded their service sectors, which use less energy than manufacturing. Second, imports are getting greener due to regulatory and market pressures to green global supply chains. The reported decoupling is a positive trend which needs to be sustained in times of energy crisis, political instability and weakening of major economies.

The United Nations Environmental Program (UNEP) defines a green economy as one that leads to "improved human well-being and social equity, while significantly reducing environmental risks and ecological scarcities." UNEP outlines the characteristics of a green economy as "low carbon, resource-efficient, and socially inclusive." UNEP states that "In a green economy, growth in income and employment should be driven by public and private investments that reduce carbon emissions and pollution, enhance energy and resource efficiency, and prevent the loss of biodiversity and ecosystem services" (UNEP, 2022). Such growth would surely require a careful balance between policy–practice interface which is focused on developing effective instruments to stimulate public, business and societal engagement with inclusive and sustained green growth.

There is an emerging literature associating green growth with transformation and change. In fact, the terminology of *green transformation* started to appear in the academic literature (Amundsen & Hermansen, 2021) which evolved around the concept of transformation in the context of the climate change (O'Brien, 2012; Pelling et al., 2015). Scholars argue that the approach to addressing the climate change challenges has to be transformative and is likely to meet challenges of governance and policy (Patterson et al., 2017).

When it comes to linking transformation and sustainable economic growth, there is an emergent discourse of *greener growth* (Amundsen & Hermansen, 2021) which is linked to Dryzek's discourse of sustainability (Dryzek, 2013). In this view, economic growth is seen as a positive, productive force which needs to be sustained but adequately regulated to avoid, prevent and deal with negative environmental externalities, while simultaneously maximizing economic profits. This view supports what is termed as *shallow* transformation where business-as-usual is incrementally modified incorporating new solutions and practices contributing to the ecological footprint reduction.

Alongside the opportunities presented by the green growth, there are challenges around politics of green transformations (Scoones et al., 2015), path dependencies and preservation of business-as-usual while communicating green growth aspirations (Karlsson & Hovelsrud, 2021), a need for interactive policy-engaged research (Læssøe et al., 2013) and technological and resource challenges of green innovation (Song et al., 2019). In business context, firms experience difficulties in accessing green funding and finance (Baranova et al., 2022); they lack green skills and competences to innovate and change toward sustainable business models (IEMA-Deloitte, 2022) and find engagement with multi-stakeholder dialogue toward finding sustainable solutions problematic (Gray & Purdy, 2018).

The theoretical and empirical literature outlines the challenges of engagement with green growth which can be grouped by the topics presented in Table 5.1.

Despite a number of challenges emerging from the literature, there is a lack of contextual insights into green growth practices. Moreover, considerations about business support toward green growth are lacking theoretical and empirical developments and are often omitted from the mainstream literature. Provided small businesses are the dominant organizational form around the world, effective pro-environmental enterprise support is critical to building capabilities toward green growth.

Table 5.1.   Challenges of Engagement with Green Growth.

| Topic | Challenge |
| --- | --- |
| Low-carbon infrastructure | Lack of infrastructure to support sustainability transition including the achievement of the net zero targets by 2030 |
| Green skills | Lack of green skills to support business engagement with green growth |
| Green jobs | Although increasing at pace, green jobs are still more prevalent in large rather than small businesses and in manufacturing sectors rather than services |
| Green funding and financing | Rapidly growing over the last few years, there is now a wide range of financial products available. However, poor referral networks, a lack of specialist advisers, signposting and accessible information are the main barriers to the uptake of green finance |
| Innovation in green products and service | Insufficient support for innovation at regional and national levels. Lack of technological advancements in materials, processes and operational models to deliver levels of innovation required |
| Low-carbon technologies | Insufficient support and funding of the low-carbon technologies |
| Supply chain constraints | Lack of or undeveloped supply chains to deliver green products and services. |
| Policy–practice gap | Confusing policy landscape with multiple targets, timescales and priority areas that are not synchronized |

## Business Support Toward Green Growth: A Fragmented Landscape

Despite a significant role played by small- and medium-sized enterprises (SMEs) in national and global economies, they are "disproportionately affected by market failures, and barriers and inefficiencies in the business environment and policy sphere" (OECD, 2017, p. 5). Academic literature acknowledges a range of common SME problems associated with access to finance, staff skills and other resources and identifying new commercial and technological opportunities (Mason & Brown, 2013). They often hinder SMEs progress toward realizing their full potential (Cravo & Piza, 2019) and are linked to SMEs failure (Williams, 2014). Government policies and programs with a remit of supporting businesses to overcome resource shortages and to build SMEs competitive potential toward fulfilling their economic role are being recognized as important institutional interventions (O'Neill & Viljoen, 2001; Ribeiro-Soriano & Galindo-Martın, 2012).

The importance of seeking external business assistance has been extensively considered in the mainstream small business literature. Bennett and Robson (2003) report the importance of external assistance in obtaining strategic knowledge and overcoming knowledge gaps for SMEs. Provided that external advice is contextual and evidence based, it has a higher chance of supporting the firm's competitive advantage (Chrisman & McMullan, 2004). Several studies report a positive relationship between external advice and firm's performance (Bennett & Robson, 2003; Berry et al., 2006), but this trend is not for any form of advice. The studies find that external advice on business strategy and staff recruitment is associated with higher performance.

A range of typologies attempting to explore the nature of business support is growing. The enterprise support literature articulates well the distinction between formal assistance, delivered through private sector consultants, professional organizations and business support programs and informal assistance delivered in an informal setting such as family, friends and business associations (McDonald & Westphal, 2003; Rigby & Hayden, 2013). Another evident distinction in the literature is between generic business advice, for example, about funding streams and tax reliefs, and more context-dependent support involving bespoke support packages tailored to the needs of individual SMEs (Chrisman & McMullan, 2004).

The *transactional* versus *transformational* role of business support is also explored in the literature with a distinction being drawn between assistance focused on SME's day-to-day operational issues and those emphasizing enterprise growth strategies as well as change initiatives attempting radical step change and those focused more on incremental change paradigms (Alexiev et al., 2010; North et al., 2011). The transactional–transformational continuum is a useful way of categorizing enterprise support services. Often the initial contact between a business owner-manager and business adviser is more likely to be about a generic advice to resolve an operational issue. The relationship might evolve toward more bespoke and potentially more transformational advice as trust between the parties develops (Mole et al., 2014).

Despite a wealth of empirical evidence about the benefits of the enterprise support to business growth and development, the enterprise scholars report limited uptake of enterprise support. Uptake of support can be related to SME characteristics such as size and sector, as well as external influences, such as the state of the economy (Mole et al., 2016). A study by Bager et al. (2015) suggests, for example, that program enrollment may be subject to selection bias leading to SMEs with the most growth potential being overlooked. Support providers may recruit unsuitable participants who do not always fulfill the target criteria, and SME owners from, for example, craft/practical backgrounds may be less interested if the training is in formal setting rather than in informal or workplace-based settings.

Scholars exploring the role of policymakers in the design and implementation of enterprise support programs commented on a mismatch in the "hierarchy of choices" concerned with who delivers the support, the type of support offered, how it is allocated and how the support is funded (Mole & Bramley, 2006). The reluctance of support providers to focus "… more intensive assistance on appropriate beneficiaries" or match enterprise support to a specific business problem facing the SME has also been a criticism of enterprise support (Mole et al., 2009, p. 20). More successful outcomes emerge, therefore, when a knowledge gap is addressed within the SME through problem-based enterprise support. Indeed, support in the form of general business advice is unlikely to have the same impact as, for example, specialist support sought from environmental management professionals, accountants, and other established professions.

In terms of the focus of the enterprise support, the literature is largely concerned with the configuration of support for SMEs for business growth. This is not surprising as business support policy has often been an extension of national industrial policy with a traditionally dominant focus on economic development and growth, especially at a regional level (Huggins et al., 2015). In the United Kingdom, Business Links, a decentralized network of business support services established in late 1990, became a prototype for the LEP network operating currently. Business Links were supported by the Industry Ministry and funded on performance. The most important performance indicators were the amount of "market penetration" and the "satisfaction rate" (Mole et al., 2011). In contrast, the government funding of LEPs supports "capacity building" within LEPs and "supports the development and delivery of their strategic plan" (HM Treasury, 2012). LEPs are also invited to bid for funding from a number of national and EU funding streams, including Growing Places Fund, the Single Local Growth Fund and Growth Deals and EU structural and investment funding.

When it comes to supporting SMEs' environmental ambitions and capitalizing on green growth opportunities, the enterprise support available to SMEs is limited. Although clean growth has been recognized as one of the strategic priorities for many LEPs (DBIS, 2018) and the low-carbon economy is one of the four current investment priorities for ERDF funding (ERDF, 2020), the policy discourse outlining actions toward addressing the challenge is rather vague. Historically, operationalization of this priority has been limited to energy efficiency measures and carbon reduction interventions. Only a very few LEPs offer enterprise support that attempts to combine cost reductions through improved environmental performance while boosting low-carbon pro-environmental niches, for example, Greater Manchester Growth Hub, LoCase in Kent and Low Carbon Business Network at the University of Derby. In the same vein, the Carbon Trust has recently launched the START2ACT program for start-ups and young SMEs offering free energy efficiency consulting and mentoring in contrast with the more common focus of nongovernmental organizations (NGOs) on corporate and public body clients.

Although such initiatives are encouraging, they are still outside the scope of the mainstream enterprise support programs. Traditionally, business support initiatives have targeted the achievement of the evidence-based economic outcomes. Environmental and social outcomes, although growing in prominence, remain an afterthought still when it comes to understanding the purpose of an enterprise, and the funding streams often do not deviate greatly in scope and in reach of the business support. The policy and regulatory landscapes are, therefore, far from being conducive to the development of a sustainability-focused enterprise.

Our evidence confirms that, overall, only a handful of enterprise support programs across England attempt to balance SMEs' growth and development aspirations with reduction in environmental impact. Support programs toward environmental performance of SMEs are largely similar to those of large companies and offer little appreciation of SMEs' specifics. They often lack a place-based focus (Baranova et al., 2020), and few are based on localized understanding of the SME community, in terms of the firm's size, sector, urban/rural and domestic/international dimensions, LCEGS scope and outcomes and environmental impact trends.

## Study Design and Methods

The research is underpinned by a pragmatist ontology in which the value of the knowledge is understood through its power to inform action. The guiding principle of pragmatism is to change the relationship between cognition and reality, and as Joas puts it, "truth is no longer to do with getting a correct representation of reality in cognition"; "rather, it expresses an increase of the power to act in relation to an environment" (Joas, 1993, p. 21). This position recognizes that reality can only be accessible through the plurality of individual experiences and perceptions and representations (Blaikie & Priest, 2019; Seale, 1999). Such plurality is of importance, as in pragmatism terms "all our theories are instrumental, are mental modes of adaptation to reality, rather than revelations" (James quoted in Mills 1966, p. 227).

In line with the pragmatism of epistemology, the study is designed to provide knowledge and understanding into the green growth phenomenon and at the same time enable action across the multiple agencies to accelerate green growth. The study design involved two stages:

Stage 1: As part of the ongoing collaborative work with the regional Chamber of Commerce, the survey was developed and launched as part of the Economic Quarterly Survey mechanism. The survey was distributed to the businesses operating in the Midlands. It aimed to explore engagement of the businesses with green growth and to identify the policy–practice gaps. The survey had five main sections: socio-demographic characteristics, green growth performance, policy and support for green growth, green growth strategy and green growth skills. The survey was launched in February 2022 across the three counties: Derbyshire, Leicestershire and Nottinghamshire. The first survey of this sort was launched back in 2015. Since then, the survey was launched six times in 2017, 2018, 2020, 2021 and 2022. This resulted in a significant longitudinal data collection on green growth in the region over a seven-year period.

Stage 2: The results of the survey were presented at a number of regional forums, including Sustainability Summit in September 2022, and briefings for policy and business support agencies which prompted discussions documented in the field notes.

Survey was analyzed using descriptive statistics functionality in MS Excel. Documentary analysis was undertaken using thematic analysis (TA) approach, defined as an appropriate method for identifying, analyzing and reporting patterns (themes) within data. Its application is deemed to be valuable in gaining insights into people's experiences and in enabling the construction of "particular phenomena in particular contexts" (Braun & Clarke, 2013, p. 121).

Ethics and moral standards are integral to research studies (Mertens & Ginsberg, 2009). Research ethics protocols and compliance with the University of Derby research ethics policy and regulations were observed throughout the study.

## Results and Analysis

### Green Growth Trends

The survey yielded a response from 372 businesses operating across the three counties with 40% of businesses from Derby and Derbyshire, 28% from Leicester and Leicestershire, 30% from Nottingham and Nottinghamshire and the remaining 2% from outside the region; 27% of responses came from engineering and manufacturing sectors followed by professional services (18%); retail (8%); and construction, public and voluntary and education and training at 5% each; with the remaining sectors, from transportation and logistics to tourism and hospitality, agriculture and health, representing under 5% of the responses. Micro businesses provided 42% of survey responses, 32% came from small businesses, 20% from medium and 6% from large.

When asked about the share of the GGSs in the company's turnover, 45% of businesses stated they generate some part of the turnover from GGSs in the Q1 of 2022, 8% up from 37% in 2021. More than a third of the businesses responded to the survey did not generate any GGS turnover. The 1–19% turnover category remains the most frequent rate of green growth strategy adoption across the businesses surveyed. Fig. 5.1 illustrates a breakdown of business responses by firm size.

Further analysis shows that larger companies have more flexibility to commit fully to the green growth. This is evidenced by the highest proportion of large

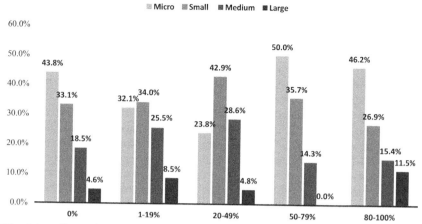

Fig. 5.1.   Green Growth Performance by Firm Size, February 2022.

companies reporting turnover in the 80–100% category. SMEs, on the other hand, show a mixed performance across the turnover categories with small-sized businesses leading in two out of four turnover categories.

A similar survey exploring the green growth trends was carried in 2015, 2017, 2018, 2020 and 2021. Fig. 5.2 shows the percentage of businesses deriving GGS turnover during the last seven years. There is a fourfold increase, from 7.5% to 28.5%, in the businesses reporting 1%–19% turnover from GGSs over the last seven years. Such a sustained and continuing increase in this category shows a positive growth trajectory and proliferation of the green diversification. As the majority of survey respondents are small businesses, this is a significant trend that shows sustained green diversification strategies by small businesses over time.

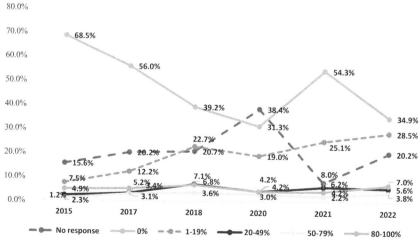

Fig. 5.2.   Green Growth Performance, 2015–2022.

Despite each of the remaining turnover categories (20–49%, 50–79% and 80–100%) reported by less than 10% of the businesses surveyed during 2015–2022, these strategies are on the rise too. The number of businesses in the 20–49% turnover category has doubled over the last seven years, and more than doubled in the 50–79% turnover category. The number of businesses reporting 80–100% GGS turnover increased one and a half times during 2015–2022. The inclusion of "no response" in the trends analysis shows the respondents' attitude toward the question and could mean unawareness about the turnover breakdown in the businesses concerned. The "no response" figures have risen since 2015 with a surprising drop in 2021. The 2021 drop could be explained by the effect of the COVID-19 pandemic and the COP26 impact on regional businesses in the way of intensifying the attention to the green issues and engaging with the Quarterly Economic Survey (QES) survey. The 2022 figures registered 20.2% for "no response" category which signal the return to the previous trend.

### Green Growth and Business Strategy

The number of businesses considering green growth as part of their business strategies has more than doubled over the last four years, increasing from 9.7% in 2018 to 21.5% in 2022. Similarly, the number of companies that had never considered green growth has decreased from 36.2% in 2018 to 14.2% in 2022. Less positively, there is an increase in businesses that could not see the opportunities presented by the green growth, an increase of 7.4% over the last four years from 13.6% in 2018 to 21% in 2022.

Analysis of the responses confirms the fragmented picture concerning the integration of green growth ambitions and business strategy and reflects trends described in the academic literature (Baranova et al., 2020). Namely, that larger companies appear to be well in advance of their smaller counterparts, in respect of their strategic approach to green growth, with 88% of large companies either incorporating green growth or developing green growth strategies compared with only 36% of micro, 56% of small-sized and 61% of medium-sized businesses (see Fig. 5.3).

All of the large businesses surveyed saw clean growth as a growth opportunity, while 25% of micro, 22% of small-sized and 17% of medium-sized businesses had considered and dismissed it as an opportunity for growth. These contrasting positions signal differences in the way large and small businesses recognize business growth opportunities linked to green growth. These findings highlight that despite the potential to lead on green growth, SMEs are significantly lagging behind larger firms.

### Skills and Information Gaps

The survey data indicated 35% of businesses still aren't engaged with green growth with reasons cited such as gaps in information, shortage of green skills and access to finance. Only 17% of the businesses said the current policy landscape allows them to fully engage with green growth. These findings paint a challenging picture

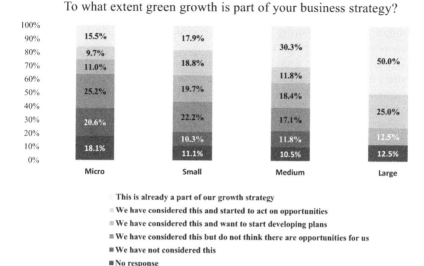

To what extent green growth is part of your business strategy?

This is already a part of our growth strategy
We have considered this and started to act on opportunities
We have considered this and want to start developing plans
We have considered this but do not think there are opportunities for us
We have not considered this
No response

Fig. 5.3.   Green Growth Strategy by Firm Size.

where the skills and information gaps constrict the green growth potential of the regional businesses.

When asked which of 18 listed areas businesses need to capitalize on green growth opportunities, efficiency-focused areas dominated the responses. Resource efficiency, energy efficiency and use of renewables were considered the most important areas to be strengthened. With leadership for sustainability, environmental strategy and sustainable purchasing and procurement following closely behind.

The top four skill sets remain largely unchanged from the 2021 QES data apart from the waste management which dropped from third to sixth place in 2022. The biggest change in the demand for green skills is in the area of supply chain management moving up from the 13th to the 9th place. This signals an intensifying engagement of the regional businesses in supply chains as part of the competitive strategy in the expanding green market niches. Altogether, businesses demand skills that help them achieve energy and resource efficiency internally and as part of the green supply chains. Businesses recognize leadership for sustainability and environmental strategy as important competences to harness the green growth opportunities.

### *Manufacturing Versus Service Engagement with Green Growth*

At the backdrop of the positive trend of the triple rise in businesses selling GGSs in the Midlands, there are striking differences in how manufacturing and service companies feature in the trend; 37% of service companies surveyed have no green offer on their portfolio when compared with the manufacturing businesses at 32%. Manufacturing companies lead in every single turnover category for green products and services; 1–19% turnover category is the most popular position reported by both manufacturing and service companies with manufacturing leading by 10% to services. The biggest difference is in the 20–49% turnover category where the number of manufacturing companies reporting green products and service turnover is almost triple of services.

In terms of the green growth strategy adoption, 26% of the manufacturing companies already have green growth ambitions as part of the business strategy when compared with 19% of the services. Only 12% of the manufacturing companies have not considered green growth as a viable strategic growth option when compared with 16% of service companies. Whilst environmental strategy is already part of the business strategy in half of the manufacturing companies; only 40% of the service companies we have surveyed confirmed this being the case. There is an emerging picture of manufacturing companies being more proactive in integrating and pursuing the green growth opportunities when compared with the service counterparts.

Although service companies feel they are better informed about the business support available, they are less likely to access business support than their manufacturing counterparts. One in four manufacturing businesses currently access business support when compared with one in five of the service firms. Only a third of service and manufacturing companies surveyed reported that they have a good understanding of policy for clean growth in the locality. More manufacturing companies are confident in their knowledge of how to access the business support when compared with services.

There is a difference in skills demands for green growth from the manufacturing and service companies. The biggest difference is in the areas of supply chain management, waste management, product design and development and innovation support and knowledge management. For example, the demand for supply chain skills is double that of from the service companies. Waste management skills are in demand from half of the manufacturing companies we surveyed when compared with 36% of service companies. Lastly, a reverse trend in relation to green marketing and branding skills: more service companies signified their importance to green growth than manufacturing companies.

## Discussion

Although study findings signal a positive trend in the engagement of regional businesses with green growth, it is important to recognize that such an engagement is dependent on firm size, sectoral specifics, regulatory environment and business support mechanisms. It is clear that for some companies, it is much easier to integrate the green growth aspirations with the business strategy, and for others far less so.

The significance of firm size in relation to growth is well recognized in the literature (Bentzen et al., 2012). The study confirms such a significance in relation to growth in emerging green market niches. While a number of micro businesses solely trading with green products and services are growing, it is small businesses that are most likely to adopt a "hybrid" approach to the portfolio of green products and services.

Green skills development and upskilling is essential to business engagement with green growth. Study shows the largest demands for skills development are in the areas of energy and resource efficiency, renewables, leadership for sustainability, environmental strategy and access to green finance. As businesses become more confident operating in green markets, they are looking for skills that would sustain competitive success long term. Such skills are not "readily available" and need to be developed over time as they rely on internal capabilities for renewal, agility and quality.

Manufacturing and service companies differ in the way they engage with green growth, policy and business support programs. Sectoral specifics, namely the policy and the regulatory environment, play an important part in stimulating the pro-environmental business behavior. Manufacturing industries have more established and regulated practices that drive positive environmental performance. Supply chain pressures for environmental performance and demands for green products and services are another stimuli for manufacturing companies to green their operations and business performance. Although such pressures are growing in the service sectors, they are far less pronounced.

As the service industries accounted for 78% of total UK economic output (gross value added) in April–June 2022 and 82% of employment in January–March 2022 (UK Parliament, 2022), services are an important part of the solution to the net zero challenge. They seem to be legging behind their manufacturing counterparts in strategic approach and operationalization of the green growth ambitions. What is important to realize is that their needs for skills development and business support are different to manufacturing companies. Policy and business support instruments need to be more attuned to the specifics of manufacturing and service companies when designing support packages and policy interventions.

In light of the study findings, the following considerations should inform the enterprise support to catalyze the engagement with green growth:

- *Broadening the purpose of the enterprise support* is necessary to encourage the growth aspirations that go beyond just an economic rationale and include commitments toward environment, community and place. Such a shift in purpose would require understanding of the business challenges in addressing the conflicting priorities when it comes to balancing economic and environmental logics and development of the approaches to resolving such tensions. Some of them might include use of the digital collaborative and partnership platforms similar to Zellar (2022) and effective techniques in stakeholder management and relationship building. Business support professionals and agencies have to demonstrate clear and consistent commitments toward the delivery of the business support programs that support green growth and its broader contribution to sustainable development. A comprehensive program of training and development for Business Advisers that places the pathway toward green growth at the heart of the business advice would help scale up transition and radically increase the engagement of business with green growth.
- *Broadening the scope of the enterprise support* is necessary to accommodate the broadening of the purpose. The broadening of support interventions should

go beyond the traditional focus on energy efficiency and renewables. It includes development of the competences in the areas of competitive strategy, responsible management and leadership, green funding and finance, collaborative working and stakeholder management to name just a few. Competence development should reflect specifics of manufacturing companies when compared to services and include support packages to NGOs and charities to support development of the ecosystem for pro-environmental business support in the regions and nationally.

- *Business-led interventions*: there needs to be a careful balance when it comes to generic versus customized business support. Often pro-environmental business support programs offer "generic" competence development and networking opportunities. When it comes to balancing the economic and environmental challenges, businesses require confidence building and degree of green competence development before they are ready to invest in and pursue the green growth opportunities. Although a generic green competence building could be a first step to building green competences, a business-led, bespoke interventional and consultancy tend to yield higher results (Chrisman & McMullan, 2004).

- *Access to diverse learning opportunities*: understanding business support provision as *learning experience* and business support interventions as *learning opportunities* provides a useful rationale for the ethos and the design of business support programs. Small businesses favor diversity of learning opportunities and experiential learning through connection with other businesses and wider stakeholder groupings (Baranova, 2022). Diversity should be reflected not only in the content and scope of the business support interventions but also in the learning mechanisms and styles of the business support delivery. For example, a use of digital platforms, interactive and bite-size materials and podcasts is particularly effective for small businesses. Thinking of business support as a learning experience brings considerations about the value and the outcomes of the learning experience as well as the endeavors of how such experience can be enhanced further. In the context of green growth, a learning perspective can also encourage long-life learning aspirations from owner/managers and support development of the businesses as learning organizations toward a more sustainable way of life.

- *Transformative ethos and action*: transformative rationale for pro-environmental business support has important implications in the way the support interactions are designed and undertaken. This is a radically different approach to transactional, short-term business support interventions prevailing across the pro-environmental business support programs. In the context of green growth, a transformative approach to business support should go beyond strategic rationale and include transformative experiences that would support behavioral change toward a more sustainable way of living. The support programs should empower a shift in personal and professional behaviors through awareness building, experiential and collaborative learning (Kolb, 2014; Sadler-Smith et al., 2000). Programs similar to carbon literacy training (Carbon Literacy Project, 2022) are useful examples of how such interventions can be constructed. The transformative ethos and actions toward addressing the climate change concerns through business support could offer opportunities for collaborative action and accelerate transition to a low-carbon economy.

## Conclusion

Business support programs framed and supported by the regional and national industrial policy are important elements of the business support eco-system for green growth. As businesses are increasingly focusing on green market niches across the domestic and international markets, the broadening of the scope and availability of the support is becoming critical. The broadening of support interventions should go beyond the traditional focus on energy efficiency and renewables. It includes development of the competences in the areas of competitive strategy, responsible management and leadership, green funding and finance, collaborative working and stakeholder management to name just a few. Such skills need to be developed over time and require a *transformative approach* in the delivery of business support. The ethos of such support is about *empowering* businesses to face the vision of their role in addressing the climate challenges and *enabling* proactive and positive actions that strengthen the contribution of business toward sustainable development.

Policy community is advised to develop support mechanisms which reduce skills and information gaps. This includes financial support and programs to reskill and upskill the existing workforce as well as to invest in innovation toward net zero. Collaborative networks of local government, businesses, policymakers, university and public should be part of the solution to bridge the information gaps, to accelerate the problem-solving toward sustainability and to intensify the green growth opportunities in the region and nationally.

## References

Alexiev, A. S., Jansen, J. J., Van den Bosch, F. A., & Volberda, H. W. (2010). Top management team advice seeking and exploratory innovation: The moderating role of TMT heterogeneity. *Journal of Management Studies, 47*(7), 1343–1364.

Alrasheedi, M., Mardani, A., Mishra, A. R., Streimikiene, D., Liao, H., & Al-nefaie, A. H. (2021). Evaluating the green growth indicators to achieve sustainable development: A novel extended interval-valued intuitionistic fuzzy-combined compromise solution approach. *Sustainable Development, 29*(1), 120–142.

Amundsen, H., & Hermansen, E. A. (2021). Green transformation is a boundary object: An analysis of conceptualisation of transformation in Norwegian primary industries. *Environment and Planning E: Nature and Space, 4*(3), 864–885.

Bager, T. E., Jensen, K. W., Nielsen, P. S., & Larsen, T. A. (2015). Enrolment of SME managers to growth-oriented training programs. *International Journal of Entrepreneurial Behaviour and Research, 21*(4), 578–599.

Baranova, P. (2022). Environmental capability development in a multi-stakeholder network setting: Dynamic learning through multi-stakeholder interactions. *Business Strategy and the Environment, 31*(7), 3406–3420.

Baranova, P., Paterson, F., & Gallotta, B. (2020). Configuration of enterprise support towards the clean growth challenge: A place-based perspective. *Local Economy*, *35*(4), 363–383.

Baranova, P., Paterson, F., & Gallotta B. (2022). Green growth trends in the East Midlands 2022. University of Derby.

Bassetti, T., Blasi, S., & Sedita, S. R. (2021). The management of sustainable development: A longitudinal analysis of the effects of environmental performance on economic performance. *Business Strategy and the Environment*, *30*(1), 21–37.

Bennett, R., & Robson, P. (2003). Changing use of external business advice and government supports by SMEs in the 1990s. *Regional Studies*, *37*(8), 795–811.

Bentzen, J., Madsen, E. S., & Smith, V. (2012) Do firms' growth rates depend on firm size? *Small Business Economics*, *39*(4), 937–947.

Berry, A. J., Sweeting, R., & Goto, J. (2006). The effect of business advisers on the performance of SMEs. *Journal of Small Business and Enterprise Development*, *13*(1), 33–47.

Blaikie, N., & Priest, J. (2019). *Designing social research: The logic of anticipation*. John Wiley & Sons.

Bowen, A., & Hepburn, C. (2014). Green growth: An assessment. *Oxford Review of Economic Policy*, *30*(3), 407–422.

Braun, V., & Clarke, V. (2013). Teaching thematic analysis: Overcoming challenges and developing strategies for effective learning. *The Psychologist*, *26*(2), 120–123.

Carbon Literacy Project. (2022). *The Carbon Literacy Project*. Retrieved January 9, 2022, from https://carbonliteracy.com/

Chrisman, J. J., & McMullan, W. E. (2004). Outsider assistance as a knowledge resource for new venture survival. *Journal of Small Business Management*, *42*(3), 229–244.

Cravo, T. A., & Piza, C. (2019). The impact of business-support services on firm performance: A meta-analysis. *Small Business Economics*, *53*(3), 753–770.

De Angelis, E. M., Di Giacomo, M., & Vannoni, D. (2019). Climate change and economic growth: The role of environmental policy stringency. *Sustainability*, *11*(8), 22–73.

Department for Business, Innovation and Skills (DBIS). (2018). *Local industrial strategies, policy prospectus*. Retrieved February 22, 2020, from https://www.gov.uk/government/publications/local-industrial-strategies-policy-prospectus

Dinda, S. (2014). A theoretical basis for green growth. *International Journal of Green Economics*, *8*(2), 177–189.

Dryzek, J. S. (2013). *The politics of the earth. Environmental discourses* (3rd ed.). Oxford University Press.

*Economist*. (2022). Economic growth no longer requires rising emissions: Now this decoupling must accelerate, leaders – Debunking degrowth. *Economist*, November 10.

ERDF. (2020). *European Regional Development Fund*. Retrieved February 26, 2020, from https://ec.europa.eu/regional_policy/en/funding/erdf/

Fernandes, C. I., Veiga, P. M., Ferreira, J. J., & Hughes, M. (2021). Green growth versus economic growth: Do sustainable technology transfer and innovations lead to an imperfect choice? *Business Strategy and the Environment*, *30*(4), 2021–2037.

Gray, B., & Purdy, J. (2018). *Collaborating for our future: Multistakeholder partnerships for solving complex problems*. Oxford University Press.

Gupta, J., & Vegelin, C. (2016). Sustainable development goals and inclusive development. *International Environmental Agreements: Politics, Law and Economics*, *16*(3), 433–448.

HM Treasury. (2012, December). *Autumn statement 2012, Cm 8480*, p. 41.

Huggins, R., Morgan, B., & Williams, N. (2015). Regional entrepreneurship and the evolution of public policy and governance. *Journal of Small Business and Enterprise Development*, *22*(3), 473–511.

IEMA-Deloitte. (2022). *A blueprint for green workforce transformation*. Retrieved January 7, 2022, from deloitte-uk-a-blueprint-for-green-workforce-transformation.pdf

Joas, H. (1993). *Pragmatism and social theory*. University of Chicago Press.

Karlsson, M., & Hovelsrud, G. K. (2021). "Everyone comes with their own shade of green": Negotiating the meaning of transformation in Norway's agriculture and fisheries sectors, *Journal of Rural Studies, 81*(2021), 259–268.

Kolb, D. A. (2014). *Experiential learning: Experience as the source of learning and development*. FT Press.

Læssøe, J., Feinstein, N. W., & Blum, N. (2013). Environmental education policy research–challenges and ways research might cope with them. *Environmental Education Research, 19*(2), 231–242.

Mason, C., & Brown, R. (2013). Creating good public policy to support high-growth firms. *Small Business Economics, 40*(2), 211–225.

McDonald, M. L., & Westphal, J. D. (2003). Getting by with the advice of their friends: CEOs' advice networks and firms' strategic responses to poor performance. *Administrative Science Quarterly, 48*(1), 1–32.

Mertens, D. M., & Ginsberg, P. E. (2009). *The handbook of social research ethics*. SAGE Publishers.

Mills, C. W. (1966). *Sociology and pragmatism: The higher learning in America*. Oxford University Press.

Mole, K., Baldock, R., & North, D. (2016). Which SMEs seek external support? Business characteristics, management behaviour and external influences in a contingency approach. *Environment and Planning C: Government and Policy, 35*(3), 476–499.

Mole, K. F., & Bramley, G. (2006). Making policy choices in nonfinancial business support: an international comparison. *Environment and Planning C: Government and Policy, 24*(6), 885–908.

Mole K., Hart M., & Roper S. (2014). When moving information online diminishes change: Advisory services to SMEs. *Policy Studies, 35*(2), 172–191.

Mole, K., Hart, M., Roper, S., & Saal, D. (2009). *Broader or deeper? Exploring the most effective intervention profile for public small business support* [Working Paper No. 105, CSME Working Papers, University of Warwick].

Mole, K. F., Hart, M., Roper, S., & Saal, D. S. (2011). Broader or deeper? Exploring the most effective intervention profile for public small business support. *Environment and Planning A, 43*(1), 87–105.

North, D., Baldock, R., & Mole, K. (2011). *Research to understand the barriers to take up and use of business support* [Report for the Department for Business Innovation and Skills, Department of Business Innovation and Skills].

O'Brien K. (2012). Global environmental change II: From adaptation to deliberate transformation. *Progress in Human Geography, 36*, 667–676.

OECD. (2011). *Towards green growth*. Organisation for Economic Co-operation and Development.

OECD. (2017). *Enhancing the contributions of SMEs in a global and digitalised economy*. OCED.

O'Neill, R. C., & Viljoen, L. (2001). Support for female entrepreneurs in South Africa: Improvement or decline? *Journal of Family Ecology and Consumer Sciences, 29*, 37–44.

Patterson, J., Schulz, K., Vervoort, J., van der Hel, S., Widerberg, O., Adler, C., Hurlbert, M., Anderton, K., Sethi, M., & Barau, A. (2017). Exploring the governance and politics of transformations towards sustainability. *Environmental Innovation and Societal Transitions, 24*, 1–16.

Pelling, M., O'Brien, K., & Matyas, D. (2015). Adaptation and transformation. *Climatic Change, 133*, 113–127.

Reilly, J. M. (2012). Green growth and the efficient use of natural resources. *Energy Economics, 34*, S85–S93.

Ribeiro-Sorianoa, D., & Galindo-Martın, M. (2012). Government policies to support entrepreneurship. *Entrepreneurship and Regional Development, 24*(9/10), 861–864.

Rigby, J., & Hayden, J. (2013). Financing Europe's innovative SMEs with public-private partnerships: John Rigby and Jennifer Hayden. In *Innovation policy challenges for the 21st century* (pp. 143–162). Routledge.

Rodrik, D. (2014). Green industrial policy. *Oxford Review of Economic Policy*, *30*(3), 469–491.

Sadler-Smith, E., Gardiner, P., Badger, B., Chaston, I., & Stubberfield, J. (2000). Using collaborative learning to develop small firms. *Human Resource Development International*, *3*(3), 285–306.

Scoones I., Newell P., & Leach M. (2015). The politics of green transformations. In I. Scoones, M. Leach, & P. Newell (Eds.), *The politics of green transformations* (pp. 1–24). Routledge.

Seale, C. (1999). Grounding theory. *The Quality of Qualitative Research*, *1*, 87–105.

Song, M., Fisher, R., & Kwoh, Y. (2019). Technological challenges of green innovation and sustainable resource management with large scale data. *Technological Forecasting and Social Change*, *144*, 361–368.

Stoknes, P. E., & Rockström, J. (2018). Redefining green growth within planetary boundaries. *Energy Research & Social Science*, *44*, 41–49.

UK Parliament. (2022). Service industries: Key economic indicators, research briefing. House of Commons Library, November 11.

UNEP. (2022). *Green Growth – UNEP UN environment programme*. Retrieved November 20, 2022, from https://www.unep.org/es/node/20880

Williams, D. A. (2014). Resources and failure of SMEs: Another look. *Journal of Developmental Entrepreneurship*, *19*(1), 1450007.

World Bank. (2012). *Inclusive green growth – The pathway to sustainable development*. The World Bank. http://siteresources.worldbank.org/EXTSDNET/Resources/Inclusive_Green_Growth_May_2012.pdf

Zellar. (2022). *The sustainability score for every business*. Retrieved January 9, 2023, from https://www.zellar.com/

Chapter 6

# Exploring Organizational Responses to Nonmarket Institutional Pressures: The Case of the EU Taxonomy Regulation

*Michelle Palharini, Matthias Fertig and Peter Wehnert*

*Friedrich-Alexander-Universität, Germany*

## Abstract

Published in June 2020, the European Union (EU) Taxonomy Regulation is an important tool for the reorientation of capital flows toward sustainability, establishing a classification system that enables investors to identify green economic activities. Confronted by the reporting demands of this regulation, companies are caught in a sustainability economic revolution. This study seeks primarily to understand firms' responses to the EU taxonomy, and whether they recognize value creation opportunities by aligning market and nonmarket strategies with the taxonomy goals. For that, we conducted expert interviews and adopted a conceptual framework based on institutional theory, dynamic capabilities view and nonmarket strategy research. Our findings indicate that most firms respond reactively, while firms with sustainability-driven business models tend to respond in an anticipatory way, and firms with high greenhouse gas (GHG) emissions and low taxonomy eligibility in a defensive way. We also find evidence for mimetic isomorphism related to the influence of consulting and auditing services. Further, high levels of uncertainty, ambiguity and lack of clarity has a great impact on firms' responses and motives. Finally, this study highlights the EU taxonomy considering a paradigmatic shift toward sustainability, which is not recognized by most firms. To this end, we find that most companies have not identified opportunities arising from nonmarket integration and, rather, see the taxonomy only as an extra regulation to be

Sustainable and Resilient Global Practices:
Advances in Responsiveness and Adaptation, 99–147
Copyright © 2024 by Michelle Palharini, Matthias Fertig and Peter Wehnert
Published under exclusive licence by Emerald Publishing Limited
doi:10.1108/978-1-83797-611-920241006

compliant with. Hence, we argue that it is crucial that firms contextualize the taxonomy within its larger institutional paradigmatic shift to capture the importance of going beyond mere compliance.

*Keywords*: EU taxonomy; dynamic capabilities; nonmarket strategy; paradigmatic shift; sustainable finance; European green deal

## Introduction

Global sustainability issues have been increasingly gaining space in political agendas, sparking several discussions on environmental crises and international efforts to tackle them. In this respect, the Paris Agreement and the 2030 Agenda for Sustainable Development stand out, placing environmental, social and corporate governance (ESG) issues at the forefront. Against this background, the European Commission (EC) has devised a set of policy initiatives called the European green deal, which includes substantial measures to transition to a low-carbon, resilient and resource-efficient economy (TEG, 2020). Launched in December 2019, the European Union (EU) green deal provides an action plan to restore biodiversity, cut pollution and support a more efficient use of resources (EC, n.d.).

Notably, such green transition requires financing toward sustainable production and consumption patterns, with the reorientation of capital flows toward sustainability (FSFSCMU, 2020). As the Organization for Economic Co-operation and Development (OECD) (2017) predicts, a total of 6.35 trillion euro a year will be necessary to achieve the goals of the Paris Agreement by 2030. A key challenge is the identification of sustainable activities, to which the EU has responded through a reform of its financial system (Och, 2020). To this end, the EC established the Technical Expert Group (TEG) on sustainable finance to develop a classification, resulting in the development of the EU Taxonomy Regulation (hereafter TR) – a tool that allows market participants to identify and invest in sustainable assets.

Seen from an institutional perspective, the TR represents a coercive pressure for sustainability development to which affected firms must react. Seen from the perspective of firms, the TR exerts a compelling nonmarket pressure that affects strategic management, calling for the analysis and understanding of firms' responses to the TR. Such analysis is important to scrutinize the efficacy of the efforts toward a green economy since companies' responses can reveal the extent to which they are committed to substantive sustainability development or just engaged in symbolic/ceremonial responses.

Considering the novelty of the TR, existing research on this topic is still in its infancy. However, given the topic's relevance for businesses and its significance for the success of the transition to a green economy, the present academic research aims to contribute to the understanding of how firms react in the face of pressures exerted by the TR by targeting the following research question: *how do firms respond to the requirements of the new EU TR?* To this end, the present work seeks to mainly contribute to the emerging literature on the TR.

For that, we adopt the perspective of dynamic capabilities view (DCV) and nonmarket strategy research, also drawing on the theoretical lens of institutional theory. Despite an increased popularity in the research on nonmarket strategies, little has been investigated in terms of regulatory pressures for sustainability development. Given that the TR will continue to evolve in the years to come, shaping the economy toward sustainability development, it seems logical at first that firms should embed TR-related goals into their business strategies in order to leverage sustainability while creating value at a market level. Hence, the present study also seeks to explore if and how companies have been integrating market and nonmarket strategies in the case of the EU TR.

We adopt a qualitative approach with the use of semi-structured expert interviews as the main method. Regarding the organization of this chapter, we have structured it as follows: We first provide an overview of the TR as well as a review of relevant literature. Next, we show the main concepts and theories that compose the theoretical framework. Then, we explain the chosen methodology, followed by the findings and interpretations thereof. A further discussion is then provided along with theoretical and practical implications. Finally, we present our conclusion along with limitations to our study as well as suggestions for future academic research.

## Overview of the EU Taxonomy for Sustainable Finance

Published in June, the TR sets a regulatory framework with a list of economic activities to help differentiate which investments support the environmental objectives of the EU. This unified approach should provide harmonization, helping "(...) investors and companies make informed investment decisions on environmentally friendly economic activities" (TEG, 2019). Essentially, the TR installs six environmental objectives, as follows: (1) climate change mitigation, (2) climate change adaptation, (3) sustainable use and protection of water and marine resources, (4) the transition to a circular economy, (5) pollution prevention and control, and (6) the protection and restoration of biodiversity and ecosystems (TEG, 2019). It is worth noting that taxonomy alignment is determined based on economic activity rather than entity, sector or industry (TEG, 2020). For that, the TEG utilizes the NACE (Nomenclature des Activités Économiques dans la Communauté Européenne) industry categorization, as well as its own mapping for additional classification systems not covered by the NACE (TEG, 2020).

### *The EU Taxonomy Requirements and Its Target Audience*

The TR classification relies on the Technical Screening Criteria (TSC), which determines performance thresholds for economic activities. Accordingly, in order to be considered sustainable, economic activities will have to align with three requirements: "make a substantive contribution to one of six environmental objectives; do no significant harm (DNSH) to the other five, where relevant; and meet minimum safeguards" (TEG, 2020, p. 2).

*Economic activities that make a substantial contribution.* The TR acknowledges two kinds of substantial contribution: "green" and "enabling activities." The first are economic activities carried out in an environmentally sustainable way, such as "low carbon energy production" or "energy efficient manufacturing processes" (TEG, 2020, p. 15). The latter are activities that enable the substantial contribution of other economic activities, such as the "manufacture of low-carbon technologies and information and communications technology for climate change mitigation" (TEG, 2020, p. 15).

Furthermore, the TR also acknowledges transition activities which are those that do not comply with climate neutrality, and regardless of adherence with current thresholds, they would still not be climate neutral.

*The "do no significant harm (DNSH)" principle.* According to §2 of Article 17 of the TR 2020/852, the assessment of an economic criteria against the principle of DNSH must consider the environmental impact of the activity itself as well as the environmental impact of the products and services based on their life cycle.

*Meet minimum safeguards.* To be taxonomy aligned, firms must meet some minimum social safeguards set in Article 18 of the TR (2020/852) as follows: These are the OECD Guidelines for Multinational Enterprises, the UN Guiding Principles on Business and Human Rights and the Declaration of the International Labour Organization on Fundamental Principles and Rights at Work and the International Bill of Human Rights.

Finally, there are three main target groups: financial market participants that offer financial products on the EU market; non-financial firms that are already listed under the Non-Financial Reporting Directive (NFRD) regulation; and the EU and Member States who are responsible for setting public measures, standards or labels (TEG, 2020). The present work focuses on non-financial market participants.

### TSC: Climate Change Mitigation and Adaptation

The EC is responsible for installing TSC through delegated acts (Och, 2020). According to the TEG, the TSC determines substantial contribution and DNSH (TEG, 2019, p. 3). In April 2021, the EC introduced the EU Taxonomy Climate Delegated Act with the first set of TSC related to climate change mitigation and adaptation (EC, 2021). According to the Intergovernmental Panel on Climate Change (IPCC), mitigation refers to "an anthropogenic intervention to reduce the sources or enhance the sinks of greenhouse gasses" (2001, p. 379). In turn, adaptation is defined as the "adjustment in natural or human systems in response to actual or expected climatic stimuli or their effects, which moderates harm or exploits beneficial opportunities" (IPCC, 2001, p. 365).

All firms subject to the company disclosure requirements must describe how, and to what extent, their economic activities are taxonomy aligned. Non-financial firms must include their disclosures in their non-financial statement (IPCC, 2001). Such company-level disclosures must contain information on the proportion that each TR-aligned economic activity contributes to the firm's performance according to turnover, capital expenditure (CapEx) and, if relevant, operating expenses

(OpEx) (Lucarelli et al., 2020). Turnover provides clarity on the firm's progress against the TR, while CapEx equips investors with an awareness of a firm's direction and strategy for how they target environmental performance. OpEx, in turn, can give an overview of short-term expenses linked to the TR.

## Review of Relevant Literature on the EU Taxonomy and Firms

In this review, we include both peer and non-peer reviewed articles, with the quality of the articles playing a secondary role (Peters et al., 2015, p. 142). Although this is not intended as a systematic literature review, the selection of relevant papers was guided by the Joanna Briggs Institute (JBI's) systematic reviews three-step method.[1] First, a search for the keyword "EU Taxonomy" was conducted in three databases (EBSCOhost, ProQuest and SSRN). Because the TR was first introduced in 2018, the inclusion criteria encompassed only papers published between 2018 and 2022 and only in English. Overall, the three databases generated 338 articles, with 44 articles remaining upon scanning their titles. In the second step, we scrutinized the respective abstracts, leaving out papers targeting less relevant areas adjacent to the TR, channeling our results down to 17 articles, which were then read in full. Finally, in the third step, backward and forward searches were conducted following Xiao and Watson's (2019, pp. 103–104) recommendation, but to little avail (only one extra relevant source found), given that TR literature related to companies' responses is still very limited, bringing the final number of selected articles to 18.

From the 18 selected papers, 13 display only an indirect relationship to the present research (summarized in the Appendix). Two articles were selected as relevant literature because they strongly relate to the view of the TR within the context of a new institutional paradigmatic shift for sustainable development. These two articles are summarized in Table 6.1. The remaining three articles comprise the core relevant literature for this study because of their direct relationship to our topic (Table 6.2).

## Review of Relevant Theories and Concepts

### *Dynamic Capabilities View*

Given the demands and dynamic nature of today's fast-changing market and nonmarket environments, we pose DCV as one of the theoretical lenses to compose our framework. DCV stems from the resource-based view approach, which sees them as "bundles of resources" that are "heterogeneously distributed across firms" (Eisenhardt & Martin, 2000, p. 1105). To this end, resources are defined as anything that could be imagined as a strength or weakness of a given firm (Wernerfelt, 1984).

---

[1]The JBI's method includes the following phases: (1) selecting studies using predefined criteria, (2) appraising selected studies and (3) examining selected papers' reference lists (Peters et al., 2017, pp. 13–14).

Table 6.1. Articles About the TR as a New Paradigm Shift.

| Authors | Type | Purpose | Relevant findings and/or main arguments |
|---------|------|---------|------------------------------------------|
| Bond and Dusík (2022) | Discussion | To show how taxonomies can change the mindset around sustainable development connected with policy tools such as Environmental Impact Assessment (EIA) | They pose that emerging taxonomies such as the TR offer an improved framework based on theory and, thus, are better equipped than EIA to achieve sustainable development. To this end, they suggest that sustainable taxonomies can profit from the integration with current EIA systems and vice versa. Furthermore, they argue that taxonomies for sustainable development depict a revolutionary paradigmatic shift from an "economic" to an "ecologic" mindset |
| Howard (2022) | Reaction paper | Reaction paper to Bond and Dusík (2022) | Howard suggests that Bond and Dusík's depiction of the TR as a revolutionary paradigmatic shift should be placed in a bigger context as the evolution of ecological values that have risen to prominence with environmental awareness and activism since the 1960s. To this end, he argues that EIA is a "tool of its time" (Howard, 2022, p. 111) and, likewise, taxonomies for sustainable development also reflect the recent developments and prioritization of sustainability of the present |

Table 6.2.   Overview of Relevant Literature on the EU Taxonomy.

| Authors | Title | Type | Purpose | Relevant Findings and/or Main Arguments |
| --- | --- | --- | --- | --- |
| Schütze and Stede (2020) | EU Sustainable Finance Taxonomy – What Is Its Role on the Road Towards Climate Neutrality? | Mixed-methods research | The authors propose an interesting discussion on the TR's scope and technical performance thresholds applied to economic activities that are still not green | In a first moment, they find that the sectors covered by the TR amount to a lower portion of employment and gross value added than emissions, showing that "labour intensity is not a good indicator for carbon intensity" (p. 5). In a second moment, based on a large-scale examination of the official EU consultation on the interim report released by the TEG in June 2019, they find that the thresholds for transition activities are not appropriately designed to foster progress toward a net-zero GHG. They argue that innovative sustainable technologies for high-emission activities are capital intensive, but with the current thresholds of the TR, there is no incentive for these innovative technologies to be pursued" (p. 15) |
| Och (2020) | Sustainable Finance and the EU Taxonomy Regulation – Hype or Hope? | Discussion | Och outlines the structure of the TR, stressing the key areas of debate and latest developments | Some of the key challenges are (1) ESG data gaps and costs; (2) lack of full ESG taxonomy, since the TR does not address social and governance areas as independent criteria; (3) scope for greenwashing (financial products could be marketed as 50% taxonomy compliant, for example, even if the other 50% is composed of environmentally harmful activities). For these challenges, Och proposes an enhanced disclosure of ESG data, a consistent and complete ESG framework, and the extension of the scope of the TR to include the level of sustainability of companies |

*(Continued)*

Table 6.2.  (*Continued*)

| Authors | Title | Type | Purpose | Relevant Findings and/or Main Arguments |
|---|---|---|---|---|
| Fischer et al. (2022) | The New EU Sustainable Strategy and Accounting Practice – Ex ante Corporate and Auditor Perspectives from Germany | Qualitative research with in-depth interviews | This paper presents an ex ante evaluation of practitioners' perception on the implementation of the TR and the Corporate Sustainability Reporting Directive (CSRD) | Fischer et al. argue that despite supporting the TR, practitioners perceive that the challenges brought by the implementation can hamper its achievement in praxis. This is mostly due to high complexity and a lack of clarity. Additionally, they also find that practitioners lack experience with non-financial KPIs. Ultimately, the authors suggest that these findings can help policymakers identify means to adjust reporting practices and support preparers and auditors to better plan for the TR requirements |

Teece et al. (1997) define DCV as "the firm's ability to integrate, build, and reconfigure internal and external competences to address rapidly changing environments" (p. 516). Kindström et al. (2013) complement this definition, broadly defining DCV as a set of "routines within the firm's managerial and organizational processes that aim to gain, release, integrate and reconfigure resources" (p. 1064). Furthermore, dynamic capabilities can be dissected into three components: (1) the capacity of sensing and shaping opportunities and threats, (2) the capacity of seizing opportunities, and (3) the capacity to sustain competitiveness by transforming, that is, "enhancing, combining, protecting, and, when necessary, reconfiguring the business enterprise's intangible and tangible assets" (Teece, 2007, p. 1319).

Overall, the DCV stands out as a lens to explore firms' responses to political regulations (such as the TR) because it highlights their ability to develop and use their competencies to align with the demands of changing environments (Oliver & Holzinger, 2008).

### Nonmarket Strategy and Integrated Strategy

Nonmarket strategy has attracted the attention of scholars for more than four decades. It contends that the choice of nonmarket strategy is influenced by a variety of factors both internal and external to the firm, and that the business environment comprises market and nonmarket components. The market environment is driven by market forces and contracts (Baron, 2006), influencing the choice of nonmarket strategy (Wrona & Sinzig, 2018). The nonmarket environment is defined as "the legal, political, and social arrangements in which the firm is embedded," determining "the rules of the game for the market environment through government policies and public expectations" (Baron, 2006, p. xxix). In this respect, nonmarket pressures such as the TR are a formal coercive source of the "rules of the game" and a firm's success depends on its management of the nonmarket environment.

Based on the above premises, institutional pressures could be managed by firms through the integration of market and nonmarket strategies, from which synergies can be gained (Baron, 1995, 1997). This is even more relevant when firms are highly dependent on the nonmarket component (Marquis & Qian, 2014), such as the case of EU sustainability regulations because the pressures exerted by them can also create difficulties (Schaltegger, 2011), threatening firms' stability.

Furthermore, firms can also use institutional pressures for sustainability development as an opportunity to enhance their influence on the market environment (Kotler et al., 2005). Baron (2006) argues that anticipation to changes is crucial in preparing the firm to "take advantage of opportunities as they arise and address issues before they become problems" (p. 14), which also aligns well with DCV's concepts of sensing capabilities.

### Institutional Theory and Its Relationship to Nonmarket Strategy

Institutional theory has made important contributions to the understanding of institutional processes by seeking to explain how they affect organizational conformity. Scholars in this field have produced valuable insights into the character and array of institutional pressures (DiMaggio & Powell, 1983; Meyer & Rowan, 1977; Zucker, 1977, 1983, 1988), as well as into the scope of the pressures exerted on organizations (Meyer et al., 1983; Scott & Meyer, 1987; Singh et al., 1986). As Doh et al. (2012) contend, institutional theory lends itself as an overarching unifying structure, helping organize and position research on nonmarket environment and strategy (p. 4).[2] Notably, institutional theory shares some premises from nonmarket strategy research. For example, it proposes that firms are affected by the external context (the nonmarket environment) and must adjust to changes in the external environment to maintain themselves competitive (DiMaggio & Powell, 1983). Besides, it is also argued that, in the worst case, firms' survival can be at stake if they neglect changes in the nonmarket environment (Teo et al., 2003).

Furthermore, institutional theory sees nonmarket strategy as a way of obtaining and strengthening legitimacy, thereby gaining reputational capital (Bansal & Clelland, 2004; DiMaggio & Powell, 1983; Zucker, 1988). At its core, it suggests that institutional processes lead to isomorphism, increasing the likelihood of long-term survival through stability and permanence at the cost of long-term efficiency (DiMaggio & Powell, 1983; Meyer & Zucker, 1989; Scott, 1987; Zucker, 1987). DiMaggio and Powell (1983) propose three types of institutional processes: coercive, mimetic and normative. Coercive processes result from both formal and informal pressures exerted on organizations while mimetic processes stem from uncertainty, encouraging imitation, or "modeling." Normative processes, in turn, derive mainly from professionalization and, as Sarkis et al. (2011) argue, can lead firms to conform in order to appear as carrying out legitimate activities (p. 7).

Regarding coercive processes, most relevant for the present work are the formal pressures (legal and political nonmarket pressures), which is the case of the TR. From the perspective of institutional theory, this type of pressure is seen mainly as a constraint (or cost) on firms (DiMaggio & Powell, 1983; Pfeffer & Salancik, 1978). However, coercive processes are important to encourage the management of environmental issues (Kilbourne et al., 2002). Given that sustainability development pressures in international contexts are often limited by the lack of administrative enforcement (i.e., Kyoto Protocol), compliance can also be difficult (Rugman & Verbeke, 1998). In this sense, institutional theory helps understand how such scenarios might lead to coercive processes, such as the case of the TR – that is, through the installment of new "rules of the game" as a way of tackling market failures related to environmental issues.

Notwithstanding, sustainability development pressures may also prompt firms to respond proactively as strategic adaptation (Freeman, 1984). In this respect, Oliver and Holzinger (2008) suggest that firms can gain advantage by allocating organizational resources so as to improve their adaptability to the political

---

[2]Research on nonmarket strategy has been highly fragmented, with scholars drawing on theoretical perspectives from economics, management and sociology (Doh et al., 2012; Hotho & Pedersen, 2012; Mellahi et al., 2016).

environment (p. 506). Additionally, in alignment with the logics of market and nonmarket strategy integration and with the DCV, firms could potentially proactively respond as a source of competitive advantage (Hockerts, 2015).

### Responses to Institutional Pressures: Cross-Relationship Between DCV, Nonmarket Strategy and Institutional Theory

We argue that the cross-relationship between DCV, nonmarket strategy and institutional theory lends itself as a useful lens to analyze the management of nonmarket environments. More specifically, this study aligns with the argument that DCV, nonmarket strategy research and institutional theory are complementary in the analysis of firms' responses to sustainability development pressures (Escobar & Vredenburg, 2010). DCV casts light on the dynamic nature of regulatory activities, and very importantly, it helps investigate the fundamental role of firms' internal processes and capabilities when responding to such regulations. To this end, dynamic capabilities are important elements of nonmarket strategies, enabling the analysis of possible integrated strategies. Institutional theory, in turn, serves as a bridging mechanism to understand the link between nonmarket strategy and organizational outcomes (Mellahi et al., 2016).

This theoretical cross-relationship has been previously explored by Oliver and Holzinger (2008), who have developed a typology for alternative political management strategies (Fig. 6.1). They propose four strategic responses: reactive, defensive, anticipatory and proactive, composing a valuable tool for the investigation of firms' strategic responses, as well as for the analysis of any deployed capabilities and how these play a role in capitalizing on political opportunities (Oliver & Holzinger, 2008, p. 506).

Value aspect

|  | Maintenance | Creation |
|---|---|---|
| **Compliance** | **Reactive strategy**<br><br>- Use of internal capabilities<br><br>Example: swift realignment of structure | **Anticipatory strategy**<br><br>- Use of internal capabilities<br><br>Example: set up best practices in anticipation of regulation |
| **Influence** | **Defensive strategy**<br><br>- Use of external capabilities<br><br>Example: lobbying | **Proactive strategy**<br><br>- Use of external capabilities<br><br>Example: initiate standards that influence regulation |

Strategy

Fig. 6.1.   Oliver and Holzinger's Typology for Alternative Political Management Strategies. *Source*: Adapted from Oliver and Holzinger (2008, p. 506).

### Symbolic, Avoidance and Acquiescence Responses

This study also draws on three further types of responses highlighted in the institutional literature: symbolic, avoidance and acquiescence. These have emerged during the process of abductive reasoning (for further details, see section on "data collection"), revealing their relevance as data were collected and analyzed.

Meyer and Rowan (1977) differentiate between genuine institutional practice and symbolic practice, whereby a firms' strategic approach is to adopt responses without carrying out substantive modifications to align with a sustainability development pressure (Delmas & Montes-Sancho, 2010). Such firms seek to maintain legitimacy by appearing to conform without having to bear the costs of substantive modifications (Figge & Hahn, 2005). For example, firms might try to buffer their technical core[3] from external pressures and uncertainty (Poisson-de Haro & Bitektine, 2015). Hence, the greater the technical core rigidity, the more firms may try to delay substantial changes to it by first attempting to manage stakeholders' expectations through discursive and symbolic means (Poisson-de Haro & Bitektine, 2015, p. 338).

Oliver (1991) also posits that firms might use avoidance as a response, whereby firms seek to avoid conforming "by concealing their nonconformity, buffering themselves from institutional pressures, or escaping from institutional rules or expectations"[4] (p. 154). She also poses the use of acquiescence, whereby firms might comply by mimicking institutional models (Oliver, 1991, p. 154). Most relevant for the present work are imitation tactics, which relate to the concept of mimetic isomorphism, also referred to as "modeling" by DiMaggio and Powell (1983), whereby companies can respond by mimicking prosperous firms and/or taking advice from consultants or professional associations (p. 151).

### Integrative Conceptual Framework

First, it is important to highlight that the present integrative conceptual framework is the result of an abductive approach, which was shaped by the analysis made during the two coding cycles (for further information, see the section on "data analysis").

The concepts contained in the present literature review form the basis of our integrative framework. In short, we look at firms' internal influencing factors, their motives, as well as market and nonmarket environment influencing factors as an attempt to uncover any insights related to firms' responses to the TR. The analysis of firms' responses to the TR draws on the seven types of responses presented in the literature review, namely the four management strategies of Oliver

---

[3]The authors base themselves on Thompson's (1967) definition of technical core, that is, "elements of the firm's structure responsible for transforming the inputs into outputs, from external impacts and uncertainty" (Poisson-de Haro & Bitektine, 2015, p. 327).
[4]Escaping tactic is when a firm moves its activities to a different region where institutional pressures are less stringent or when it changes its activities to escape the institutional pressure (Oliver, 1991).

and Holzinger's (2008) typology as well as on symbolic, avoidance and acquiescence (see conceptual framework in Fig. 6.2).

## Methodology

To investigate firms' responses to the TR and any possible market and nonmarket integration strategies, we take on a qualitative approach by using semi-structured expert interviews. As Silverman (2010) points out, "research methods should be chosen based on the specific task" (p. 9). In this respect, a qualitative approach is suitable to explore firms' responses to the TR as a new and ongoing phenomenon.

The choice of semi-structured expert interviews is based on its suitability for exploration (Bogner & Menz, 2002, p. 37). As the review on relevant literature on the EU Taxonomy reveals, little is known about firms' responses to the TR. To this end, the use of semi-structured interviews allows us to access experts' experiences and knowledge specific to praxis and exploration, while also keeping the interview process "flexible and adaptable to change" (Saunders et al., 2016, p. 175). Such flexibility is important in accessing participants' insights that go beyond and above those foreseen by the researcher, which, according to Saunders et al. (2016), is a necessary element in explorative research (p. 175).

### *Sample and Data Collection*

For the selection of participants, we used cluster sampling as it offers a simplified way to deal with large, fragmented groups and geographical areas (Hair et al., 2016, p. 182). Such is the case of firms affected by the TR, which belong to diverse sectors and industries, and are geographically scattered. This sampling

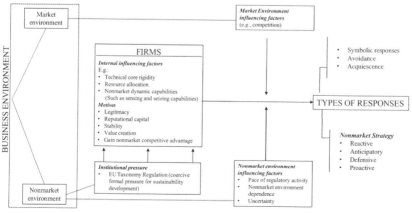

Fig. 6.2.    Conceptual Framework.

method enables the selection of participants from different sectors and countries, allowing a broader sample.

Two groups were targeted: firms (Group 1), which generated more specific data related to their unique experience responding to the requirements of the TR; and experts (i.e., consultancies, auditors, business network forums, etc.; Group 2), who could provide a broader perspective on firms' responses while also serving as a means of comparison with firms' answers (as to increase validation). Based on the cluster criteria in Table 6.3, we used the following criteria to select firms (Group 1): the sector of the company, the company size (in terms of revenue and number of employees) and the rating in sustainability-related rankings (e.g., Morgan Stanley Capital International (MSCI), Sustainalytics, among others) to account for differences in the level to which companies had addressed sustainability prior to the introduction of the TR. The final clusters included 93 public-listed companies and 15 consulting firms based in the following countries: Belgium, Denmark, France, Germany, Hungary, Italy, Netherlands, Sweden, Switzerland and Portugal. Most companies were contacted via email, telephone or LinkedIn, with some stemming from personal networks.

The first interview guide was derived from the initial theoretical framework (which at this point did not include symbolic, avoidance and acquiescence types of responses) and composed of 14 questions. Additionally, two versions of the interview guide were created to cater to the two different groups identified during sampling. After the first round of interviews, weaknesses were identified, as well as the need for further concepts to be included (at this point, symbolic, avoidance and acquiescence responses emerged). This generated a second interview guide containing 17 questions. Moreover, each incremental interview added further insights that were then embedded in subsequent interviews in the form of spontaneous follow-up questions. It is worth noting that this process reflects the nature of abductive reasoning in this study, which allows us to handle data collection and analysis in a dynamic manner, making room for new key constructs to emerge (Dubois & Gadde, 2002).

Table 6.3.    Sampling Criteria.

| Respondent | Criteria 1 | Criteria 2 |
| --- | --- | --- |
| Firms | Respondent must work for a firm affected by the TR | Must work directly with the implementation of TR |
| Other experts (consultancy firms, business network forums, policymakers) | Must be involved in providing consultancy/ services to firms affected by the TR | Must work directly with the topic of TR or sustainable finance |

In order to tap into the areas outlined in the integrative conceptual framework and give room to new insights, the interview guideline was structured as follows: the first part contained introductory questions, which allowed participants to introduce themselves and tell about their relationship with the topic of TR; the second part contained questions to explore firms' organizational structure in response to the TR, such as the creation of any departments, functions, team projects, task forces, etc. These questions were linked to both *RQ1* and *RQ2*, supporting the exploration of any dynamic capabilities through the understanding of how firms initially allocated resources to embed the workload of the TR into their structure, while at the same time allowing room for participants to address any challenges in the initial stages of implementation. The third and final part of the interview contained questions to tap deeper into firms' responses (*RQ1*) as well as motives (*RQ2*), while also leaving room for participants to share unforeseen insights in relation to their experience with the TR. These questions were essential in exploring some areas that might have an impact on their responses to the TR, such as the relationship with the institutional environment, engagement with public consultations, attempts to shape the regulation or to set the pace in their industries, use of dynamic capabilities, the motivation behind their responses and a deeper understanding of challenges brought by the TR.

The sample size was determined based on theoretical saturation, that is, "[t]he point in category development at which no new properties, dimensions, or relationships emerge during analysis" (Strauss & Corbin, 1998, p. 143). As such, the dataset was considered sufficient once data redundancy took place. Altogether, 15 interviews (see Table 6.4) ranging from 30 to 120 minutes were carried out between the period of early October 2021 and late June 2022, encompassing both the stages before the first round of TR disclosure as well as the immediate period after the first TR disclosure. This was an important step to answer the research questions because it could enable us to tackle possible antecedent strategic responses related to political engagement, or even mimetic isomorphism. The interviews were entirely anonymous, and because of COVID19, they were conducted online, recorded and transcribed verbatim using MAXQDA. Some of them were carried out in Portuguese and then translated into English.

### Data Analysis

Following Miles et al. (2020), data collection and data analysis were processed concurrently, with analysis taking place on an ongoing basis (p. 62). This was important in managing the high data volume while ensuring that each incremental interview could be enriched through the analysis of prior interviews. Further, this process also reflects abductive reasoning, the best explanation for the phenomenon of study is sought, while allowing room for developing or changing concepts at any point of the research process (Dubois & Gadde, 2002, p. 558).

For the analysis we used coding, for "coding is deep reflection about and, thus, deep interpretation of the data's meanings. (…) coding is analysis" (Miles et al., 2020, p. 63). This was conducted in two cycles (Saldaña, 2013). In the First Cycle Coding, we derived a list of codes deductively from the conceptual framework

Table 6.4.  Sampling Overview.

| Respondents | Country | Type | Sector | Number of Respondents | Position |
|---|---|---|---|---|---|
| C1 | Denmark | Consultancy | Consulting services | 1 | Consultant |
| C2 | Germany | Consultancy | Consulting services/buildings | 1 | Consultant |
| E1 | Germany | Firm | Manufacturing/sports | 1 | Sustainability spokesperson |
| E2 | Germany | Firm | Chemical, energy and power | 1 | Sustainability reporting |
| E3 | Germany | Firm | Manufacturing/automotive | 1 | Sustainability reporting |
| E4 | Germany | Firm | Medical technology | 1 | Head of sustainability |
| E5 | Germany | Firm | Pharmaceutical/life sciences | 1 | Sustainability reporting |
| E6 | Germany | Business forum | Forum | 1 | Sustainable finance expert |
| E7 | Italy | Firm | Utilities | 2 | Sustainability manager (both respondents) |
| C3 | Netherlands | Consultancy | Consulting services | 1 | Consultant |
| E8 | Portugal | Firm | Energy | 2 | Sustainability consultant/sustainability reporting |
| E9 | Portugal | Firm | Food Retail | 3 | Financial legal manager/head of environmental relations/consolidation manager |
| E10 | Portugal | Firm | Information/communication | 1 | Investment analyst |
| E11 | Portugal | Firm | Energy | 2 | Sustainability manager/strategy and sustainability |
| E12 | Germany | Firm | Industrial manufacturing | 1 | Environmental protection expert |

(Table 6.5), a method called "provisional coding," "which can be revised, modified, deleted, or expanded to include new codes" (Saldaña, 2013, p.144).

Transcripts were analyzed immediately after the interviews by using MAX-QDA, allowing emerging insights to be brought into subsequent interviews while also allowing new codes to be determined inductively. As a result, the First Cycle Coding generated further 175 codes/subcodes in the form of short phrases that captured the essence of the emerging insights. These were further analyzed to establish patterns which were then labeled with an extended thematic statement, a process referred to as "theming the data" (Saldaña, 2013, p. 175).

Next, we re-analyzed the data to create categories in order to better reorganize the initial codes and themes toward the direction of the study. This was done concurrently with the Second Cycle Coding in the form of an iterative analysis, where categories were narrowed down further in line with the research questions, and new insights were condensed as new key constructs. Finally, data triangulation was conducted (Patton, 1999, p. 1192) in order to strengthen the credibility and validity (Noble & Heale, 2019) on "defensive strategy," with which only one firm in the sampling aligned.

## Findings and Interpretation of Collected Data

Our findings are divided into three parts. First, we present key insights on nonmarket environment aspects that influence firms' responses, more specifically, a

Table 6.5.   List of Deductively Derived Codes.

| Codes | Abbreviation |
| --- | --- |
| Seizing dynamic capabilities (allocation of resources) | SEIDC |
| Sensing dynamic capabilities (allocation of resources) | SENDC |
| Strategic response/acquiescence | SRAC |
| Strategic response/symbolic | SRS |
| Strategic response/avoidance | SRAV |
| Motives/legitimacy | ML |
| Motives/stability | MS |
| Motives/value creation | MVC |
| Gain nonmarket advantage | GNA |
| Nonmarket environment influencing factors | NEIF |
| Market environment influencing factors | MEIF |
| Firm's internal influencing factors | FIIF |

high level of uncertainty stemming from the TR. We then address findings that are directly related to firms' responses to the TR. Finally, we show findings related to firms' motives.

### High Level of Uncertainty

One of the key insights emerging from the data refers to the high degree of uncertainty that firms have been facing in the process of implementing the measures stipulated in the TR. Overall, the data reveal two main aspects, namely, ambiguity and lack of clarity in the TR and uncertainty related to the pace of regulatory changes in the TR.

*(1) Ambiguity and lack of clarity in the TR.* Regarding any differences in the interpretation of the TR, most participants reported ambiguity and lack of clarity (see Table 6.6), stating that it is "not black and white" (E11). For example, a participant says that "no one knows what substantial means" in substantial contribution (E2). Regarding OpEx, many criticize its use as an environmental key performance indicator (KPI), claiming that "OpEx is a lot of things" (E11) and difficult to interpret and that "many companies are still struggling with the bizarre OpEx definition in the EU taxonomy, which is not linked basically to any normal economic managerial interpretation of OpEx because it's just very abstract" (E3). The topic of OpEx also seems to puzzle consultants, as one participant explains: "when we are talking about the definition of what OpEx is (…) still today there are some doubts between us and the consultants" (E9).

*(2) Uncertainty related to the pace of regulatory changes in the TR.* Furthermore, as the data show, uncertainty is also closely related to the pace of the TR (see Table 6.7) because of the timeline in the first round of disclosures and, most notably, because of the TR's dynamic nature which can be seen in the many

Table 6.6.   Quotes from Respondents Who Experienced Ambiguity and Lack of Clarity in the TR.

| Respondent | Quotes |
| --- | --- |
| E11 | "And what happened was we had a lot of questions in some of our activities, *[name of consultancy firm]* also had, and *[name of consultancy firm]* had to contact their international network to debate our doubts and help us on the clarification." |
| E2 | "There are heaps of things, so to say, not clarified yet. I mean, so, on certain criteria they mention 'substantial contribution' and no one knows what 'substantial' means. (…) You have in the description, even in the description of the activities, there are- you have stated – we have the activity 'manufacturing of plastics in primary form' and the description starts with describing three specific product groups and then it refers to a NACE code called 20.16, which has a broad range of polymers and not only these three." |

*(Continued)*

Table 6.6.    (*Continued*)

| | |
|---|---|
| E3 | "I also see that a lot of companies are still struggling with the bizarre OpEx definition in the EU taxonomy, which is not linked basically to any normal economic managerial interpretation of OpEx because it's just very abstract and I think OpEx is a bit of a weird word to use it. And I've heard that a lot of- there have been a lot of calls to exclude the OpEx KPI because people will not understand that really, I think, and it's extremely difficult also to get that KPI because for turnover and CAPEX every company has specific financial processes in place to get that data, but for that specific OpEx definition of the EU taxonomy, we're just linked to absolutely nothing else. We just don't have that, so it's something completely new that will not be used for anything but the EU taxonomy, so to me that doesn't make sense, and that's also what I've heard from – what I hear from other companies, it's very a great challenge" |
| E5 | "Now for EU taxonomy, yeah, every single product was differently described, and so you you're not talking with the whole industry, but you're only talking about one product with the company that really is affected. So, you need to discuss it with 40 companies, and no one is listening to 40 companies." |
| C2 | "There are always some 'How do you interpret the different aspects?'. And I give you an example – if you build a new building, you must reply to the water topic and all your showers are only allowed to use six litters per minute. And that's not much to be honest, that's like a really- that's not too comfortable. And this applies to all buildings which are not for residential buildings, which makes sense at one point. However, a hotel is also not a residential building." |
| E6 | "I also think that the technical screening criteria and the do no significant harm criteria (...) what I've heard and what I've experienced is that those are complex and hard to figure out. Especially breaking them down on each activity level of the company and then doing the assessment or potentially next year then doing the assessment, but also being compliant with the do no significant harm criteria that this is not always very straightforward." |

changes and amendments that are published (sometimes very close to disclosure deadlines). To this end, companies report having "too little time to implement" (E6) and that, although much of the work will be done in the first screening, firms' "processes might not be relevant anymore or as the criteria changes [firms] have to change their assessment too" (C1).

Table 6.7.   Quotes Concerning Uncertainty Related to the Pace of TR: Key Quotations.

| Respondent | Main Statements |
| --- | --- |
| E3 | "(…) there's just not on every topic a clear interpretation that is seen as the standard to be applied (…) And even now, I mean, it's December now, so we basically must report from one month on forward. Even yesterday we got news that something has changed again – and like material changes that still come up in like the general leading interpretation of material matters one month before we're supposed to report – so it's extremely challenging." |
| E6 | "I think that there was some ambiguity beforehand, and the companies then had too little time to implement this (…) And that a lot of expertise is needed to do that, and especially in the short amount of time maybe that there was no time to, like, reconcile this with all the stakeholders to, you know, give that a proper check-up in order to have a good implementation on that." |
| C1 | "I mean, a lot of the work will be done in the first screening, of course, but you will need to update your financials every year at least for sure. And then you might also have to update, and processes criteria might not be relevant anymore or the criteria changed, and you have to change the assessment too, so you need a system that can keep up with something dynamic." |
| E2 | "So, criteria can change six times and we have no transparency [on] how they will change. So, in an extreme case – and I mean that's now a black and white example, but to make it transparent – I report always green CapEx but I never show green sales because the criteria will have changed in the meantime and this is, for investors, a nightmare." |
| C3 | "So, the starting point might be compliance (…) I think that also because of the very pressing timelines, the starting point is in 90% of the time compliance." |
| E5 | "(…) the practical doing is a major challenge – the legal requirements come out today and you need to fulfil them tomorrow." |
| E7 | "I think one big challenge is about climate change adaptation, because in general the requirement of the taxonomy is really challenging (…) We already have a risk management approach that take into account climate change adaptation, but there are, like, every time pieces to add to the way we conduct the study." |

## Firms' Responses to the TR and Related Aspects

In this section, findings are arranged according to the types of responses in the conceptual framework. During the interviews, we asked participants about how resources were allocated regarding the organizational structure when implementing the necessary measures of the TR, the processes they needed to create or extend, as well as specific questions about any processes they have in place to scan the nonmarket environment. Answers to these questions gave us an understanding of the types of dynamic capabilities deployed by companies, indicating not only how swiftly they react to new regulations and how these are kept in their radar but also the level of political engagement and impact on resource allocation.

Furthermore, we also asked questions about the possible influence of any dominant organizations on the implementation of the TR requirements as well as engagement with the institutional environment. These questions generated data more specific to possible imitation (acquiescence). The findings reveal that most firms respond in a reactive way, and mostly only front-running firms with extensive sustainability business strategies present a response closer to the profile of anticipatory response. Moreover, the high level of uncertainty inherent to the TR triggers companies to acquiesce (although this response does not reveal to be mutually exclusive with other responses in the case of the TR). Regarding a defensive type of response, this was also identified in the case of sectors where controversy and low alignment with the TR can be noted, displaying a cross-relationship with symbolic response. Finally, in terms of avoidance and proactive strategies, it was not possible to identify any patterns related to these two types in the dataset. In the following subsections, we present these results in more detail along with key quotations from interview participants to support the credibility of the findings.

### Reactive Type of Response

As mentioned in the last section, most firms' responses resonate with a reactive type of response, whereby firms seek compliance while prioritizing value maintenance. Overall, the data reveal four aspects related to this response, as follows:

*(1) Reaction speed of scanning capabilities (sensing capabilities).* Firms that align with reactive responses claim that the first time the TR came to their attention was when the TEG published its first draft in 2020, contrary to firms that participated in the very early stages of the TR conception by shaping the regulation through active engagement or lobbying. One premise is that "it's simple resource matter [...] and courageous to start preparing" too soon (E4). One of the consultants claims that the TR "just came into force and people now are just realizing that it really is there" (C2).

*(2) Different functions scanning nonmarket environment (sensing capability).* Another aspect is having "multiple different functions looking from different angles" (E4) when it comes to scanning the environment, instead of one function or department. In some cases, the sustainability department shares this task with a "centralized regulatory office" (E3). As one participant metaphorically explains,

"it's a soup with many ingredients" (E9), where sustainability, legal and financial play a part in the scanning.

*(3) Creation of a task force in the early stages (seizing capability).* In our findings, the creation of task forces is a common process in the early stages (see key quotations in Table 6.8). Contrary to companies that have a long history of holding departments exclusively responsible for political engagement, firms that respond reactively seem to first create a task force. Although not a process extension exclusively used by companies that respond reactively, it highlights the ad hoc nature with which these firms respond to the new regulation as a low resource, effective strategy to accomplish organizational goals (Newton & Levinson, 1973). This resonates with Oliver and Holzinger's (2008) argument that reactive responses usually rely on rapid and low-cost reconfiguration of processes (p. 507).

*(4) Creation of functions responsible for the TR (seizing capability).* Some participants also report external hires to deal with regulations (including the TR). Such is the case described by a participant: "when you want to know how it [the TR] directly affects me, is that my entire job is implementing the EU taxonomy. So, in terms of my position, it wouldn't exist if the EU taxonomy didn't exist" (E3). Likewise, one of the consultants also claimed to see external hires happening as way of dealing with uncertainty or in their own words:

> several of the companies we work with say "Well, this is too much," either it's too much additional work, we cannot also take this on, we don't have the in-house expertise (...) So we see more and more vacancies now going online specifically for EU taxonomy or kind of sustainable finance reporting specialist. So, yeah, external hiring is also happening more. (C3)

In the case of another firm, they have created a group through internal hire composed partly by senior staff, described as a "small start-up in the big corporate [...] to take external requirements like TCFD or the EU taxonomy, but also internal ones to translate them into our organization" (E2). In both cases, the aim is to work on compliance while aiming at maintaining value.

### Acquiescence Type of Response

The dataset reveals that acquiescence (or modeling) types of responses are directly related to high levels of uncertainty. Three aspects stand out: influence from consulting and/or auditing firms, influence from front-runners, and influence from first movers through their voluntary disclosures.

*(1) Influence from consulting and/or auditing firms.* Most firms report contacting consulting and/or auditing firms. Also, the interviewed consultants reported having clients from a broad range of sectors and company sizes. Against this background, the first firms that had to disclose reported the most uncertainty, resorting to consulting firms to reduce such uncertainty. For some participants, such influence is very clear, as indicated by E5, who said "I

Table 6.8.    Quotes from Respondents on the Creation of Task Forces.

| Respondent | Quotes |
|---|---|
| C3 | "Well, what we've seen in quite a few companies is that they set up task forces." |
| E1 | "At least for our financial year 2021, we have built quite a loose, let's say, working group but we will further, stabilize this with the upcoming reporting requirements as of 2022 and 2023 onwards, depending on the deadlines as they are going to be set." |
| E9 | "So, we're mandated internally by the group to work together so that we can find the solutions to better accommodate the requirements from the taxonomy." |
| E10 | "We decided to develop a project dedicated to the taxonomy and lead by our two departments (CFO and Sustainability)." |
| E12 | "Researcher: And how has the firm organized the implementation of the requirements of EU taxonomy in terms of team structures? Have there been project teams, task forces or any other creative structures? Respondent: All of them, all of them." |
| E6 | "In my personal experience, many companies work in some kind of dedicated project organizations with representatives from many different departments." |

guess we are strongly influenced by just applying the regulation very closely, because our auditor is very strict on applying a literal interpretation of the EU taxonomy regulation." In the case of other firms, consultancy was used as training "for some key focal points at the company" (E11), as an additional input to their own self-study (E5), as an initial help with the remainder done internally (E10) and as support in processing data manually (E2). For another participant, consultancy is "the quickest path forward, or the easiest path forward to get preparation done" (E4). This is reflected in the statements from consultants, such as C1, for example, who claims that whereas a few companies simply want some guidance, most of them "are just lost" and expect the consulting firm "to do most of the work."

*(2) Influence from front-runners.* Many participants report having other companies (in some cases from diverse sectors) looking up to them as role models and contacting them to exchange insights on the interpretation of the TR. Table 6.9 displays the main statements from these firms.

*(3) Influence from first movers through their voluntary disclosures.* Finally, our dataset also reveals influence from the few voluntary disclosures by early first movers. As one of the consultants explains, "[there are] a few companies that have already voluntarily disclosed EU taxonomy requirements" (C3), and these have served as a guide for many companies searching for examples. Another participant also shared the influence of such early disclosures, as follows:

Table 6.9.   Main Statements from Respondents on the Influence from Front-Runners.

| Respondent | Main Statements |
|---|---|
| E3 | "I have noticed that in discussions with other companies, almost no one was as far along as we were, and we are constantly being contacted by other companies who are asking us for opinion on how we implement certain – or how we deal with certain issues that arise when implementing the EU taxonomy." |
| E8 | "[other companies] have contacted us (…) [we are seen] as a frontrunner company. I think in Portugal there are no companies that have disclosed against the Taxonomy, especially in terms of KPIs, like we have. No one does what we do." |
| C3 | "I think I should mention the larger consulting firms that are also an auditor – so all the Big Four and then some others– we're also in a group together to also kind of align our thinking on how to implement this so that we have one voice." |
| E2 | "We are getting direct requests from peer companies." |
| E1 | "[the firm] has been at the forefront (…) and we even have informed other business peers what is coming up from their side to help them to build the necessary awareness as well as to prepare for this as well." |
| E7 | "I can say that in some cases we have been a best practice if you want because we also publish the alignment." |
| C2 | "There are some [big companies]. They're driving the market as role models." |

we look at the work they [the company] did and it was well done because they provide a consolidation of the taxonomy, their opinion about certain exclusion of activities (…) and they also provide a description of the steps they have taken to make the report. (E7)

It is likely that these three identified influences will increase in future rounds of disclosure once best practices have been established, leading to further mimetic isomorphism. This can already be observed in our last round interview which was conducted in late June 2022 (after most companies had already published their reports in the first round). According to one participant, their consultancy firm has already consulted many companies in the past year, and thus, they "have already identified those elements that are negotiable or at least subject to interpretation" (E12), exerting a much stronger influence on the interpretation of the TR.

### *Anticipatory Type of Response*

This section deals with the few responses which can be attributed to an anticipatory type of strategy. First, it is worth highlighting that firms aligning with this type of response in our sample were large multinational companies that possess strong public relations capabilities, innovation drive and a business model built on sustainable products. This is further supported through the statement of a senior consultant who reported working with

> front-running companies that already have quite an extensive sus-
> tainability strategy and now see themselves confronted with all sorts
> of regulation and they want to ensure that their strategy is still in
> line with the regulation that is coming their way and how to best
> profit from these regulations and make the most out of it. (C3)

Against this backdrop, we have identified three sensing capabilities that differentiate this type of response, which are discussed in more detail in the following paragraphs.

*(1) Scanning and predictive capabilities to anticipate changes (sensing capability).* Regarding this area, one of the interviewed firms established a "Sustainability Board" for a timely and continuous scanning of the nonmarket environment. As such, they first started occupying themselves with the TR around the year of 2016 with the first EU talks about sustainable finance, that is, "when the first documents cropped up, and the TEG was formed to prepare these documents" (E8). In the case of another firm, significant importance is placed "on the topic of shadowing and observing (or watchdogging) political developments" (E1), treating regulatory developments with priority. In the participant's own words, "as we actually see the entire agenda from the EU becoming more important, I think we have intensified our efforts and resources to better track and shadow everything which is coming from the EU side" (E1). In this case, a senior top manager is in the lead to deal with sustainability policy. To this end, the engagement of senior management in sensing the political environment stands out in comparison to other types of responses.

*(2) Emphasis on effective communication across business units (sensing capability).* Regarding the questions on organizational structure, one of the greatest challenges identified is that the implementation of the TR involves liaison with a wide range of functions and expertise (see Fig. 6.3). In this respect, firms that align with an anticipatory type of response stand out for their ability to effectively communicate across business units.

As such, the data reveal that what differentiates anticipatory responses from other responses is the involvement of business units in the early stages, as claimed by participant E8:

> (…) from 2018 to 2021, we had two moments influenced by the
> public consultations (…) and, simultaneously, through an involve-
> ment with the business units (…) in the processes of public consul-
> tation, very specifically on the climate [mitigation and adaptation]
> (…) when it is to do with very specific/technical subjects, we have
> always made sure to involve the specific business units to support
> us in the correct interpretation. (E8)

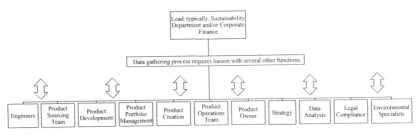

Fig. 6.3.    Overview of Most Quoted Functions for the Implementation of the TR.

Yet another participant reported an emphasis on cross-functionality through a matrixed structure. For them, involving other business units enables them "to make sure that [their] response back to the platform [EU] is robust, fact-based, and is honest" (E1). For them, a matrixed structure allows them to be nimble when responding to external challenges such as the TR.

*(1) Engagement with decision-makers and regulators (sensing capability).* Furthermore, the data also reveal that companies presenting an anticipatory type of response are prone to direct and/or indirect political engagement. In the case of one firm, for example, a very senior manager is responsible for direct engagement, as reported in the interview in the following statement:

> This is also in particular one of my core roles, building a close dialogue to the decision makers and to the regulators, not just related to the taxonomy, but also to all the other concepts and legal initiatives as they are in the pipeline. Because we think the earlier we know the earlier we can influence, and as earlier we can prepare. (E1)

For E8, such engagement took place more indirectly through associations and forums. As the participant claims, the firm has invested much attention to the process leading up to the TR. In their words,

> in 2018 we responded to the public consultation, in 2019 we responded again, that is, around 10 public positions that we took part in during 2018 and 2019. This increase in the period of 2020 and 2021, so we can talk about forty individual participations (as a company) in public consultations. (E8).

### Defensive Type of Response

First, we stress that only a very small part from the sample aligns with this type of response. Without intending to generalize from a few sources, we still consider these findings relevant since they present a stark contrast to the rest of the results. This response is marked by a narrative to protect the status quo and thwart the new regulation, as proposed by Oliver and Holzinger (2008, p. 507). Overall, the data reveal two main aspects shown in the following paragraphs.

*(1) Resistance to make the leap from older regulations.* In this respect, we observed resistance to adhere to the new institutional logics against which the EU green deal and the TR are developed, which integrates market goals with sustainability goals. To this end, the stringency of the TR is compared to the less demanding requirements of existing frameworks with which the company is already compliant, as can be seen in the participant's statement as follows:

> all our products are subject to stringent regulations in every country.
> (…) the EU taxonomy is not aligned with the other legal requirements
> because the EU taxonomy, from the normative evaluation, goes far
> beyond what is legally required. And this is the challenge. (E5)

Although other participants have also reported tensions between the TR and existing legal and voluntary frameworks, the difference is that this aspect is marked by a defensive narrative, as can be seen in Table 6.10. For firms that align with an anticipatory response, the narrative emphasizes the harmonization of different frameworks, whereby the TR is understood as part of an "economic revolution" toward sustainability. In the case of firms aligning with a defensive

Table 6.10.   Different Narratives on the Leap From Established Legal/ Voluntary Frameworks and the TR.

| | Firm From Renewable Energy Sector Aligning With Anticipatory Response | Firm From Chemicals Sector Aligning With a Defensive Response |
| --- | --- | --- |
| Direct quotation | "(…) the tension that exists relates to the difficulty in visualising the harmonisation of the several pieces in the bigger picture. We are watching an economic revolution where companies distinguish themselves based on their sustainability. And the regulation is much ahead than companies' resources and capacity to adapt to such changes. (…) We find that, in the next couple of years, they might complement each other (…) as to become harmonised and yield something like the financial statements from the IFRS framework." (E8) | "Well, I'm not a psychologist, but usually you're not going to convince anybody, and normally you're bringing up a resistance against this. Why? I assume that many companies will at one point in time do what is required from the EU Taxonomy on the reporting base, but they will not change their behaviour. They will not change a product because it's too far away and this is exactly what it is for [us]. If I would talk to decision-making colleagues in North America and South America, Brazilians, US Americans, they would say, are you crazy?" (E5) |

response, on the other hand, these tensions are perceived in a negative light, in which the TR represents an unwelcome challenge to the current regulatory landscape. Thus, we observe a resistance to make the leap to the TR and a desirability to protect the current status quo.

*(2) Firm leans on its own idea of sustainability.* Following the same argument in the last aspect, here we identify a degree of opposition to the TR's definition of what is sustainable and a general belief that the company's idea of sustainability is more accurate to their sector's needs. This can be seen in the following statement:

> It's a bit annoying because where we have a real impact on something (…) will never be reflected in there [the TR]. (…) we have a big project that means we want to reduce the carbon footprint of agriculture by 30% and again until 2030. And not in the smallest ways, but in big agriculture, so let's say, uh, producing corn or canola or soy in North and South America and (…) this will never be reflected by the EU taxonomy. If this really works – what we are working on – there will be a huge positive impact reducing greenhouse gas emissions, but it will not be due to the methodology of EU taxonomy. (…) Just because it's not part of their methodology to understand. (E5)

This has also been acknowledged by one of the consultants when asked about conflicts between the TR and the goals and interests of firms. As the participant reported, "the goal might be similar, but the way to get there is different," leading some firms to "follow their own path that they've sometimes already started, and then explain why that doesn't align with what the EU taxonomy asks from them" (C3). These findings have been previously reported by a detailed analysis of key sectors regarding lobbying on the TR's green criteria by the think tank InfluenceMap. As their report shows, "[a] common theme has been industry lobbyists pushing for definitions of environmental sustainability based on current, more lenient, regulatory approaches instead of the science-based recommendations of the TEG" (InfluenceMap, 2020, p. 10).[5]

### Firms Motives and Integration of Market and Nonmarket Strategies

In this section, we present the findings related to questions about the motives behind firms' chosen strategy to implement the requirements of the TR. Additionally, we also analyzed the collected data for any further related insights.

---

[5]According to the same report from InfluenceMap, some key sectors that have pushed for concessions in the criteria include "gas (asking for alignment with the Clean Energy Package), bioenergy (asking for alignment with the Renewable Energy Directive (RED II)), agriculture (asking for alignment with the Common Agricultural Policy (CAP))." (InfluenceMap, 2020, p. 10).

The findings indicate that the main motive for most participants is related to the coercive nature of the TR and the resulting legitimacy and reputational capital, while for a very few, also value creation, stability and competitive advantage (Table 6.11).

Table 6.11.   Overview of Identified Motives Behind Firms' Responses.

| | Key Quotations | Motive |
|---|---|---|
| E1 | "The motivation is simply driven by the fact that we must prepare for a regulation. (…) Because I think we are subject of an external assurance processes, and as we fall under the law, we want to make sure a hundred percent that we are reporting and disclosing information in the correct way. So, this is the main motivator. There isn't any other motivator." | Reputation, legitimacy |
| C3 | "Some companies just say 'Alright, we have to be compliant, tick the box, that's it'. And some companies say, 'Well, we must be compliant, this is something that is asked from us, but we want to link it to our sustainable direction that we're pursuing anyway. And then let's see how we can use the taxonomy, how we can benefit from all the work that's been put into it to strengthen our own strategy (…) And then of course reputation (…) 'we cannot not be compliant.'" | Reputation, legitimacy <br><br> Value creation (mid-long term) |
| C2 | "Motivation factor – in the end it's about what they need to do (…) that one thing they need to comply with it and to report, and the other one they also set like these sustainability goals and have to achieve them also." | Reputation, legitimacy |
| E5 | "It's just to fulfil the legal requirements. And to fulfil the legal requirements means that it needs to be the evaluation of the products and services offered and then there would need to be the numbers calculated and that's it." | Legitimacy |

(Continued)

Table 6.11.    (*Continued*)

| Key Quotations | Motive |
|---|---|
| E12 "I don't think that this is genuine willingness to save the world. (…) At least I haven't seen evidence on that top level, you know, for being more environmentally compliant or more environmentally proactive, let's put it this way." | Legitimacy |
| E9 "If we talked about sustainability in general, our motivation is (…) to do our path and make sure we're doing it right." | Reputation |
| C1 "Compliance is the main, and then there's also reputation and risk management, access to finance, assessing sustainable impact and future proofing your business (…) branding and image." | Legitimacy, reputation, competitive advantage |
| E2 "(…) I mean, there's no way on not displaying any figures. So, whatever might happen, and that's when it comes also in the personal motivation for me, is whatever might happen we will deliver reliable figures end of the year for our annual report." | Legitimacy |
| E8 "I think we have no doubts in this sense. [Our] strategy in terms of sustainability will always be classified as proactive. In 1991, no one was talking about or seeing these issues, and we had already formed an environmental council. Around 1994 we already had a prevention and security policy and we put together an environmental policy and so, our sustainability history is very old (…) and the market in Portugal only started talking about socially responsible investing very recently. And that explain why sometimes we are ahead; it has to do with it." | Sustainability pioneer (regardless of the TR) |

Nonetheless, the findings show that part of the reason for the lack of integration of market and nonmarket strategies is the pace of the regulatory framework. That is, the initial tight deadlines and the pace at which the EU has released delegated acts and Q&A information for firms in the first round of disclosure. As one participant states,

> [t]here are all these Q&A every three months (…) and now the latest Q&A will come mid-December for reporting. Mid of December almost all companies say are closed in terms of the concept. (…) Let's assume they come next week. I mean, we are, so to say, close to finish, do I now have to rebuild my whole IT system because there is a different interpretation of it? (E2)

One of the consultants explains that "because of the very pressing timelines, the starting point is in 90% of the time compliance," complementing that "sometimes we do bring it up, you know, more kind of this strategic angle, but most companies are just not ready for it, they cannot take it on at this moment, it's just kind of overwhelming, I think" (C3).

Moreover, this is a bigger problem in the case of firms with a high technical core rigidity, and whose activities are considered transition activities by the TR. This is particularly the case for companies in critical sectors (e.g., chemicals), where the costs of phasing out huge plants would be a necessary step in order to steer the measures of the TR into business strategy. For example, as one participant states,

> We have many transitional activities. These will be phased out. (…) I know only that criteria revision will be every three years, but I do not know how it changes. So, (…) if I have an idea for an investment, I check on the EU taxonomy alignment, I propose to my board (…) Then I get the final approval before I start working (…) I report green CapEx to my investors, and the plant runs for ten years, fifteen years, maybe twenty years. And within these twenty years (…) criteria can change six times and we have no transparency how they will change. So, in a really extreme case (…) I report always green CapEx but I never show green sales because the criteria have changed in the meantime and this is, for investors, a nightmare. (…) And this is what honestly prevents me from integrating that deeply into processes, because there's so much changing. (E2)

In this example, the pace of changes in the TR, the firm's core rigidity, and the investors' expectations are all critical factors.

Finally, firms with a stronger sustainability focus and/or stronger innovation strategy harnessing sustainability aspects (such as those aligning with an anticipatory type of response) saw an opportunity in the TR to strengthen their own approach. One way this was done was by early and voluntarily implementing reporting requirements even before the TR turned into effect. Another way was the early adaptation of internal business processes such as risk management processes or the consideration of TR-related criteria in the setup of strategic projects. However, this also reflected that sustainability was a core part of these companies' strategy before. However, as C3 reports, in the future, more companies might perceive opportunities to strengthen one's position in the market as a possible next step by at least half of the companies that provide consultancy for taking a more proactive approach after basic compliance with the law has been ensured.

## Implications

In the last section, we presented the findings along with some interpretations, revealing insights that are relevant both to the new literature on the TR and to the theoretical field proposed in our integrative conceptual framework. In this section, we provide further reflections on our findings, linking them to existing literature and discussing implications for research and for management.

### *Theoretical Implications for EU Taxonomy-Related Research*

The present study contributes mainly to the literature on the EU Taxonomy, while also offering insights to a more general understanding of how firms react to non-market institutional pressures. Overall, the findings suggest that the TR represents an important next step in sustainability reporting, challenging firms to re-think their capital expenditures and operation expenses within a new institutional logic marked by sustainability development. This follows recent research related to the EU Taxonomy, as argued by Bond and Dusík (2022), who state that taxonomies for sustainable development depict a paradigmatic shift from an "economic" to an "ecologic" mindset. At the same time, we contend that this also taps into the question of whether firms' responses are more substantial or ceremonial, and in this respect, our findings show that high levels of uncertainty related both to ambiguity and the pace of the regulation have a great impact on firms.

Some of the main challenges identified include interpreting a complex (often ambiguous) and stringent new regulation and dealing with the high level of granularity required while trying to effectively combine financial, sustainability, legal, environmental, strategic and technical expertise from multiple functions in diverse business units in the data-gathering process. In special, the data-gathering process is particularly challenging, as already identified by Och (2020) who discussed the problem of data gaps before the first TR round of disclosures.

Furthermore, our study complements Fischer et al.'s (2022) ex ante study of German practitioners' perspectives of the TR where they identify complexity and lack of clarity as obstacles in implementing the TR. Our study confirms their findings not only in the case of German firms but also firms in other EU countries. Additionally, we contribute by identifying different types of responses to such challenges and how different types of sensing and seizing capabilities have been so far deployed according to these different responses. To this end, we propose that future research could further explore sector-specific dynamic capabilities through case studies for a more detailed understanding of capabilities deployed in response to the TR.

Our study also supports Schütze and Stede's (2020) predictions on the negative impacts of the TR thresholds for transitioning activities on firms' motivation to "greenify." This was especially the case for firms in sectors with high greenhouse gas (GHG) emissions (e.g., chemicals) and supply chains. However, we make an extra contribution by finding that uncertainty related to the pace of the TR has a considerable impact on steering TR-related goals into business strategy, such as reconfiguring CapEx toward investing in newer assets to foster "green" economic activities. Given the perceived short-time frame for the implementation of TR-related requirements and the feared risks for businesses' reputation and legitimacy, companies might engage in lobbying and ceremonial responses, weakening the objectives of the TR. To this end, we suggest future research to explore corporate political activities of companies related to the TR (Hillman et al., 2004; Mellahi et al., 2016). Moreover, it would be interesting to explore shareholders' awareness of the TR as well as whether and the extent to which shareholders enact pressure on firms to transition into green activities based on the TR.

### *Theoretical Implications for DCV, Nonmarket Strategy Research*

In addition to the contributions to TR-related research, the present study also makes a small contribution toward linking the topic of sustainability development regulation with DCV and nonmarket literature under the prism of institutional theory. As the findings show, nonmarket environment influencing factors related to the TR are characterized by high uncertainty and a very dynamic pace. Teece et al. (1997, p. 509) propose DCV to investigate how firms can develop and maintain their resources to achieve and sustain competitive advantage in the market environment. Thus, our findings reinforce the pertinence of this logic in the case of the TR, especially considering its dynamic nature with several expected changes and amendments taking place as it develops (e.g., the inclusion of new delegated acts and screening criteria for the remaining environmental objectives).

Oliver and Holzinger (2008) further contend that DCV can be extended to the realm of nonmarket strategy. The present study aligns with this contention, contributing by extending its application to the context of regulation for sustainability development. As our study shows, the TR has posed the need for firms to reconfigure some of their internal resources as well as to adapt and extend their processes. Future research could focus on understanding firms' use of external capabilities in the case of TR by, for example, further investigating lobbying practices and the incident of external hire of government experts and/or members of green parties.

Furthermore, by analyzing and understanding how companies respond to the TR, we contribute to DCV and nonmarket research with an insight into the interplay between (1) internal influencing factors like resource allocation, processes utilized and motives, (2) nonmarket external influencing factors such as high degree of uncertainty and ambiguity or the pace of TR regulation and to a lesser degree (3) industry affiliation as a market influencing factor. As our analysis shows, such interplay has an impact on firms' responses, revealing varying degrees of deployment of dynamic capabilities (see Fig. 6.4).

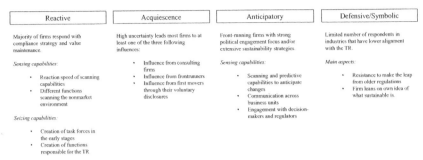

Fig. 6.4.    Identified Responses to the TR and Their Core Aspects.

These findings reinforce the relevance of Oliver and Holzinger's (2008) typology of nonmarket strategies for the analysis of firms' responses to sustainability regulations. Additionally, they also point to potential areas of improvement for firms if they are to enhance their responses to harness synergies from market and nonmarket integration and create long-term value. This is important considering that the TR will likely shape the way investors choose their financial products, creating further pressure for firms to prove their sustainability strengths. Thus, these institutional pressures might require firms to continuously "integrate, build, and reconfigure internal and external competences to address rapidly changing environments" (Teece et al., 1997, p. 516).

In terms of market and nonmarket integration, the present study makes a hypothetical inference based on the examination of motives behind firms' responses. We find that the TR does not significantly alter the strategy of firms that already operate within the logics of sustainability – these have already been for some time coordinating their interests with those of sustainability-related nonmarket institutions and frameworks because it brings value to their strategy. However, an interesting finding is that firms that are not sustainability driven do not seem to see market and nonmarket integration opportunities and, instead, are mostly motivated by keeping their reputation and gaining legitimacy (as suggested by the institutional theory), focusing on compliance only. As such, for these firms, the likelihood of integrating their strategies might only be triggered if their business performance is threatened by, for example, competitors who have been able to develop sustainable innovations and, thus, attract more clients and investment in an environment that is transitioning toward a green economy. If this would be the case, these firms' stability would be at stake. To this end, Baron's (1995) assertions around the importance of integrating market and nonmarket strategies would be germane to gain competitive advantage.

### *Implications for Practice*

Our findings also have direct implication for firms and policymakers. In terms of the high level of uncertainty experienced by firms, we contend that the TR and its challenges should be framed in the context of the identified paradigmatic shift and not only faced as an extra regulation that firms must comply with. As demonstrated in the Appendix, there is increasing research in the understanding of the impacts of the TR on current existing sustainability frameworks (legal and voluntary). These studies include arguments around the alignment of different green initiatives with the TR to increase transparency (Beerbaum, 2021), and the contention that the TR could set the pace globally due to its higher level of refinement (Zetzsche et al., 2021), shaping international sustainability standards (Rant, 2022). As such, the right contextual framing could help shape firms' responses toward reconfiguring their capabilities on an ongoing basis, fostering the development of best practices in TR disclosure. As firms progress into subsequent TR disclosures in the coming years, the initial high level of uncertainty might also become less relevant, and the scope for business strategy within the background of the TR might also increase.

However, if the high levels of uncertainty remain, firms could focus on working on the microfoundations of their dynamic capabilities by sharpening their sensing capabilities to continuously scan both nonmarket and market environments in order to capture further regulatory developments and best practices (Teece, 2007).

Moreover, we also highlight the importance of including business strategy units in the process of responding to the requirements of the TR. By framing the current paradigmatic shift and including business strategy, firms could more effectively align their motives with the developments of the TR and, on a wider context, with the EU Green Deal.

Lastly, we contend that the current study also has implications for policymakers, as follows:

*(1) Reactive responses.* These can be a sign of suboptimal reactions to the regulation which should be tackled by policymakers. This could help them adjust where weaknesses exist, such as ambiguity, lack of understanding about industry-specific sustainability (as well as innovation) best practices, adjusting the pace of regulation and ensuring more support in the interpretation of the delegated acts. To this end, we contend that public consultations targeted at understanding sector-specific best practices could greatly improve the TR framework and how it applies to different sectors.

*(2) Defensive responses.* These, in turn, can be sign decoupling in sectors with high GHG emissions and low TR eligibility. This could have great implications for policymakers by helping them identify more nuanced aspects that stop these firms from making meaningful investments toward innovative sustainable technologies. On a deeper level, it could also support policymakers in the iteration of less efficient TR requirements, such as adjusting the thresholds for transition activities to incentivize sectors with high GHG emissions to take substantial action toward 11 sustainability goals.

*(3) Acquiescence responses.* In this respect, particularly modeling responses stemming from the influence of consultants and auditors can signal the need for policymakers to consider the influence that the consulting and auditing community have on how firms react. To this end, liaison could foster a more precise interpretation of the regulation.

## Conclusion

The main purpose of the present study was to explore firms' responses to the new TR through the lens of DCV, nonmarket research and to some extent also institutional theory and to investigate if firms have been integrating their market and nonmarket strategies. To achieve that, we have conducted semi-structured expert interviews, analyzing internal influencing factors such as resource allocation and processes that needed to be extended, identifying possible influences from any patterns of perceived challenges stemming from the nonmarket environment and examining the motives behind firms' responses.

Our results show that most firms align with a reactive type of response, whereby their motives are related to legitimacy, reputation and stability. In turn, sustainability pioneering firms are more likely to align with anticipatory types of responses, harnessing existing sensing and seizing dynamic capabilities which help them anticipate the evolution of the TR as part of their routine scanning of sustainability developments. For firms with higher GHG emissions, the results are more complex. We identify the tendency to align with a defensive type of response, whereby firms show a resistance toward the more stringent requirements of the TR in favor of less demanding established regulations. For these firms, the motivation is only legitimacy and reputational capital. We also find that acquiescence responses are not mutually exclusive with the other types of responses but, yet, more prominent in reactive types of responses, stemming from the influence of consulting and auditing services. Furthermore, we find that, as of now, firms have not considered the integration of market and nonmarket strategies in their responses to the TR. In the case of companies that respond in an anticipatory manner, although at first they might appear to seek the integration of market and nonmarket strategies, we identify that their orientation is more connected to their strong sustainability focus rather than being related to the TR.

Regarding influences from the nonmarket environment, our expert interviews show that firms' responses have been impacted by a high level of uncertainty related both to ambiguity and lack of clarity in the interpretation of the TR, as well as to the dynamic pace of the regulation. The latter seems to have the most impact on the possibility of TR-related goals being embedded into business strategy, with firms refraining from making meaningful capital expenditures toward new environmentally friendly assets because they fear that the regulation might change and these investments could soon not be TR-aligned anymore.

Finally, our expert interviews reveal that the TR is an important step in sustainability reporting, and which develops against a paradigmatic shift leading to a stronger integration of an economic and ecological mindset. This insight is of great relevance to the perception of how firms should respond to the TR in terms of business strategy. Firms that have not yet realized this paradigmatic shift will likely continue to face the TR as a mere instrument of compliance to gain legitimacy, reputation and stability. However, firms that understand this shift could face the TR as an instrument of sustainability development to create value and gain competitive advantage.

Despite the efforts in following a systematic approach, there are still limitations to the present study. The main limitation relates to the sample. We acknowledge that participants belonged to firms that had the resources to take part in the interview (personnel and time availability), as well as the willingness to do so when most firms are struggling with the first TR disclosure. As such, the sampling does not capture a complete picture of the broad spectrum of sectors and industries in the EU. To overcome that, we increased drastically the number of companies contacted across the EU, but we still only had very few responses (and no financial institutions willing to participate). As such, the impact of this limitation on the present study was mitigated by approaching the dataset homogeneously (instead of emphasizing unique responses per sector), as Yin (2011) suggests when examining cross-cutting issues (p. 240).

Another limitation refers to subjectivity. Despite leaning on scientific methods for conducting the expert interviews and analyzing the data, the impact of the researcher is still predominant during the interviews, most notably when spontaneous exchanges take place, giving space for subjective opinions. To this end, more efforts were channeled toward reflexivity and the examination of one's own beliefs during the research, as well as conscious efforts to diligently follow the chosen methods as neutrally as possible.

Furthermore, we had an exceptionally low response from firms in sectors that are more GHG-emission intensive. This would have been important to increase the validity of our findings related to a defensive type of response. To overcome that, we resorted to triangulation by researching documents that report on the level of lobbying from firms with high GHG emissions. In this respect, we suggest that future research could concentrate on sectors with high GHG emissions and with low TR eligibility to further investigate their motives and whether the TR is likely to become only a ceremonial element in their routine disclosures.

On a broader level, although the credibility of this study may be somewhat affected by the limitations presented in this section, this also opens a window for future research to explore sector-related responses in greater detail once a higher number of companies have disclosed against the TR and are more confident to take part in academic research. Moreover, as more firms disclose against the TR in the years to come, future research would also have the chance to investigate what best practices have been installed, the influence from consultants in such best practices and potential resulting isomorphic processes. To this end, the present study fulfills an exploratory purpose, laying out the first insights on firms' responses to the TR which can serve as a basis for further research.

Finally, although we contend that DCV and nonmarket research is suitable to analyze companies' responses to the TR, it also comes with a small caveat. This is mostly related to the fact that, as of now, firms' have only started to disclose and explore their capabilities to respond to the pressures stemming from the TR. While this has allowed us to delve into sensing and, less so, seizing capabilities, it is still too early to investigate any transforming capabilities. As such, future research could also engage in exploring whether firms will be using or developing any transforming capabilities as the requirements of the TR become more complex.

# References

Bansal, P., & Clelland, I. (2004). Talking trash: Legitimacy, impression management, and unsystematic risk in the context of the natural environment. *Academy of Management Journal, 47*(1), 93–103.

Baron, D. P. (1995). Integrated strategy: Market and nonmarket components. *Californian Management Review, 37*(2), 47–65.

Baron, D. P. (1997). Integrated strategy, trade policy and global competition. *California Management Review, 39*(2), 145–169.

Baron, D. P. (2006). *Business and its environment* (5th ed.). Pearson.

Beerbaum, D. O. (2021). *Green Quadriga? – EU – Taxonomy, non-financial reporting directive, EBA pillar III ESG risks and IFRS foundation.* https://ssrn.com/abstract=3934765

Bogner, A., & Menz, W. (2002). Das theoriegenerierende Experteninterview. Erkenntnisinteresse, Wissensfonnen, Interaktion. In A. Bogner, B. Littig, & Menz, W. (Eds.), *Das Experteninterview* (pp. 33–70). Leske and Budrich.

Bond, A., & Dusik, J. (2022). Environmental assessments and sustainable finance taxonomies – A riposte. *Impact Assessment and Project Appraisal, 40*(2), 123–128.

Brühl, V. (2021). *Green finance in Europe – Strategy, regulation and instruments* [Working Paper No. 657, Center for Financial Studies]. https://ssrn.com/abstract=3934042

Delmas, M. A., & Montes-Sancho, M. J. (2010). Voluntary agreements to improve environmental quality: Symbolic and substantive cooperation. *Strategic Management Journal, 31*(6), 575–601.

DiMaggio, P. J., & Powell, W. W. (1983). The iron cage revisited: Institutional isomorphism and collective rationality in organizational fields. *American Sociological Review, 48*(2), 147–160.

Doh, J., Lawton, T., & Rajwani, T. (2012). Advancing nonmarket strategy research: Institutional perspectives in a changing world. *Academy of Management Perspectives, 26*(3), 22–39.

Dubois, A., & Gadde, L. E. (2002). Systematic combining: An abductive approach to case research. *Journal of Business Research, 55*, 53–60.

Dumrose, M., Rink, S., & Eckert, J. (2022). Disaggregating confusion? The EU taxonomy and its relation to ESG rating. *Finance Research Letters, 48*, 102928. https://doi.org/10.1016/j.frl.2022.102928

Eisenhardt, K., & Martin, J. (2000). Dynamic capabilities: What are they? *Strategic Management Journal, 21*(Special Issue), 1105–1121.

Escobar, L. F., & Vredenburg, H. (2010). Multinational oil companies and the adoption of sustainable development: A resource-based and institutional theory interpretation of adoption heterogeneity. *Journal of Business Ethics, 98*, 39–65.

European Commission (EC). (2021, April 21). *Sustainable finance and EU taxonomy: Commission takes further steps to channel money towards sustainable activities.* https://ec.europa.eu/commission/presscorner/detail/en/ip_21_1804

European Commission (EC). (n.d.). *A European green deal.* https://ec.europa.eu/info/strategy/priorities-2019-2024/european-green-deal_en

Figge, F., & Hahn, T. (2005). The cost of sustainability capital and the creation of sustainable value by companies. *Journal of Industrial Ecology, 9*(4), 47–58.

Financial Stability, Financial Services and Capital Markets Union (FSFSCMU). (2020, August 5). *Renewed sustainable finance strategy and implementation of the action plan on financing sustainable growth.* Retrieved April 7, 2021, from https://ec.europa.eu/info/publications/sustainable-finance-renewed-strategy_en

Fischer, F., Habermann, F., & Scheucher, I. (2022). The new EU sustainable strategy and accounting practice – Ex-ante corporate and auditor perspectives from Germany. *SSRN Journal.* https://ssrn.com/abstract=4026250

Freeman, R. E. (1984). *Strategic management: Stakeholder approach.* Pitman.

Gortsos, C. (2020). The taxonomy regulation: More important than just as an element of the capital markets union. *European Banking Institute Working Paper Series, 80.* https://ssrn.com/abstract=3750039

Hair, J. F., Celsi, M., Money, A. H., Samouel, P., & Page, M. (2016). *Essentials of business research methods* (3rd ed.). Routledge.

Hillman, A. J., Keim, G. D., & Schuler, D. (2004). Corporate political activity: A review and research agenda. *Journal of Management, 30*(6), 837–857.

Hockerts, K. A. (2015). Cognitive perspective on the business case for corporate sustainability. *Business Strategy and the Environment, 24*(2), 102–122.

Hotho, J. J., & Pedersen, T. (2012). Beyond the "rules of the game": Three institutional approaches and how they matter for international business. In M. Demirbag & G. Wood (Eds.), *Handbook of institutional approaches to international business.* Edward Elgar.

Howard, R. A. (2022). Response to: Environmental assessments and sustainable finance frameworks: Will the EU taxonomy change the mindset over the contribution of EIA to sustainable development? *Impact Assessment and Project Appraisal, 40*(2), 110–112.

Hummel, K., & Jobst, D. (2022). *The current state and future of corporate sustainability reporting regulations in the European Union.* https://ssrn.com/abstract=3978478

InfluenceMap. (2020). *Lobbying on the EU taxonomy's green criteria December 2020.* An InfluenceMap report. https://influencemap.org/EN/report/Lobbying-on-the-EU-Taxonomy-s-Green-Criteria-9fa94d19d713248426018f89410d2fbd

IPCC. (2001). *Climate change 2001: Synthesis report.* In R. T. Watson & the Core Writing Team (Eds.), *A contribution of working groups I, II, and III to the third assessment report of the intergovernmental panel on climate change.* Cambridge University Press.

Kilbourne, W. E., Beckmann, S. C., & Thelen, E. (2002). The role of the dominant social paradigm in environmental attitudes: A multinational examination. *Journal of Business Research, 55*(3), 193–204.

Kindström, D., Kowalkowski, C., & Sandberg, E. (2013). Enabling service innovation: A dynamic capabilities approach. *Journal of Business Research, 66*(8), 1063–1073.

Kotler, P., Wong, V., Saunders, J., & Armstrong, G. (2005). *Principles of marketing.* Pearson Education.

Loew, E., Erichsen, G., Liang, B., & Postulka, M. L. (2021). Corporate social responsibility (CSR) and environmental social governance (ESG) – Disclosure of European banks. *European Banking Institute Working Paper Series, 83.* http://dx.doi.org/10.2139/ssrn.3778674

Lucarelli, C., Mazzoli, C., Rancan, M., & Severini, S. (2020). Classification of sustainable activities: EU taxonomy and scientific literature. *Sustainability, 12*(6460), 1–25.

Marquis, C., & Qian, C. (2014). Corporate social responsibility reporting in China: Symbol or substance? *Organization Science, 25*(1), 127–148.

Mellahi, K., Frynas, G., Sun, P., & Siegel, D. (2016). A review of the nonmarket strategy literature: Toward a multi-theoretical integration. *Journal of Management. 42*, 143–173.

Meyer, J. W., & Rowan, B. (1977). Institutionalized organizations: Formal structure as myth and ceremony. *American Journal of Sociology, 83*(2), 340–363.

Meyer, J. W., Scott, W. R., & Deal, T. E. (1983). Institutional and technical sources of organizational structure: Explaining the structure of educational organizations. In J. W. Meyer & W. R. Scott (Eds.), *Organizational environments: Ritual and rationality* (pp. 45–67). Sage Publications.

Meyer, M., & Zucker, L. (1989). *Permanently failing organizations.* Sage Publications.

Miles, M. B., Huberman, A. M., & Saldaña, J. (2020). *Qualitative data analysis: A methods sourcebook* (4th ed.). Sage Publications.

Newton, P. M., & Levinson, D. J. (1973). The work group within the organization: A socio-psychological approach. *Psychiatry: Journal for the Study of Interpersonal Processes, 36*(2), 115–142.

Nipper, M., Ostermaier, A., & Theis, J. (2022). *Mandatory disclosure of standardized sustainability metrics: The case of the EU taxonomy regulation.* https://ssrn.com/abstract=4123423

Noble, H., & Heale, R. (2019). Triangulation in research, with examples. *Evidence-based Nursing, 22*(3), 67–68.

Och, M. (2020). *Sustainable finance and the EU taxonomy regulation – Hype or hope?* Jan Ronse Institute for Company & Financial Law Working Paper No. 2020/05. https://ssrn.com/abstract=3738255

OECD. (2017). *Investing in climate, investing in growth.* OECD Publishing. http://dx.doi.org/10.1787/9789264273528-en

Oliver, C. (1991). Strategic responses to institutional processes. *Academy of Management Review, 16*(1), 145–179.

Oliver, C., & Holzinger, I. (2008). The effectiveness of strategic political management: A dynamic capabilities framework. *Academy of Management Review, 33*(2), 496–520.

Pacces, A. M. (2020). *Sustainable corporate governance: The role of the law* [European Corporate Governance Institute – Law Working Paper No. 550/2020]. https://ssrn.com/abstract=3697962 or http://dx.doi.org/10.2139/ssrn.3697962

Pacces, A. M. (2021). Will the EU taxonomy regulation foster sustainable corporate governance? *Sustainability, 13*(21), 12316. http://dx.doi.org/10.3390/su132112316

Patton, M. Q. (1999). Enhancing the quality and credibility of qualitative analysis. *HSR: Health Services Research. 34*(5), Part II.

Peters, M., Godfrey, C., Khalil, H., McInerney, P., Parker, D., & Soares, C. (2015). Guidance for conducting systematic scoping reviews. *International Journal of Evidence-based Healthcare, 13*(3), 141–146.

Peters, M., Godfrey, C., Khalil, H., McInerney, P., Soares, C., & Parker, D. (2017). Guidance for the conduct of JBI scoping reviews, *International Journal of Evidence-Based Healthcare, 13*(3), 141–146.

Pfeffer, J., & Salancik, G. R. (1978). *The external control of organizations: A resource dependence perspective.* Harper & Row.

Poisson-de Haro, S., & Bitektine, A. (2015). Global sustainability pressures and strategic choice: The role of firms' structures and non-market capabilities in selection and implementation of sustainability initiatives. *Journal of World Business, 50*(2), 326–341.

Rant, V. (2022). *Regulating the green transition and sustainable finance in the European Union.* https://ssrn.com/abstract=4108232

Rugman, A., & Verbeke, A. (1998). Corporate strategies and environmental regulations: An organizing framework. *Strategic Management Journal, 19*(4), 363–375.

Saldaña, J. (2013). *The coding manual for qualitative researchers* (2nd ed.). Sage Publications.

Sarkis, J., Zhu, Q., & Lai, K. H. (2011). An organizational theoretic review of green supply chain management literature. *International Journal of Production Economics, 130*, 1–15.

Saunders, M., Lewis, P., & Thornhill, A. (2016). *Research methods for business students* (7th ed.). Pearson Education.

Schaltegger, S. (2011). Sustainability as a driver for corporate economic success. *Society and Economy, 33*(1), 15–28.

Schuetze, F. & Stede, J. (2020). EU Sustainable Finance Taxonomy – What Is Its Role on the Road towards Climate Neutrality? DIW Berlin Discussion Paper No. 1923, Available at SSRN: https://ssrn.com/abstract=3749900 or http://dx.doi.org/10.2139/ssrn.3749900

Scott, W. R. (1987). The adolescence of institutional theory. *Administrative Science Quarterly, 32*(4), 493–511.

Scott, W. R., & Meyer, J. W. (1987). Environmental linkages and organizational complexity: Public and private schools. In H. M. Levin & T. James (Eds.), *Comparing public and private schools* (pp. 128–160). Fulmer Press.

Silverman, D. (2010). *Doing qualitative research. a practical handbook* (3rd ed.). Sage Publications.

Singh, J. V., Tucker, D. J., & House, R. J. (1986). Organizational legitimacy and the liability of newness. *Administrative Science Quarterly, 31*(2), 171–193.

Siri, M., & Zhu, S. (2019). Will the EU Commission successfully integrate sustainability risks and factors in the investor protection regime? A research agenda. *Sustainability, 11*(22), 6292. http://dx.doi.org/10.3390/su11226292

Strauss, A., & Corbin, J. (1998). *Basics of qualitative research: Techniques and procedures for developing grounded theory.* Saga Publications.

Teece, D. J. (2007). Explicating dynamic capabilities: The nature and microfoundations of (sustainable) enterprise performance. *Strategic Management Journal, 28*(13), 1319–1350.

Teece, D. J., Pisano, G., & Shuen, A. (1997). Dynamic capabilities and strategic management. *Strategic Management Journal, 18*(7), 509–533.

TEG. (2019). *Using the taxonomy (supplementary report).* European Commission.

TEG. (2020). *Taxonomy: Final report of the Technical Expert Group on Sustainable Finance.* European Commission.

Teo, H. H., Wei, K. K., & Benbasat, I. (2003). Predicting intention to adopt interorganizational linkages: An institutional perspective. *MIS Quarterly, 27*(1), 19–49.

Thompson, J. D. (1967). *Organizations in action: Social science bases of administrative theory.* McGraw-Hill.

Wernerfelt, B. (1984). A resource-based view of the firm. *Strategic Management Journal, 5*(2), 171–180.

Wrona, T., & Sinzig, C. (2018). Nonmarket strategy research: Systematic literature review and future directions. *Journal of Business Economics, 88*(2), 253–317.

Xiao, Y., & Watson, M. (2019). Guidance on conducting a systematic literature review. *Journal of Planning Education and Research, 39*(1), 93–112.

Yin, R. K. (2011). Case Study Research: Design and Methods. *The Modern Language Journal, 95*(3), 474–475.

Zetzsche, D. A., & Anker-Sørensen, L. (2022). Regulating sustainable finance in the dark. *European Business Organization Law Review, 23*, 47–85.

Zetzsche, D. A., Bodellini, M., & Consiglio, R. (2021). *The EU sustainable finance framework in light of international standards.* https://ssrn.com/abstract=3984511

Zucker, L. G. (1977). The role of institutionalization in cultural persistence. *American Sociological Review, 42*(5), 726–743.

Zucker, L. G. (1983). Organizations as institutions. In S. B. Bacharach (Ed.), *Research in the Sociology of Organizations* (Vol. 2, pp. 1–47). JAI Press.

Zucker, L. G. (1987). Institutional theories of organization. *Annual Review of Sociology, 13*, 443–464.

Zucker, L. G. (1988). Where do institutional patterns come from? Organizations as actors in social systems. In L. G. Zucker (Ed.), *Institutional patterns and organizations: Culture and environment* (pp. 23–49). Ballinger.

## Appendix – Overview of EU Taxonomy Literature With an Indirect Relationship to the Present Study

| Authors | Title | Source | Type of Source | Purpose | Relevant Findings and/ or Main Arguments |
|---|---|---|---|---|---|
| Siri and Zhu (2019) | Will the EC Successfully Integrate Sustainability Risks and Factors in the Investor Protection Regime? A Research Agenda | *Sustainability* | Discussion | Analysis of global sustainable finance regulations with a more comprehensive view on the EU Action Plan | Although commendable, the EU sustainability reform proposal risks underestimating the complexity of financial sustainability if practical implications on each type of financial operators are not considered |
| Gortsos (2020) | The TR: More Important Than Just as an Element of the Capital Market Union | European Banking Institute Working Paper Series | Discussion | Thorough analysis of the TR legislative act, looking at the system of rules and the TR's field of application | The TR will also be important for companies that are not in the TR's scope of application, especially in the form of a benchmark |

| | | | | | |
|---|---|---|---|---|---|
| Pacces (2020) | Sustainable Corporate Governance: The Role of Law | The European Corporate Governance Institute (ECGI) | Discussion | This paper examines the part that the EU legislation conceivably plays in endorsing sustainable corporate governance | Sustainability may be pursued by institutional investors via corporate governance, but whether this happens is unclear. Author argues that frameworks like the TR can promote this alignment |
| Beerbaum (2021) | Green Quadriga? – EU – Taxonomy, Non-Financial-Reporting Directive, EBA Pillar III ESG Risks and IFRS Foundation | SSRN | Discussion | Assessment and discussion of four green initiatives (TR, NFRD, EBA Pillar III ESG risks and IFRS Foundation) | Beerbaum notes that there is a lack of alignment across the four green initiatives, arguing that they must be coordinated and reconciled to each other as a precondition to be attained by regulators to increase transparency |

*(Continued)*

Appendix – (*Continued*)

| Authors | Title | Source | Type of Source | Purpose | Relevant Findings and/ or Main Arguments |
|---|---|---|---|---|---|
| Brühl (2021) | Green Finance in Europe – Strategy, Regulation and Instruments | Center for Financial Studies at the Leibniz Information Centre for Economics | Discussion | Extensive overview of different EU regulatory initiatives and the frameworks for disclosure for financial institutions and companies. Paper shows areas for mobilizing capital to advance the EU Green Deal | In order to improve sustainability regulatory frameworks, Brühl proposes the installation of tax incentives for green investments in the business sector. Additionally, he suggests a reform in top management's compensation by linking it to factual reduction goals for GHG (e.g., by using the TR's metrics as benchmark) |

| Hummel and Jobst (2022) | The Current State and Future of Corporate Sustainability Reporting Regulations in the European Union | SSRN | Theory-based discussion | Succinct overview of the EU sustainability disclosure regulation and suggest possible paths for future research. With that, the authors aim at helping corporate decision-makers better understand present EU regulatory developments | They argue that current regulatory developments in the EU reveal what the future could look like while, at the same time, allows ample room for the study of the "rationale, nature and consequences of sustainability reporting" (p. 45) |
| Loew et al. (2021) | Corporate Social Responsibility (CSR) and Environmental Social Governance (ESG) – Disclosure of European Banks | Europe Banking Institute Working Paper Series | Quantitative research | This paper examines how well CSR activities are disclosed by banks under the NFRD. It does so through statistical analysis of multiple influencing factors | They argue that regulators should ponder the efficacy of non-financial disclosure regulations in the banking sector and contemplate the possible need to adopt guidelines and regulations that are specific to the banking sector |

*(Continued)*

Appendix – (*Continued*)

| Authors | Title | Source | Type of Source | Purpose | Relevant Findings and/ or Main Arguments |
|---|---|---|---|---|---|
| Nipper et al. (2022) | Mandatory Disclosure of Standardized Sustainability Metrics | SSRN | Quantitative research | The authors hypothesize that investors are more inclined to invest in companies that disclose much green revenue (rather than little) or who have higher sustainability rating (rather than none) | Their findings support their hypothesis. They also find that a high sustainability rating influences investment probability regardless of whether it is combined with much or little green revenue (indicated on TR disclosure) |
| Pacces (2021) | Will the EU Taxonomy Regulation Foster Sustainable Corporate Governance? | *Sustainability* | Theory-based discussion | This paper examines the capacity of the new EU rules on sustainability disclosure to enact a sustainable corporate governance | For Pacces, due to the inability of institutional investors to fully avoid unsustainable investments, they will likely slowly pursue sustainable corporate governance through voice (instead of exit) |

| Zetzsche et al. (2021) | The EU Sustainable Finance Framework in Light of International Standards | European Banking Institute e.V. | Qualitative (content analysis) | This article looks at the relationship between the EU sustainable finance framework (EU SF framework) and mainstream ESG standards | The TR displays a higher level of refinement than international ESG standards, potentially setting the pace globally. However, it brings additional costs to EU firms as well as "political resistance against the overly detailed EU approach" (p. 31), which could cripple international perception of the EU SF framework |

*(Continued)*

Appendix – (*Continued*)

| Authors | Title | Source | Type of Source | Purpose | Relevant Findings and/ or Main Arguments |
|---|---|---|---|---|---|
| Rant (2022) | Regulating the Green Transition and Sustainable Finance in the European Union | SSRN | Discussion | The author provides an overview of EU sustainable finance regulation and its motivation to bridge the EU green financing gap through redirecting private capital flows toward sustainable investments | Rant notes there is an essential financial metamorphosis in the EU toward sustainability objectives, with strong implications for the financial sector, policymakers and research. To this end, the EU sustainable finance framework could shape international sustainability standards |
| Dumrose et al. (2022) | Disaggregating confusion? The EU Taxonomy and Its Relation to ESG Rating | Finance Research Letters | Quantitative research | The authors discuss the TR considering ESG ratings, arguing that the taxonomy can aid in the reduction of discrepancies across different ESG data providers | Although they find a positive relation between ESG ratings and firm taxonomy performance, the potential for reducing discrepancies is not yet fully materialized |

| Zetzsche and Anker-Sørensen (2022) | Regulating Sustainable Finance in the Dark | The European Business Organization Law Review (EBOR) | Discussion | The authors analyze what kind of financial regulation should be adopted under the EU Green Deal and the Sustainable Finance Strategy 2021 | They argue that a rational, data-driven approach to redirecting investment toward sustainability is too premature. Regulators should have a deep understanding of the impacts of sustainability finance regulation on financial intermediation and investment streams |

Chapter 7

# Corporate Responsiveness and Sustainability Transition: Insights from a Danish–Malaysian Palm Oil Multinational*

*Frederik Hejselbjerg Vagtborg*

*Copenhagen Business School, Denmark*

## Abstract

This chapter explores the strategic responsiveness of commodity multinationals operating in developing countries to the uncertainties raised by the emergent European Union (EU) sustainability regulation. The study applies deductive theory triangulation to derive five response propositions, subsequently contrasted with inductive insights from an exploratory single-case study. The research involves in-depth interviews with a mix of senior and middle management and numerous external stakeholders. Empirical findings are discussed through storytelling and retrospective sensemaking and cross-checked against corporate documents, archive material, and online articles for added validation. This chapter concludes that an authentic commitment to corporate social responsibility and creating shared value can enhance the multinational enterprise (MNE)'s resilience and responsiveness to regulatory uncertainty, especially when combined with early signal scanning and real options reasoning. Through varied, first-hand insights, the case study demonstrates the role of reputation, core values, and ethical leadership in support of effective stakeholder engagement capabilities and the MNE's ability to develop viable collaborative solutions to uncertainties implied by evolving sustainability regulation and

---

*Based on a bachelor thesis submitted to the BSc International Business Program at the Copenhagen Business School in May 2023.

---

Sustainable and Resilient Global Practices:
Advances in Responsiveness and Adaptation, 149–191
Copyright © 2024 by Frederik Hejselbjerg Vagtborg
Published under exclusive licence by Emerald Publishing Limited
doi:10.1108/978-1-83797-611-920241007

stakeholder expectations. Taking an evolutionary view, this chapter introduces a process perspective on sustainability transition, relevant to firms seeking a shift in focus from mere compliance toward strategic responsiveness founded on adaptability and renewal.

*Keywords*: Adaptability; corporate social responsibility; EU sustainability regulation; exploratory case study; multinational enterprise; strategic responsiveness

## Introduction

The sustainability transition of multinational enterprises (MNEs) is among the most prominent contemporary issues in international business today. It has sparked interest in concepts such as corporate social responsibility (CSR), Environmental, Social, and Governance (ESG) reporting, sustainable finance, and the notion of a "triple bottom line" as corporations seek to develop sustainable relations with their stakeholders, the broader business environment, and society at large. Drawing on the 2030 United Nations (UN) Agenda for Sustainable Development, the European Union (EU) is set to introduce a new wave of regulatory initiatives to accelerate businesses' sustainability transition. Similar initiatives are being proposed in other developed country jurisdictions, but the EU is generally recognized as a frontrunner in leading the way for progressive sustainability regulation (Neslen, 2023). In December 2022, the European Parliament and Council approved the Regulation for Deforestation-Free Supply Chains (hereafter Deforestation Regulation) targeting six agricultural commodities, including palm oil, which is the sector of focus in this chapter. The open public consultation on the Deforestation Regulation resulted in over 1.2 million inputs – the second most in EU history – showing overwhelming support from both citizens and firms (European Commission (EC), 2022). In contrast, it triggered adverse reactions from developing country governments, including Malaysia and Indonesia, who labeled it "crop apartheid and discriminatory" and responded by threatening to ban palm oil exports into the EU (Hancock et al., 2023), raising political risks in the process. A similar outright blanket ban – The Forced Labor Ban – is also proposed by the EU for labor-related issues (EC, 2022c; Think Tank European Parliament, 2023), which is also expected to impact commodity MNEs in developing countries. The EU has further proposed the Corporate Sustainability Due Diligence Directive, which will make firms increasingly responsible for the sustainability of their own and extended supply chains. It has been described as "one of the most ambitious corporate laws reforms to ever be proposed" (Gottlieb, 2022), suggesting its implications may be far-reaching. This may especially be true for commodity MNEs operating in developing countries, dependent on natural resources and local suppliers that do not necessarily share the same views toward social–environmental standards or the means necessary for compliance.

In parallel, a comprehensive framework named the EU Taxonomy for Sustainable Activities (hereafter EU Taxonomy) is being developed. The EU Taxonomy is a classification system founded on the logic of sustainable finance, which will make it clear what percentage of a firm's economic activities are socially and environmentally sustainable based on standardized criteria and Key Performance Indicators (KPIs) (KPMG International Entities, 2022). The Taxonomy and its related Corporate Sustainability Reporting Directive (hereafter CSRD) are unprecedented in their attempt to introduce a new integrative corporate performance reporting structure that incorporates social–environmental dimensions along with the financial dimensions. This is envisaged to impact more than 50,000 companies by 2025 (Gottlieb, 2022).

Collectively, these regulations introduce new layers of uncertainty to businesses' sustainability transition. This is particularly relevant for commodity MNEs based in developing countries subject to intense public scrutiny. Commodity-linked deforestation has in the media been singled out as a significant contributor to biodiversity loss and global greenhouse gas (GHG) emissions (Ritchie & Roser, 2021), and agricultural commodities are among the sectors frequently criticized for forced labor and other social irregularities (Jong, 2023). While parts of the EU's sustainability regulation (hereafter EU regulation) are approved and scheduled, other parts of the framework are still at the proposal stage or under preliminary discussion. Thus, the regulatory environment is envisaged to evolve dynamically in scope, reach, and enforceability over the coming decade. In addition to tackling immediate compliance demands, the MNE must, therefore, enhance its strategic responsiveness and adaptivity to a business environment characterized by interconnected uncertainties in evolving regulation and movements in stakeholder expectations pressuring its sustainability transition. To the best of my knowledge, corporate responsiveness to the uncertainties associated with the new and evolving EU regulation is yet to be studied from the perspective of commodity multinationals in developing countries. This chapter attempts to address this void by exploring the following research question: *How should a commodity multinational operating in developing countries enhance its responsiveness to uncertainties associated with emergent EU sustainability regulation in the context of its sustainability transition?*

A combination of theory triangulation and contextual empirical research is adopted. The theory triangulation offers five deductive response propositions, to be understood as normative recommendations based on theoretical rationales established in prevailing literature. This is followed by an exploratory, single-case study on *United Plantations Berhad*, a Danish–Malaysian palm oil multinational demonstrating effective responsiveness throughout its history and current practices. The case study offers inductive, empirical insights with which the propositions are contrasted and synthesized to establish an abductive answer to the research question. Finally, key conclusions are extended through managerial implications applicable to other firms seeking a more competitive sustainability transition through a nuanced perspective on corporate responsiveness.

## Literature Review

This section uses *deductive theory triangulation*, exploring the issue through five complementary perspectives and concepts. The literature review aims to establish theory-based propositions on effective responsiveness by commodity MNEs faced with uncertainties induced by the EU regulation. Beyond ambiguities in the shape, scope, and form of future regulation, the dynamic nature of stakeholder expectations that often underlie and foreshadow regulatory movements constitutes a key source of uncertainty. Proactive stakeholder management is arguably an important avenue through which the MNE achieves legitimacy and preemptively adapts to regulatory changes. In contexts of regulatory uncertainty, effective stakeholder management becomes an integral aspect of organizational resilience.

*Stakeholder Theory* is an overarching perspective because it motivates the discussion around the implications for MNEs broadening their orientation from shareholder-value-maximization to one of multi-stakeholder alignments. It is a building block for the integrative ("triple bottom line") value perspective of sustainable finance and thereby links to the broader purpose of the EU Taxonomy, which integrates financial, social, and environmental value creation. Stakeholder theory on its own, however, lacks actionability, which calls for incorporating CSR and *creating shared value* (CSV) as supplementary concepts and tangible tools through which stakeholder alignment and legitimacy are pursued. In addition, the environmental uncertainty induced by regulatory changes heightens the importance of strategic flexibility in the MNE's response. *Real Options Reasoning* may offer a valuable approach to incorporating flexibility into CSR and CSV initiatives when responding to evolving stakeholder expectations and regulatory uncertainty. Finally, the *Sensemaking Perspective* is included to examine the role of managerial attributes, complementing the first four perspectives for applicability in firm-specific contexts.

### Setting the Scene for Effective Responsiveness

Research shows that environmental regulation induces firms to respond by altering and implementing environmental strategies (Aragón-Correa et al., 2020). Such strategies are, however, characterized by significant heterogeneity (Aragón-Correa & Sharma, 2005) and may, under some circumstances, become a source of competitive advantage, particularly when assessed in aggregate rather than to single regulatory initiatives (Aragón-Correa et al., 2020; Hart, 1995; Weigelt & Shittu, 2016).

Sustainability transition is arguably a matter of long-term corporate survival, a process under which evolving regulatory landscapes and stakeholder expectations challenge the commodity MNE's longevity. It is argued that effective responsiveness goes far beyond mere regulatory compliance and, importantly, lies in the MNE's ability to continuously adapt and renew itself to emerge from these evolving conditions as more competitive (Andersen & Young, 2020). This encapsulates the concept of *sustainable resilience* (Andersen & Young, 2020) and is complemented by the related dynamic capabilities concept (Teece, 2007; Teece et al.,

1997). Dynamic capabilities refer to the organization's ability to adapt, integrate, and reconfigure internal and external competencies and resources to address rapidly changing environments (Teece, 2007; Teece et al., 1997). This chapter illustrates a case for dynamic capabilities as an antecedent for effective responsiveness in contexts of evolving sustainability regulation. Though conceptually elastic, it remains an important indirect lens through which the response actions discussed in the following perspectives are weighed and assessed.

### Stakeholder Theory

Classical economists argue that the sole goal of firms should be shareholder-value maximization (Friedman, 1970). Conversely, stakeholder theory proposes that firms have wider accountability beyond shareholders and emphasizes how value is created in the interactions between management and the firm's customers, suppliers, regulators, financiers, and communities (Donaldson & Preston, 1995; Freeman, 1984). The theory argues that corporations become more successful when they establish healthy relationships with their stakeholders, as each stakeholder group "can affect or is affected by the achievement of an organizational objective" (Freeman, 1984, p. 46). Commodity MNEs in developing countries are subject to potentially more complex stakeholder dynamics than the average firm. The labor intensity and inherent natural resource dependency of upstream activities heighten the interests of host governments and local communities. If poorly managed, such stakeholders may impede the MNE's social license to operate and exacerbate liabilities of foreignness (Zaheer, 1995). The sensitivity extends into product markets where the commodity MNE is subject to significant attention among (typically developed country) nongovernmental organizations (NGOs) and regulators, which could restrict market access through direct sanctions or indirectly through negative publicity.

The stakeholder literature distinguishes between descriptive, normative, and instrumental theories (Donaldson & Preston, 1995). While normative stakeholder theory holds that stakeholder interests are ends rather than means, the instrumental perspective views stakeholder interests in a more strategic light as a means to support the achievement of corporate goals (Freeman, 1999). Although it recognizes the importance of ethical business behavior, the instrumental perspective does not only advocate such behavior because it is ethical in itself but because it can contribute to enhancing firm efficiency, competitiveness, and profitability (Freeman, 1999). An instrumental perspective is advocated because the MNE should respond to regulatory uncertainties and pressures for sustainability transition not only for the mere interests of its stakeholders but also to enhance its adaptive capacity and competitiveness.

The basic ideas underlying an instrumental stakeholder approach can be recognized in strategic CSR and particularly CSV (Porter & Kramer, 2011). Though somewhat fluid, these concepts offer a tangible route to re-legitimize the commodity MNE and effectively incorporate wider social–environmental interests into its business model. The intangible aspect takes form in the very process of stakeholder engagement, serving not only as an antecedent to the effective implementation of the tangible tools in CSR and CSV but also encompasses value in itself. The instrumental perspective holds that a relational rather than transactional stakeholder engagement approach produces better results (Jones, 1995), consistent with Strand and Freeman's (2015) argument that "long-term profitability is a by-product of a well-run company that engages efficiently with its stakeholders." Stakeholder engagement capabilities may, thus, offer a supportive element in MNE's response repertoire and are explored in more depth later in the section.

### Corporate Social Responsibility

The abundant and varied literature on CSR reflects its conceptual elasticity, having no universally agreed definition. However, a content analysis of 37 CSR definitions by Dahlsrud (2008) concluded that CSR encompasses five common dimensions: the stakeholder dimension, the social dimension, the economic dimension, the voluntariness dimension, and the environmental dimension.

Instrumental stakeholder theory aligns with the strand of literature concluding a positive relationship between CSR and corporate performance. These studies emphasize how CSR enhances the MNE's reputation and customer satisfaction (Kouser et al., 2021), talent attraction (Story et al., 2016), access to finance (Cheng et al., 2011), and various risk management features, particularly in times of crisis (Arora et al., 2022; Orlitzky & Benjamin, 2001). Andersen and Torp (2019) posit that CSR may contribute to increased adaptability and more sustainable performance outcome – consistent with Ortiz-de-Mandojana and Bansal's (2015) finding that companies adopting social and environmentally responsible practices benefit from lower financial volatility and stronger organizational resilience, improving chances of survival over a 15-year period. This is an interesting observation given the average lifespan of S&P 500 firms having dropped from 61 years in 1958 to less than 18 years today, shown in a 2016 McKinsey survey (McKinsey & Company, 2016; Garelli, 2016). Embracing sustainable development and more open systems through proactive stakeholder alignment thus appears increasingly relevant to corporate longevity.

However, other studies have shown contradictory results, many of which challenge the business case for CSR, emphasizing its inevitable trade-offs to economic performance and shift of focus to other aspects that do not enhance shareholder value but increase costs (Becchetti et al., 2009; Galant & Cadez, 2017). Thus, the relationship with corporate performance remains inconclusive and appears highly contextual. Nevertheless, the literature generally acknowledges CSR as the predominant means through which the MNE seeks to establish legitimacy in stakeholder relationships (Ghardallou & Alessa, 2022). Zhao and Zhou (2022) argue that firms decrease CSR activities when faced with market uncertainty but increase CSR when faced with negative-event uncertainties. Other studies similarly suggest regulation to be highly influential in determining CSR engagement (Brown et al., 2020; Mitchell et al., 1997), particularly in reputation-sensitive industries such as commodities (Visser, 2009). A study by Garcia et al. (2017) found that CSR practices by firms in sensitive industries in developing countries were likely to improve ESG outcomes. CSR may also underpin the MNE's social license to operate in developing countries (Darendeli & Hill, 2015; Porter & Kramer, 2006), which is particularly important to location-constrained commodity MNEs, highly dependent on local government and community acceptance.

Referring to Dahlsrud's (2008) "voluntariness dimension," CSR activities imply a move by the firm ahead of the regulatory curve. This provides an element of reputational insurance (Husted, 2005) and better prepares the MNE to swiftly adjust and comply once regulatory trends materialize into policy. This preemptive argument for CSR corresponds with Orlitzky and Benjamin's (2001) view that strategic CSR processes better enable the MNE to anticipate and reduce environmental risks such as governmental regulation. CSR might, therefore, constitute an important preemptive response mechanism, whereby the MNE's early attention to stakeholder signals provides a head start in responding to an uncertain and evolving regulatory landscape.

The inconclusiveness concerning CSR's performance effects, however, implies that such investments cannot be blindly recommended without contextual consideration and appreciation of the contingencies for its effective use. Dyllick and Muff (2015) advocate for organizational CSR integration since standalone or so-called bolt-on sustainability projects will not suffice. Other scholars argue that CSR commitments must be part of the organization's core and genuinely embraced at the highest levels of management for it to have any meaningful impact (Gajadhur, 2022). The very process by which such commitments are established and communicated is of equal importance – not only to facilitate internal organizational buy-in but also to maximize stakeholder alignment (Jones, 1995).

Various literature also points toward a multitude of unconstructive responses, ranging from relocating social and environmental malpractice to exploit regulatory voids in countries with weak enforcement to "symbolic" CSR responses that resemble greenwashing without any substantive effect (Asmussen & Fosfuri, 2019; Crane et al., 2014). Aragón-Correa et al. (2016) find that MNEs who communicate most aggressively about their environmental initiatives make less real progress than those who communicate less. Hence, an effective CSR response is not symbolic but of substantive nature, focused on high-impact activities and designed to maximize its alignment with stakeholder interests and the EU Taxonomy's current and future sustainability KPIs.

### Creating Shared Value

While CSR has been the more conventional response to addressing stakeholder expectations, a central challenge remains in making social–environmental investments compatible with competitive value creation, as this implies the financial sustainability of CSR (Bosch-Badia et al., 2015). To this purpose, Porter and Kramer (2011) propose the CSV concept, defined as the adoption of "policies and operating practices that enhance the competitiveness of a company while simultaneously advancing the economic and social conditions in the communities in which it operates." CSR and CSV overlap in improving the MNE's social–environmental performance. From a stakeholder perspective, CSR practices can be both normative and instrumental, although CSV is always instrumentally motivated, given its upfront focus on profitability and competitiveness (Menghwar & Daood, 2021). In a comprehensive review of 242 CSV articles, Menghwar and Daood (2021) propose three key dimensions – strategic process, societal problem alignment with the value chain, and direct economic profits – which should all be met to distinguish CSV initiatives from practices falling under the CSR umbrella. Contrary to the conventional belief of a trade-off between societal and economic performance, CSV proposes the possibility of a "win–win," making it a commercially appealing way for firms to respond to stakeholder pressures and regulatory uncertainty.

Conceptually, CSV is an extension of "Porter's Hypothesis," which postulates that strict environmental regulation incentivizes sustainability innovation and can (over time) increase firm profitability and competitiveness, such that environmental adjustment costs are offset over the long term (Porter, 1991, 1995). The hypothetical regulatory scenario described by Porter's Hypothesis resembles that of the EU regulation in its attempt to level the playing field and encourage corporate sustainability innovation to further Taxonomy alignment of business activities (KPMG International Entities, 2022). Enhancing Taxonomy alignment may constitute a strong proxy for alignment with stakeholder expectations, such that a CSV approach, which integrates social–environmental performance with corporate strategy (Menghwar & Daood, 2021), seems reasonable to consider.

Porter and Kramer (2011) state that firms can create shared values in three ways: (1) by reconceiving products and markets, (2) by redefining productivity in the value chain, and (3) by enabling local cluster development at the company's location. They specifically mention the latter's relevance in a developing country context, citing examples of supportive cluster development for the coffee bean industry, one of the six commodities in the scope of the EU Deforestation Regulation (EC, 2022c). Various scholars have found that the three ways of CSV proposed by Porter and Kramer (2011) can and do improve social–environmental performance and increase economic value (Moon & Parc, 2019; Spitzeck & Chapman, 2012). Others criticize the CSV concept for lack of originality, substantivity, and empirical validity (Crane et al., 2014; Strand & Freeman, 2015). Thus, the conceptual robustness of CSV in guiding firms toward more sustainable and profitable business models remains subject to controversy and debate. Crane et al. (2014) criticize CSV for ignoring the tensions between business and society and persuasively claim that it is naive in assuming that sustainability transition can be achieved by relying on "win–win" scenarios without any trade-offs. This view is shared by de los Reyes et al. (2017), who highlight the inevitable trade-offs and sacrifices to profit necessary to create social–environmental value.

Based on a detailed review of extant CSV literature, however, Menghwar and Daood (2021) conclude that the basic tenets of CSV are appropriate and empirically observed. Most scholars agree that the future of sustainable business relies on sustainability being addressed at the firm's strategic level and that related initiatives are integrated with core operations with minimal trade-offs (Horisch et al., 2020; Wieland et al., 2017). Nonetheless, the path toward this ideal scenario is most likely incremental, and even Porter and Kramer (2011) recognize that not all societal problems can currently be solved through shared value solutions.

It is argued that CSR, through its less stringent focus on profitability, complements CSV's innovation-driven responses to stakeholder pressures and regulatory uncertainty. The preceding literature is contextually summarized in the following response proposition:

> *P.1a.* An effective commodity MNE should adopt CSR and CSV strategies to preemptively address social and environmental concerns ahead of the regulatory curve, aligning itself with current and (anticipated) future EU Taxonomy objectives and KPIs.

The commodity MNE's CSR and CSV initiatives should not merely respond to the EU's regulatory requirements and developed country stakeholder expectations due to the interdependence of core activities with its foreign host-country context. For a commodity MNE relying on scarce natural resources in a developing country, the rationale for CSR activities could also be explained by the resource-dependence theory (Salancik & Pfeffer, 1978) and by the MNE's attempts to develop its social path to legitimacy (Darendeli & Hill, 2015). Contextualized CSR initiatives may strengthen the MNE's social capital and support local stakeholder relations that enable longevity and continued access to vital natural and human resources.

Chapple and Moon (2005), exploring CSR practices in seven Asian countries, conclude that prioritized initiatives often differ from those in developed countries. Visser (2009) finds that CSR in developing countries mostly has a social-themed focus, whereas environmental concerns dominate in developed countries. This suggests that commodity MNEs, while responding to the EU Taxonomy criteria, still may need to target part of their CSR and CSV investments to accommodate local host-country interests. The resulting local reputation often underpins the MNE's relations with local governments and communities and may constitute a hedge against political risks (Darendeli & Hill, 2015). The Malaysian and Indonesian governments' threat of a palm oil export ban into the EU following the announcement of the Deforestation Regulation exemplifies such risks. To complement *P.1a*, it is also proposed that:

> *P.1b.* An effective commodity MNE operating in developing countries ought to supplement its EU-targeted CSR and CSV strategies with initiatives supportive of local stakeholder interests to enhance its reputation and influential capacity with host governments and help alleviate political risks.

### CSV+ and Multi-Stakeholder Initiatives

Though its legitimacy-restoring feature is one of the strongest arguments behind CSV, it, by definition, falls short of addressing stakeholder expectations in situations that cannot be supported by "win–win" activities alone (de los Reyes et al., 2017). Legitimacy concerns may constitute an increasingly important component in weighted, risk-adjusted economic returns (de los Reyes et al., 2017). In some circumstances, this may rationalize social–environmental initiatives, subject to

economic trade-offs, in pursuit of enhanced legitimacy and stakeholder acceptance in contexts beyond the idealized "win–win" scenario advocated by CSV (de
los Reyes et al., 2017).

de los Reyes et al. (2017) offer a conceptual approach extending CSV into the
so-called CSV+ ethical framework. Building on the integrative social contracts
strand of stakeholder theory (Donaldson & Dunfee, 1994), CSV+ proposes that
firms proactively respond to uncertainties in regulation and stakeholder expectations by adopting voluntary regulation developed through pre-competitive multi-
stakeholder initiative (MSIs; de los Reyes et al., 2017). CSV+ advocates that
firms embrace existing legitimacy norms – a *norms-taking* approach – by proactively seeking external input to guide trade-off decisions in social–environmental
investments outside the win–win scenario. In the absence of clear norms defining
legitimacy, however, CSV+ directs firms toward *norms-making*, achieved through
active engagement in MSIs that collaboratively define and set mutually agreed
standards for legitimacy (de los Reyes et al., 2017). Such standards, enacted
through voluntary regulation, reduce the ambiguity of stakeholder expectations
and norms for legitimacy (Schouten et al., 2012). This theoretically enables the
MNE to make more informed trade-offs in its CSR and CSV strategy to maximize stakeholder alignment within available resources.

Crane et al. (2014) also propose MSI, such as roundtables, as an effective collaborative solution to address social–environmental challenges ahead of regulatory changes. Roundtables have been established for at least three of the six
commodities in the scope of the EU Deforestation Regulation (Ingram et al.,
2018). This suggests that the adoption of MSI-backed voluntary regulation may
constitute an important "hedge" for the MNE's compliance and "insurance" of
its legitimacy from negative-event risks that may emerge from future more stringent sustainability regulation and stakeholder expectations. The enhanced legitimacy provided by CSV+ enables the MNE to pragmatically handle the sensitive
points of tension between business and society, which CSV on its own is criticized
for falling short of (Crane et al., 2014). Schouten et al. (2012) also emphasize the
legitimacy-enhancing properties of roundtables, but their findings equally point
to limitations in their deliverable value. For example, roundtables are often characterized by limited industry participation. Moreover, the significant diversity of
stakeholder interests and perspectives, combined with a lack of legal sanctioning
power, may, in some cases, dilute the substantivity of the norms and voluntary
standards adopted (Schouten et al., 2012).

However, the very diversity of stakeholder perspectives embodied by roundtables may constitute a valuable source of information and early legitimacy signals beyond what is reflected in the mutually agreed standards of both voluntary
and formal regulation (Ingram et al., 2018). Roundtable engagement thus enables
the MNE to examine its sustainability transition risks through current dominant
stakeholder expectations *and* through the lens of weaker social–environmental
trends and signals, which might constitute valuable inputs to strategic scenario
planning processes (Andersen & Young, 2020). Truly benefitting from MSI and
roundtable involvement, however, seems contingent on the MNE's absorptive
capacity (Cohen & Levinthal, 1990) of these early signals and timely reconfiguring

its CSV+ resources accordingly, in line with Teece et al.'s (1997) dynamic capabilities concept. The discussion on MSI offers the following proposition:

*P2*. An effective commodity MNE should engage in MSIs and adopt voluntary regulation to establish legitimacy and guide trade-off considerations in pursuit of its CSV+ strategy. In addressing the uncertainties implied by regulatory voids and norm ambiguity, the MNE equally benefits from MSIs as sources of early stakeholder signals yet to materialize into voluntary standards or formal EU regulation.

### Real Options Reasoning

The commodity MNE does not only face uncertainty in an evolving regulatory landscape with dynamic stakeholder expectations but equally in the significant outcome ambiguity of the CSR and CSV investments themselves, whose returns often materialize over the medium long run (Bosch-Badia et al., 2015). The prevalence of multilayered, interconnected uncertainties calls for tools that enable flexibility in the MNE's CSR- and CSV-driven response. Real options theory may be useful in valuing the strategic flexibility enabled by certain investments, which traditional appraisal methods such as Net Present Value (NPV) or Discounted Cash Flow (DCF) fall short of capturing (Andersen, 2006a; Husted, 2005). Relating to operating rather than financial assets (Kogut, 1991), real options provide the decision-maker with the flexibility to delay, stage, or alter resource commitments until after more information becomes available and to pursue an outcome only if it is favorable (McGrath, 1997). In his pioneering article, Husted (2005) proposes that proactive CSR may lower ex ante business risk and enable strategic flexibility in the form of real options through the indirect benefits generated from goodwill with local communities. Such reputational goodwill may serve particularly useful in drawing on the support and resources of stakeholders in times of crisis or high uncertainty (Husted, 2005). McWilliams and Siegel (2001) characterize CSR as a form of investment that creates "opportunities to expand and grow in the future" (Kogut, 1991, p. 21). This corresponds with Bosch-Badia et al.'s (2015) argument about how real options analysis might unveil hidden opportunities, particularly for out-of-the-money real options, in which a given CSR project would have a negative NPV if initiated now, but the possibility of a positive one at a future moment of inception. This is due to the often indirect ways CSR creates value through new, possibly unexpected, opportunities that CSR investments might induce – or *shadow options*, as termed by Bowman and Hurry (1993).

Busch and Hoffmann (2009) propose a four-step integrative investment framework using real options to respond to six areas of ecology-induced uncertainties, such as "exposure to and relevance of ecology-induced institutional [regulatory] changes" (p. 302). In applying a structured, real options logic, the MNE can prevent so-called *irreversible green mistakes* (Rugman & Verbeke, 1998) – a scenario of weak flexibility and limited leveraging potential of its resource commitments.

Although a real options approach has sound theoretical foundations, its practical applicability has been challenged due to the subjectivities in assumptions that underlie outcome distributions and the *valuation of flexibility* (Brach, 2003; Copeland & Antikarov, 2001). This might particularly be the case for continuous-time options such as real CSR or CSV options (Bosch-Badia et al., 2015), where the value changes in relation to an evolving regulatory landscape and stakeholder expectations. Furthermore, managers should be cautious not to overemphasize the prospective value of shadow options (Bowman & Hurry, 1993) to the extent that such are taken as given due to the high uncertainty of whether and how these transpire.

Nevertheless, real options theory remains relevant to our context. Unlike the conventional perception that uncertainty hinders investments, real options thinking provides managers with a more proactive response to uncertainty (Trigeorgis & Reuer, 2016). This is particularly relevant in responding to early stakeholder signals, where the time horizon is long and outcome ambiguity is inherently high, which – consistent with financial options theory – increases the value of the real CSR and CSV options used (Luehrman, 1998).

The built-in real options to defer, expand, or abandon CSR and CSV investments enable strategic maneuverability and increase the MNE's responsiveness (Barnett, 2008). This is also important in the practical consideration of budgetary constraints as the MNE designs its portfolio of activities to maximize its social–environmental performance and competitiveness. It also enables responsiveness to a broader range of issues, as fewer initial resources are committed per project (Barnett, 2008). Similarly, it reduces the risk of overcommitting to a particular path before more information becomes available – which is essential in an uncertain environment because path dependencies may impede dynamic capabilities in future response options (Teece et al., 1997).

Relatedly, de los Reyes et al. (2017) argue that one weakness of CSV lies in its stringent focus on profitably linking social–environmental improvements to existing business models. This may steer investment decisions toward *sustaining CSV innovations*, where existing products and processes are refined for social–environmental performance, rather than *transformational CSV innovations* (de los Reyes et al., 2017), where new and enhanced ideas are developed. A real options approach that reduces downside risk through lower initial resource commitments while retaining upside potential through the flexibility to adjust may facilitate ambidexterity through more considerate resource allocation between exploitative and explorative CSR and CSV investments (Tushman & O'Reilly, 1996). The real options literature brings forth the third proposition, summarized as:

*P3*. An effective MNE should incorporate real options reasoning in its CSR and CSV strategies to enhance future flexibility in its response to regulatory uncertainties and to account for outcome-ambiguities, resource constraints, and path dependencies associated with sustainability-linked investments.

### Stakeholder Engagement

Within the real options literature, other strands focus on stakeholder engagement as a precursor for real option creation and argue that new options emerge as a result of the firm's stakeholder interactions (Peters et al., 2014). New option creation materializes both through enhanced scanning and sensing and in the new solutions that emerge from collaborative stakeholder relations (Peters et al., 2014). This perspective – closely associated with instrumental stakeholder theory (Jones, 1995) – posits that total integrated value comprises not only tangible benefits, or the so-called distributed justices received by stakeholders, but also intangible benefits resulting from the affiliation and interaction itself (Harrison & Wicks, 2013). Sachs and Rühli (2011) propose stakeholder networks as a resource pool from which firms benefit differently because stakeholders contribute value and resources heterogeneously to network members (Boutilier, 2009). This might be due to differences in social capital contributions and the breadth and depth of stakeholder commitment signaled by firms (Blyler & Coff, 2003). Firms that occupy structural holes (Burt, 1992), span organizational boundaries, or are highly connected are better able to appropriate rents from stakeholder networks because social capital grants credibility to their claims (Blyler & Coff, 2003). A structural hole positioning may be the case for a commodity MNE that effectively bridges its downstream EU customer networks, which are directly subject to the new regulation, with its upstream developing country supplier network. Panda and Sangle (2019) also discuss the role of stakeholders as a valuable resource that may offer new ideas for product, process, and behavioral innovations – such as in CSR or CSV. An important capability thus lies in the very methods of stakeholder engagement and the MNE's absorptive capacity, enabling it to recognize, assimilate, and apply such stakeholder resources (Cohen & Levinthal, 1990; Panda & Sangle, 2019). In appreciating the evolving nature of stakeholder relations, Panda and Sangle (2019) argue that effective stakeholder engagement is a dynamic capability (Teece et al., 1997) and may constitute a competitive advantage. This suggests that the very engagement process that precedes CSR and CSV activities is relevant to an MNE seeking enhanced responsiveness, which warrants further examination.

In discussing four progressive stakeholder response strategies, Panda and Sangle (2019) hold that a proactive engagement style, built on open and transparent dialogue, collaboration, and joint decision-making, facilitates scanning and sensing and enhanced resource contributions from stakeholder networks. Jones (1995) similarly posits that a relational rather than transactional approach to stakeholder engagement, built on mutual trust and cooperation, can reduce contracting costs and allow the firm to participate in certain economic relationships that are unavailable to opportunistic firms. This corresponds with Connor and Prahalad's (1996) argument that knowledge-based resources outweigh the benefits of opportunism over the long run. A critical element of mutually beneficial stakeholder engagement, thus, lies in the partner selection process and in terminating or rejecting contracts with stakeholders who appear opportunistic (Jones, 1995).

A key implication of the Deforestation Regulation and Corporate Sustainability Due Diligence Directive is how codes of conduct requirements go beyond the individual firm to increasingly hold it accountable for the compliance or non-compliance of its extended supply chain. This heightens the need for interfirm accountability and requires closer collaboration by the MNE, both among its EU customers and its developing country-based suppliers, to safeguard sustainability compliance. In their discussion of safeguarding mechanisms, Pedersen and Andersen (2006) emphasize goal congruence among the MNE and its suppliers, which might be of particular importance to minimize conflicts of interest in a supply chain partly based in developing countries, where the costs and benefits of compliance are unevenly distributed. The authors also highlight trust and reputation as effective safeguards, especially in long-term relationships where the supplier can benefit from future cooperation with the MNE (Pedersen & Andersen, 2006). These safeguarding mechanisms correspond with Gereffi et al.'s (2005) relational governance mode for global value chains and share common ground with the findings of Scholten and Schilder (2015), who argue for collaborative communication, face-to-face interaction, resource-sharing, and joint learning as antecedents for more resilient and responsive supply chains. Benito et al. (2019) also propose that firms can increase their learning flows and connective efficiency through trust and relations, and the interaction that follows constitutes a learning platform.

A limitation of the proactive stakeholder engagement approach and relational governance mechanisms discussed above are their time-consuming features and the potentially high short-term opportunity costs of management time devoted to such interaction rather than core activities (Cottrell et al., 2015). Nevertheless, it may mitigate the need for hierarchical monitoring or conventional control-based mechanisms, as otherwise advocated by agency theory (Eisenhardt, 1989a). It resembles the concept of quasi-internalization, where relational governance mechanisms allow for "controlling without owning" (Asmussen et al., 2022). Reputation effects and social ties establish the so-called *shadow of the future* in the prospect of a continued flow of benefits from long-term relationships (Asmussen et al., 2022; Hennart, 1993). This incentivizes collaborating firms in the supply chain to abstain from opportunism, thereby safeguarding compliance based on long-term, mutually beneficial relationships. This might be particularly relevant for a commodity MNE that may direct a portion of its CSR or CSV investments to its local supplier network to safeguard sustainability across its supply chain. Arguably, the MNE's stakeholder engagement capabilities and trust-based governance modes constitute a valuable relational asset, which is inherently difficult to imitate or substitute. This may create a competitive advantage in the MNE's responsiveness to uncertainties associated with the sustainable supply chain regulation and is summarized in the fourth proposition:

*P4.* An effective MNE should adopt a proactive stakeholder engagement style to cultivate scanning and sensing and to better influence and access its stakeholder resources. This relational capability supports supply chain resilience and helps the MNE safeguard compliance in its response to sustainable supply chain regulation.

### Organizational Sensemaking

The theoretical perspectives thus far have offered theoretical contributions to our understanding of organizational responsiveness from multiple angles but have been limited in considering the internal, more subtle firm-specific characteristics and contextual factors that underpin the effectiveness of the responses proposed in *P1–P4*.

Studies show that managerial beliefs, morals, and perceptions affect corporate responses to uncertainty in sustainability regulation (Aragón-Correa et al., 2020). This is consistent with Andersen and Young (2020), who argue that organizational culture, cognitive biases, integrity, and the morality of key executive decision-makers play a vital role in determining how firms respond to uncertainty. Basu and Palazzo (2008) posit that CSR activities are derived from organizational sensemaking, defined as a "process by which individuals develop cognitive maps of their environment" (Ring & Rands, 1989, p. 342). The authors propose a tripartite framework to express *how an organization thinks, what it says, and how it behaves*, manifested through seven dimensions that shape a firm's so-called *CSR character* (Basu & Palazzo, 2008). These dimensions comprise identity orientation, legitimacy, justification, transparency, posture, consistency, and commitment and collectively express how a firm perceives and responds to its environment (Basu & Palazzo, 2008; Peters et al., 2014). The MNE's stakeholder engagement style and CSR-CSV strategies are, thus, not only a response to external stakeholder expectations but also a reflection of internally embedded cognitive, linguistic, and behavioral processes (Basu & Palazzo, 2008; Peters et al., 2014). These sensemaking processes, which conceptually resemble Schein's (1990) "basic underlying assumptions" from his three-levels of culture model, reflect how the organization perceives its stakeholder relations, its reasons for engaging in specific activities, and the posture and consistency it adopts in the conduct of such activities (Basu & Palazzo, 2008). The attention-based structures (Barnett, 2008) that underlie organizational sensemaking cause the MNE to view and engage with its stakeholders in a particular way and drive executive decision-making (Basu & Palazzo, 2008). Taken together, it accentuates the role of leadership in cultivating the internal conditions conducive to proactive stakeholder engagement, which supports its responsiveness and organizational resilience.

Andersen and Young (2020) emphasize the importance of ethical leadership in developing an organizational climate that fosters open communication, ongoing learning processes, involvement, and trust-based stakeholder interactions. The authors argue that corporate responsiveness in dynamic and uncertain environments is best supported by organizational structures that combine decentralized information sharing with centralized coordination (Andersen & Young, 2020). Relatedly, Barnett (2008) discusses top management's willingness to listen and open information flows as important "tailwinds" for real option recognition, as many shadow options and early stakeholder signals are discovered by middle management and field staff. Peters et al. (2014) point to the link between leadership's moral values and the MNE's collaborative capabilities, which enhances its stakeholder influence capacity and access to stakeholder resources. It speaks to the importance of congruence between espoused corporate values and those actually enacted by leadership and the organization in its engagement with stakeholders (Andersen & Young, 2020). This brings forward the fifth and final proposition:

*P5.* The MNE's top management ought to be mindful of organizational sense-making in shaping its CSR and CSV strategy and stakeholder engagement style. Through value-based leadership, it should develop an organizational culture conducive to open communication, transparency, and trust-based interactions that facilitate alignment between corporate espoused and practiced values in its stakeholder engagement.

# Methodology

## *Empirical Research Approach*

The literature review offered five theory-based propositions on how an MNE should enhance its responsiveness to the uncertainties implied by emergent EU sustainability regulation. This chapter will next examine these propositions through an exploratory single-case study, presenting empirical insights through storytelling (Yin, 1994, 2009) and retrospective sensemaking (Weick, 1995). The single-case study method was adopted to allow for dynamic, in-depth observations and to offer rich, contextualized insights supportive of new theory development (Eisenhardt, 1989b; Gustafsson, 2017). The purpose is to validate and nuance the propositions through an illustrative example of effective responsiveness and organizational adaptivity, from which new managerial insights may emerge and serve to inspire other firms.

## *Case Context*

The case company is United Plantations Berhad (hereafter UP), a Danish–Malaysian palm oil multinational founded in 1906 by Aage Westenholz. The company has a planted oil palm area of 46,307 hectares in Malaysia and Indonesia and had a 2022 revenue of MYR 2.5 billion (USD 540 million), of which approximately 80% is attributable to Europe. Thus, responding to the EU regulation is strategically important to the company. UP is listed on the Kuala Lumpur Stock Exchange (KLSE), with a market cap of ca. MYR 6.6 billion (USD 1.42 billion) (August 2023) and is owned 49.98% by United International Enterprises Limited (hereafter UIE), listed on Nasdaq OMX Copenhagen. UIE is majority owned by the brothers Carl and Martin Bek-Nielsen, who are also two of the three executive directors at UP today. Having grown up on the plantations, the Bek-Nielsen brothers succeeded their father, Børge Bek-Nielsen, in 2003, who had worked in the company since 1951. He was widely praised for his honesty, integrity, hands-on leadership, and for creating an innovative oil palm plantation based on core values conducive to broader stakeholder and community alignment (Parks, 2005). Today, UP is a global leader in sustainable palm oil production and is recognized for its long-standing commitments to CSR and CSV, rooted in a legacy of corporate citizenship since its founding (Martin, 2004). This is extensively demonstrated in the numerous awards that UP has won for sustainability and responsible behavior over the past 20 years (see the Appendix).

## Data Collection and Analysis

Several data collection methods were combined, including desk research, semi-structured in-depth interviews, and obtrusive on-site observations from numerous visits to UP's headquarters in Jendarata, Malaysia. A diverse set of managers were interviewed to obtain a variety of perspectives, including members from senior management, corporate affairs, the sustainability office, and compliance. To ensure internal validity and congruence, interview answers were compared across respondents and cross-checked with corporate documents, archive materials, books, and online articles. Most interviews were recorded, and key interviews were transcribed to ensure accuracy, supplemented with notetaking to shape a holistic impression. This was complemented by numerous informal discussions with staff from various levels in the organization to validate the alignment between espoused corporate values and those observed in practice. The research also involved external interviews to obtain and contrast additional perspectives with the internal data. This included UP's holding company (UIE), European customers, members and representatives from the Roundtable on Sustainable Palm Oil (RSPO), and other industry participants. The response propositions were re-examined by exploring their consistency with empirical observations and contrasted with new, inductive insights that emerged from the interviews. Using theme-based data analysis, transcripts, hand notes, and recordings were reviewed to understand the organizational characteristics underlying UP's historical responsiveness and their intended approach to handling future regulatory uncertainty and stakeholder pressures.

## Research Limitations

A limitation of the single-case study method is the upfront bias in the case selection itself. The high contextual sensitivity implies a narrow empirical validation of the theoretical response propositions and similarly limits the generalizability of new insights that emerge from the study to other contexts. Furthermore, the heavy reliance on interviews and observations also introduces greater subjectivity, not only in how interviewees perceive questions and recall historical events but equally in how their answers are interpreted, weighted, and formed into an empirical narrative. Finally, the backward-looking empirical findings on past response actions could be questioned in the extent to which these provide a useful answer in relation to ex ante regulatory uncertainty. However, the theory suggests that effective responsiveness to uncertainty and unpredictability is an organizational capability (Andersen & Young, 2020; Teece et al., 1997), such that ex post empirical findings will remain relevant to ex ante uncertainty, even in new contexts. The interviews do not inquire into UP's Indonesian subsidiary and focus exclusively on response strategies at the Malaysian headquarters level. This is a research limitation because different interpretations of responsible behavior and possible dilution of internal values at subsidiaries may, in some contexts, impact responsiveness at the multinational level (Andersen, 2016; Andersen & Torp, 2019).

## Empirical Analysis

This section presents empirical insights from the study on UP, contrasted and discussed in relation to the five propositions developed in the theory. Through a myriad of perspectives and anecdotes, the case is described and analyzed through the lens of responsiveness and adaptivity to dynamic sustainability regulation and evolving stakeholder expectations. This section begins with a discussion of historical and recent events demonstrating the interconnectivity of CSR and CSV with UP's strategy and competitiveness. We next explore the role of MSIs, UP's stakeholder engagement style, and showcase real option reasoning applied in various contexts. Finally, we deep-dive into organizational sensemaking to illustrate the company's spirit and shed light on the more subtle managerial attributes supportive of its success.

### *CSV in Practice*

One overarching observation from the case study is that it characterizes an organization that has, since its founding, consciously embraced the core tenets of corporate citizenship, highlighted in even the earliest annual letters to shareholders since 1916 (Martin, 2004; UP Anniversary Booklet, 1967). This generational legacy has underpinned UP's corporate values for decades and has been manifested through investments in quality housing, schools, hospitals, infrastructure, and recreational facilities for their employees and local community, often going beyond the requirements of the law. In addition to supporting its corporate reputation, these initiatives have been integral in UP's local cluster development at their locations (Porter & Kramer, 2011).

UP's formal sustainability transition commenced in 2001 when the Swiss supermarket chain Migros requested UP to develop and deliver sustainable palm oil for a potential premium. They responded by becoming the world's first audited producer and processor of sustainable palm oil, in accordance with principles and criteria specified by Migros. The company's existing foundation and history of commitment to responsible behavior greatly aided this.

As stated by Martin Bek-Nielsen, Executive Director of UP:

> When sustainability interests heightened among customers, the fundamentals to respond were already there, embedded in our history and values. We just needed to document it and reconfigure some sustainability variables in our existing practices. We realized that we could actually both do something good for the environment and turn this into a commercial opportunity.

The Migros example illustrates how UP effectively took CSV into action a decade before Porter and Kramer (2011) formalized the concept, demonstrating how shared value was created through "reconceiving their products and markets" and "reconfiguring their value chain." UP effectively de-commoditized a commodity by incorporating sustainability variables into its product differentiation and business model, as communicated in its mission of being a leader in environmental performance by "integrating and operationalizing sustainability into our DNA, so that it remains built-in and not bolted-on" (UP, 2022a).

The interviewees seldom explicitly distinguished between CSR and CSV, often using the concepts interchangeably, partly explainable by the conceptual overlap. Nonetheless, it was evident that such initiatives were utilized extensively and usually implemented many years ahead of the regulatory curve, in line with the "preemptive" aspect of *P1a*. UP commenced its carbon reduction program in 2005 and published the world's first peer-reviewed environmental life-cycle assessment (LCA) in 2008 through collaboration with 2.-0 LCA consultants from Denmark. This enabled them to back-track their GHG emissions baseline to 2004, since which they have achieved industry-leading reductions of 61%, largely attributable to efficiency-improving R&D investments (UP, 2022a). Examples include their one-of-a-kind railway transportation network to replace combustion-intensive lorries and their ongoing efforts to improve crop yields through refined seed production and new cultivation practices. Much attention is also given to the utilization of by-products in operations, such as methane capture and biogas production from palm oil mill effluent and steam and electricity produced through biomass boilers running on press fibers, shells, and empty fruit bunch fibers. They have since 2010 committed to a pledge against further deforestation, some 13 years ahead of the Deforestation Regulation. Similar to the company's rainforest preservation program in collaboration with the Copenhagen Zoo, first initiated in 2007 and officially established in 2010, these commitments directly contribute to EU Taxonomy objectives. On an aggregate basis, UP's preemptive CSV strategy has been a key driver behind their competitiveness, consistently ranking them No. 1 or 2 in yields per hectare, the lowest production costs per ton, and the Return on Equity (ROE) (21% in 2022) has consistently outperformed the industry (UP, 2022a).

Ulrik Østergaard, Managing Director of UIE, emphasized that:

> UP has been exceptionally good at finding and commercializing the areas of overlap between social, environmental, and economic value creation. This has definitely been one of the reasons why they have outperformed competitors on several KPIs.

*P.1a* suggested that a commodity MNE should align its CSR and CSV priorities with EU Taxonomy objectives, though the case study did not indicate such alignment being sought for its own sake. Rather, the interviews suggested that Taxonomy alignment was driven mainly by customers' growing demands for enhanced traceability and verifiability in response to stakeholder expectations that run ahead of regulation. One customer explained that:

> You have to be horizon scanning all the time because once something becomes public, it is a big issue. It is not so much the end-consumers but more the reputational side, fears of NGOs, and risk of bad publicity for retailers and manufacturers that drive customers' sustainability requirements. We address this by working closely with suppliers like UP, who share our sustainability ethos.

UP's most recent significant CSR investment echoes this customer's perspective. In response to the uncertainties implied by the proposed EU Forced Labor Ban, UP spent millions in 2022 to reimburse their migrant guest workers for recruitment fees paid to third-party agents in the past. Recruitment fee reimbursements are not currently part of the EU's proposed Forced Labor Ban, but through close attention to evolving "best-practice" observed in other industries and in collaboration with an NGO and some of its customers, UP responded preemptively to early signals of a potential human rights issue in the future. Beyond mitigating their own reputational risk, management discussed the value-added in being able to offer guidance through "facilitating discussions with our customers even at a very early stage" – better preparing both parties once it becomes a mainstream issue. They emphasized "close and transparent communication" with their stakeholders as a prerequisite to timely responsiveness. Thus, it appeared that a combination of both "insurance" against future negative-publicity risks and opportunities to differentiate themselves as a favorable supplier are important rationales behind their CSR- and CSV-driven response to regulatory uncertainty. Overall, the interviews indicate that Taxonomy alignment by the responsive commodity MNE is most likely indirect, addressed through preemptive attention to customer needs reflective of evolving stakeholder expectations.

Nonetheless, the case study suggests that effective responsiveness largely hinges on both proactive customer dialogue to scan for early signals and – through a CSV approach – swiftly reconfiguring value chains to incorporate new sustainability variables according to dynamically evolving customer requirements. This is consistent with Teece et al.'s (1997) dynamic capability concept and doing so ahead of the competition might constitute a source of competitive advantage.

### *Responsible Behavior and Political Risks*

*P.1b* proposed that a commodity MNE in developing countries should supplement its Taxonomy-oriented CSR and CSV strategy with initiatives intended to support local stakeholder interests and enhance its reputation with host governments, among other reasons, to address political risks, such as that of the Malaysian and Indonesian governments' threat of a palm oil export ban into the EU, triggered by the Deforestation Regulation. Not surprisingly, perhaps, the case study confirmed a positive link between commitments to responsible behavior and local reputation, supportive of UP's crucially important social license to operate and political relations (Darendeli & Hill, 2015; Salancik & Pfeffer, 1978).

The findings did *not*, however, support the aspect of *P.1b*, which proposed that such (developing country-focused) CSR activities are primarily intended to increase the MNE's local influential capacity and alleviate political risks. At UP, it appeared that this type of responsible behavior was, before all else, driven by their organizational values and genuine interest in acting by good corporate citizenship in harmony with the communities in which they operate. Interestingly, the study nevertheless demonstrated that their reputation has likely been instrumental in causing the Malaysian government to recently appoint UP's Chief Executive Director, Carl Bek-Nielsen, as chairman of the Malaysian Palm Oil

Council to facilitate negotiations between the EU and the Malaysian government around the new Deforestation Regulation, among other tasks.

As stated by Martin Bek-Nielsen:

> I think the Malaysian government can see that we genuinely care for our employees and wider communities. Of course, we understand where the EU is coming from, but we are also loyal to the Malaysian palm oil industry in trying to find joint solutions with EU policymakers.

Consequently, the reputational goodwill of CSR and CSV, combined with effective stakeholder engagement capabilities, may, in some circumstances, provide access to stakeholder resources and enhance the firm's influential capacity toward emergent regulation – indirectly addressing derivative political risks. This provides some supportive evidence for *P.1b* and the aspect of *P4* relating to stakeholder engagement capabilities as a source of the MNE's influential capacity. The finding shares similarities with those of another study on Maersk by Andersen (2016), illustrating how investments in responsible behavior enhance corporate reputation and may leverage an MNE's ability to deal with unexpected adverse events. However, it also appears evident from this study that the very ability to mitigate political risks by relying on reputation and stakeholder engagement capabilities, to a large extent, is circumstantial and arises as a "shadow option" out of years of previous CSR activities, consistent with *P3*. Accordingly, it is unclear ex ante whether *P.1b* can be generalized due to the path-dependent series of prior CSR initiatives enabling this shadow option, but it was nonetheless interesting to observe at UP.

### *MSIs and Corporate Responsiveness*

The case study found supportive evidence for the role of MSIs and voluntary regulation as mechanisms to establish legitimacy with key stakeholders, in line with *P2*. This is most notably demonstrated in UP's active involvement in the RSPO. The RSPO brings together stakeholders from various sectors of the palm oil industry, including producers, processors, traders, retailers, banks, and NGOs, to set the highest agreeable and measurable standard for sustainable palm oil certification. Currently, RSPO-certified palm oil constitutes 19% of industry output and, thus, represents a valuable "quality stamp" to the producers with the means to meet its criteria. In a race against competitors, UP became the first RSPO-certified company in 2008, which management attributed mainly to their existing groundwork and learnings that emerged and expanded following the Migros customer case in 2001.

As stated by Rasmus Frederiksen, Corporate Affairs Manager:

> Having had that baseline in place for many years, UP had a better chance at responding and becoming the world's first producer of RSPO-certified sustainable palm oil.

The internal interviewees emphasized the reputational benefits of RSPO involvement and its value as a source of product differentiation, enabling them to reach increasingly climate-conscious customers, particularly in Europe. Other RSPO members and representatives similarly highlighted "risk and reputation management" and "expanded market access" as key rationales underlying sustainability certification.

Deputy Group Manager Dr Sanath Kolandai explained how "UP's longstanding history puts us in an influential position, and we see it as our duty to help safeguard the industry's image," which supports the notion of an industry-leading position assumed by UP in addressing legitimacy concerns beyond the firm-level alone.

The study did not, however, find supportive evidence for voluntary regulation playing a vital role in addressing norm-ambiguities and guiding trade-off considerations in relation to specific CSR and CSV investments, as suggested by *P2*. The fact that UP's current practices already meet or even exceed the RSPO's benchmarks on several sustainability criteria might explain this partial divergence from *P2*. Nonetheless, these "trade-off guiding features" offered by voluntary regulation may well remain relevant to producers yet to become RSPO certified, as such firms likely seek tangible criteria toward which they can steer their sustainability investments and future practices.

Although initiatives resembling CSV+ (de los Reyes et al., 2017) were not extensively discussed in the interviews, such were still observed at UP, exemplified by the recruitment fee reimbursements of 2022. This initiative links to its operations through its employees (as per CSV) but directly involves short- to medium-term economic trade-offs in pursuit of enhanced social performance (as per CSV+). Interestingly, these trade-off decisions were not guided by the RSPO's standards or the present content of current regulation but more so by early signals captured through interactions with customers and NGOs, and to preemptively hedge themselves against such issues later becoming subject to regulatory enforcement and greater stakeholder attention.

An aspect not discussed in *P2* was the extent of conceptual overlap in the EU regulation with voluntary regulation such as the RSPO. Surprisingly, several internal and external respondents mentioned a disconnect between the RSPO and EU regulators whereby such "voluntary certification schemes will not provide a green lane" that automatically qualifies RSPO-certified producers for EU Taxonomy alignment or compliance with the Deforestation Regulation. Nevertheless, both UP and other RSPO members underlined how the certification provides a significant head start in terms of understanding and adapting to the evolving EU Taxonomy and Deforestation Regulation.

As explained by Martin Bek-Nielsen:

> The EU sustainability regulation is a potential tsunami for those companies who have not yet had any standards to follow. Our experience with the RSPO provides us with a solid head start in understanding and adapting to the EU Taxonomy and similar legislation.

It seems appropriate to extend *P2* in that the learnings and experiences obtained from voluntary regulation constitute an important supplementary aspect to aid the responsiveness of commodity MNEs to evolving formal regulation.

Finally, the case study strongly supported *P2*'s claim of MSI involvement being a valuable radar for detecting early signals on evolving stakeholder expectations and social–environmental trends. While other industry participants similarly mentioned the reputation and brand-value aspects of RSPO certification, this intangible element of multi-stakeholder interaction also appeared highly valuable to UP.

As put forward by Rasmus Frederiksen:

> The RSPO, being a multi-stakeholder organization, is valuable in providing inputs and early signals on what moves on the horizon. We have to actively extend our understanding of what is coming in the future to create new opportunities and mitigate the risk of falling behind.

The diversity of stakeholders involved in the RSPO offers valuable opportunities to scan and sense emergent issues and, as such, supports responsiveness to these early signals before they become mainstream or materialize into formal regulation. UP's Sustainability Manager, Lee Kian Wei, mentioned that through their proactive interaction with NGOs present at the RSPO, they seek to be a step ahead and are better able to respond to early signals in advance. It aligns with the views of one customer, emphasizing the importance of "horizon scanning" and hints at a proactive risk management culture shared with UP.

Management also discussed the value of looking beyond short-term ESG outcomes and immediate stakeholder pressures to mitigate the risks of what several internal and external interviewees labeled "certification and compliance fatigue" from new regulatory layers. While voluntary regulation offers an avenue to preemptive stakeholder alignment through adherence to explicit minimum standards, the study points to the importance of paying enough attention to the ongoing organizational efforts and very processes through which underlying sustainability trends and signals are addressed. UP describes its own sustainability transition as an evolutionary process driven by attention to continuous improvements supportive of long-term trends and sustainability goals. By adopting a process rather than outcome-oriented view on voluntary regulation and its broader sustainability strategy, the MNE will, over time, develop dynamic response capabilities, going beyond static Taxonomy alignment and mere compliance to the known.

### *A Relational Stakeholder Approach*

*P4* posits that the MNE's stakeholder engagement capabilities are essential for its scanning, sensing, and capacity to access and influence stakeholder resources, for which the case study provides strong support. The interviews indicate that UP's stakeholder engagement style is characterized by mutual trust, collaboration, open communication, and transparency, which are synonymous with the theory's tenets of fruitful stakeholder interaction (Jones, 1995; Panda & Sangle, 2019).

As highlighted by Martin Bek-Nielsen:

> We don't want to become known as someone who only exploits our stakeholders for resources but as someone that creates value for the network we engage with. We do everything we can to foster close, mutually beneficial relations, loyalty, and collaboration.

The essence of a relational stakeholder approach was reciprocated in the customer interviews, which emphasized the importance of trustworthiness, open dialogue, and transparency to address possible compliance gaps ahead of time and "collaboratively solve sustainable sourcing." Similarly, on the local supplier side, UP's Shipping and Logistics Manager, Selvi Kasi, highlighted the use of "training, face-to-face contact, and proactively seeking to understand suppliers' compliance challenges rather than just sending a letter of requirements." On this account, while UP's sustainability efforts are largely driven by their internal values and preemptive attention to European customers' concerns, they also ensure the transferability and adaptability of these efforts to local supplier contexts, in line with the guiding principles of *trust, traceability, and transparency* mentioned in their sustainability report (UP, 2022a).

Many of the emergent sustainability challenges characterized by uncertain regulatory movements and evolving stakeholder expectations require solutions yet to be developed. As opposed to the natural inclination of handling such uncertainties through mere tick-boxing and measurable risk assessments, the study demonstrates the value of interactive processes and open, collaborative efforts in generating solutions supportive of the MNE's supply chain resilience (Scholten & Schilder, 2015). Relatedly, UP's top management discussed the importance of partner selection both upstream and downstream. Working with fewer long-term partners that share UP's value sets was mentioned as imperative for loyalty and mutual commitment, supporting their access to stakeholder resources and mitigating opportunism – consistent with Jones (1995). Through these value sets and mutual trust, UP can exert influence in addressing supply chain due diligence challenges beyond their immediate reach. An interesting response opportunity was discussed by Rasmus Frederiksen in "UP's role as a supply chain mediator in bridging joint solutions between downstream customers and the upstream supplier network." Management expected to pragmatically influence the supply chain's ability to solve due diligence and traceability challenges implied by the Deforestation Regulation and Corporate Sustainability Due Diligence Directive, placing UP in an advantageous network position, occupying a structural hole (Burt, 1992). It effectively turns their stakeholder engagement capabilities into a valuable, rare, and inimitable relational asset to constitute a competitive advantage (Panda & Sangle, 2019) and supports their ability to find new solutions and innovate in times of unforeseen events and circumstances. This was notably demonstrated during COVID-19 and in UP's ability to successfully recover from that disruptive shock.

As explained by Ulrik Østergaard:

> Particularly during Covid-19, UP stood out for two reasons. They
> invested heavily in streamlining operations and benefitted from
> employee goodwill and loyalty, which they drew on to go the extra
> mile and find creative solutions to achieve a 30% improvement in
> headcount efficiency compared with before Covid.

UP's dynamic capability of flexibly reconfiguring operational assets is complemented by its ability to draw on its stakeholder (employee) resources, which enabled them to innovate during a time of crisis. This adaptive capacity and resilience are deemed to be equally valuable in responding to uncertainties related to future regulation.

A challenge discussed in both the internal and external interviews was the uneven distribution of costs and benefits of the heightened due diligence and traceability requirements posed by the Deforestation Regulation. Chain Reaction Research (2022) estimates an additional $387–546 million in annual due diligence costs, set to be absorbed mostly by upstream Malaysian and Indonesian palm oil actors as a result of the Deforestation Regulation. This contrasts with the two-thirds of operating profits in the EU value chain for embedded palm oil earned by downstream manufacturers and retailers (Chain Reaction Research, 2022). Relying solely on relational governance mechanisms may be insufficient to solve the implied due diligence challenges imposed by the new regulation – in line with Benito et al. (2019), who also advocate for a combination of governance mechanisms in managing global value chains. UP's management and other industry participants discussed the additional importance of pre-competitive arrangements to establish shared due diligence and traceability systems as well as market-based incentives to ensure compliance by smaller, upstream local suppliers – consistent with Pedersen and Andersen's (2006) emphasis on goal congruence to safeguarding supply chain compliance.

### *Real Options in Action*

*P3* posits that the commodity MNE may benefit from real options reasoning in its approach to CSR and CSV. The study provided supportive evidence for this but also demonstrated how stakeholder engagement processes may support real option creation, in line with Peters et al. (2014). The example of UP drawing on employee goodwill during the COVID-19 crisis illustrates how previous investments in stakeholder relations provided strategic flexibility in their response to emergent uncertainties. Similarly, weak signals sensed through stakeholder interaction at RSPO meetings have enabled early responsiveness to emergent social–environmental concerns. This is an interesting observation because it links *P3* (the real options perspective) not only with *P1* (CSR-CSV strategies) but also with *P4* (stakeholder engagement). Interviews with UP's management indicated a propensity to adopt a staged-out and gradual approach to their investments in CSV-driven innovation.

As stated by Rasmus Frederiksen:

> There are many new technologies and emerging sustainability standards, but as a company, you cannot do everything at once but must consciously evaluate what [CSR and CSV] investments will give you the best return. By "having a toe in the water" and exploring options in many areas, we can remain flexible to adjust or scale up once more information becomes available – thereby adapting ourselves whilst avoiding resource-draining overcommitments.

Consistent with *P3*, the statement reflects the value of flexibility in CSR and CSV investments that enable adaptation in their responses under evolving future conditions. UP's real options reasoning was primarily justified in the context of budgetary considerations along with inherent outcome uncertainties of new CSR and CSV investments – both in terms of impact and relevance to stakeholders in the future. UP's Sustainability Manager provided several examples of CSV-driven renewable energy investments first initiated at a smaller scale, but once the technology became more promising, commitments were made to scale it up, such as solar panel systems or their biogas plants. The company's early investments in LCAs and GHG emission measurement technology, long before such became mainstream, enabled them to track and document their industry-leading progress in emission reductions, now serving as a competitive differentiator years later when increased stakeholder attention and regulatory requirements have sharpened.

A possible real option currently brewing lies in UP's collaborative efforts with some of their larger European customers to make pilot (trial) templates anticipating the requirements of emergent regulation, enabling both parties to preempt requirements and make more responsive adjustments once regulatory criteria become clearer. The real option component takes shape in the early time and resource investments going into such pilot templates, enabling transferability of their knowledge and learning experience to future customer contracts if and once formally required by regulation.

An interesting insight from the study is how many of the previously discussed CSR and CSV initiatives had, at later stages, turned out to provide unplanned but, in hindsight, valuable learnings to enhance their responsiveness. UP's learnings from the sustainability documentation related to the Migros deal in 2001 turned out to be crucial in helping them become the world's first RSPO-certified company in 2008. The learnings obtained through voluntary regulation in the RSPO now appear vital for UP's preparedness for the emergent EU regulation today. The storyline illustrates a case of options in options and may extend *P3* to incorporate the importance of ongoing learning in real option development.

In UP, real option generation and explorative learning are consciously supported by its Environmental Sustainability Committee. This is an internal task force, partly separate from the main organizational structure, to which management commits significant resources to investigate new technologies for emission reductions and new sustainability solutions. The committee provides the freedom for its members to travel around the world to meet people, establish new networks, and engage in learning platforms with inputs from other companies, industries, and scientific conferences. The purpose is to extend their understanding of emergent sustainability issues, particularly those on the three- to five-year horizon, and explore the applicability of new technologies in a palm oil context. By applying their gradual "toe in the water" approach, the most promising ideas are investigated for further internal development. The Environmental Sustainability Committee exemplifies a concrete attempt to facilitate experimental learning through structural ambidexterity (Tushman & O'Reilly, 1996), by which UP balances its optimization of existing operations while also pursuing more explorative activities supportive of its future renewal. Supported by open and upfront discussions on commitments to innovate, it extends its future options for maneuverability under changing conditions and its capacity to develop solutions to future issues yet to materialize in regulation or explicit stakeholder expectations. Relatedly, management mentioned how scenario planning helps them stay attentive to the possible long-term challenges facing UP, such as broader climate change transition risks or the implications of synthetic palm oil alternatives as a potential complement to the industry's sustainability transition. Collectively, the study finds supportive evidence of UP flexibly coping with regulatory and stakeholder uncertainty through real options reasoning – not just tangibly in the various staged-out CSR-CSV initiatives and exploratory R&D investments but also intangibly through their stakeholder engagement and the ongoing learnings that follow.

### *Sensemaking and Organizational Success*

*P5* suggested that organizational sensemaking influences how MNEs engage with their stakeholders and shape their CSR-CSV activities and that congruence between espoused and enacted values supports corporate responsiveness to uncertainty. The empirical evidence firmly validates *P5*. The interviews indicate that UP's internal values and top management's psychological connection to the company's moral legacy of commitment to responsible behavior are foundational for the CSR-CSV approach and its principles for stakeholder engagement practiced today. This resonates with Schein's (1990) argument that corporate culture is derived from founders' values and subsequent learnings and beliefs of new leaders. In fact, UP's organizational sensemaking and its internal values appear more influential in their response to uncertainties and stakeholder engagement style than the immediate pressures arising from the forthcoming EU regulation. This is consistent with Weick (1995), who proposes that organizational sensemaking plays an increasingly important role in contexts of environmental uncertainty.

Applying Basu and Palazzo's (2008) tripartite model, a "dipstick assessment" of UP's organizational sensemaking is presented in Fig. 7.1. The tripartite model is adopted because of its direct link to CSR (and supposedly CSV) and its suitability for antecedent use (Peters et al., 2014). It provides a holistic perspective on the various internal aspects that motivate UP's unique approach to CSR-CSV and underpin its stakeholder engagement capabilities and real options reasoning (Basu & Palazzo,

| Sensemaking in UP: CSR Character | | |
|---|---|---|
| **Cognitive**<br>*What UP*<br>*thinks* | Identity<br>orientation | **Relational**<br><br>• "We do everything we can to foster close, mutually beneficial relations, loyalty, and collaboration"<br>• "It is important that the results we create are shared and impactful to those we work with" |
| | Legitimacy | **Moral**<br><br>• "Throughout our history it has always been a priority to incorporate sustainable values and act morally right in dealing with our stakeholders. It comes down to treating people with respect"<br>• "It is not only about getting a green image and making money, but also the positive spiral that follows from doing what we believe is right based on our moral compass" |
| **Linguistic**<br>*What UP*<br>*says* | Justification | **Both economic and ethical**<br><br>• "Being a leader in environmental performance by integrating and operationalizing sustainability into our DNA, so that it remains 'build-in' and not 'bolted-on'"<br>• "We genuinely care to provide our employees and their families with good housing, schools, hospitals and living facilities"<br>• "We are not a charity organization, but want to do business in the right way and in a way which makes us proud" |
| | Transparency | **Balanced**<br><br>• "In UP we recognize that we are not fault-free, and know that there is always room for improvement"<br>• "We tolerate mistakes and deviations from plans but do not tolerate silence, non-communication, or hiding issues under the carpet. Our internal communication must be based on openness and respect" |

Fig. 7.1. (*Continued*)

| Conative *How UP behaves* | Posture | **Open** <br>• "We practice an open-door policy, and firmly believe that no one person at the top is stronger than the pyramid of people who supports him or her" <br>• "You must always listen to your stakeholders and partners and make a genuine attempt to understand where they are coming from" <br>• "The Executive Directors [Martin and Carl] have a personal touch with each and everyone here … They are only a WhatsApp away" |
| | Consistency | **Strategically/internally consistent** <br>• "Sustainability is part of our strategic core and embedded into our operational DNA" <br>• "The biggest challenge is to ensure that the entire organization, down to the field worker level, understands why sustainability is important and why UP needs to address these evolving [regulatory] criteria" |
| | Commitment | **Both normative and instrumental** <br>• "The founder Aage Westenholz and his successors have always set the highest welfare standards within the conditions of the day. This was one of the founding principles of UP, and remains ever important" <br>• "Whilst we are a profit-seeking company, we have always believed in a triple-bottom-line" |

Fig. 7.1. Dimensions of Sensemaking in UP.

2008). The sensemaking dimensions are expressed through quotes and statements from the interviews, informal discussions, and the annual report (United Plantations Berhad, 2021a, 2021b, 2021c).

The most important observation is the consistency between what is thought, said, and done with respect to UP's sustainability practices and stakeholder engagement. The authenticity shines through from the top management's words to what is believed and practiced at the middle management and floor level. Many employees and their families have been with the company for multiple decades, supportive of the consistency in culture developed over the years. The culture appears conducive to trust-based relations, extending its access to and influence on stakeholder resources, enhancing its ability to continuously upgrade sustainability solutions in collaboration with its partners. In their partnerships and contracts, UP looks beyond economic optimization to consciously select its customers and suppliers based on shared value sets and, where possible, alignment of sustainability interests. One customer's statement – "We share the same sustainability ethos with UP" – is a testament to this congruence, supportive of fruitful collaboration jointly aiding their responsiveness. The quotes in Fig. 7.1 suggest that UP lives and breathes sustainability and that "triple-bottom-line thinking" is ingrained in the organizational DNA and top management's attention-based structures. These structures appear quite attentive to shadow option recognition and new option creation that simultaneously support social, environmental, and economic value creation.

It was mentioned in several conversations that UP's Chief Executive Director spends time nearly every morning walking in the fields and factories to observe operations and communicate with employees. It exemplifies efforts at listening and encouraging information sharing and is in sync with management's open-door policy, signifying a perceived low power distance, as captured in one employee's comment: "The executive directors [Martin and Carl] have a personal touch with each and everyone here ... They are only a WhatsApp away." The open communication culture supports management's awareness and receptivity to early signals and the willingness of subordinates and external stakeholders to share such signals, feedback, and new ideas.

There is particular effort devoted to creating secure forums and settings for open dialogue to obtain updated information and inputs from across the organization. This often means going beyond formal office contexts to engage with employees on their "home turf" and encourage open conversation in what is perceived as psychologically safe environments by those they seek inputs from. Many unexpected problems are reportedly noticed by floor-level staff, and possible solutions often emerge through feedback loops established between and within different levels of the organization. Management consciously nurtures these feedback loops and seeks varied inputs to improve decision-making, consistent with Andersen and Torp's (2019) observation that the engagement of middle- and lower-level managers in strategic processes may enhance responsiveness. Broad involvement and open conversation ensure greater organizational buy-in and commitment to the very implementation of new solutions by the workforce – hereby aligning their intended sustainability strategy with the CSR-CSV character manifested in the sensemaking assessment.

In summary, the study illuminates a case where organizational value sets, an ethical leadership style, CSR-CSV-oriented attention-based structures, and information flows appear conducive to effective responsiveness. The study thereby supports *P5* in its entirety but equally points to the above-mentioned organizational attributes as probable antecedents for successfully applying CSR- and CSV-driven strategies in response to regulatory uncertainty and evolving stakeholder expectations.

# Conclusion

This chapter explored how commodity MNEs operating in developing countries should respond to uncertainties associated with the emergent EU sustainability regulation in the context of its broader sustainability transition. The study showed that the pursuit of CSR and CSV activities combined with voluntary regulation from MSIs might be effective ways for commodity MNEs to respond to regulatory uncertainties and movements in stakeholder expectations. Not surprisingly, perhaps, the proactive implementation of sustainability initiatives ahead of the regulatory curve pays off and creates first-mover advantages. It is illustrated that the MNE's ability to scan and respond to early stakeholder signals is a dynamic capability that preemptively enables it to circumvent adverse consequences from emergent regulation. The study indicated that voluntary regulation from MSIs plays a general role in addressing legitimacy concerns and may provide learning-based head starts in preparation for the EU Taxonomy and Deforestation Regulation in particular. Observations from the study indicated that Taxonomy alignment is pursued primarily through indirect means in its attention to European customers' requirements and value-added offered through sustainability-driven product differentiation.

Consistent with the theory, empirical findings showed that real options reasoning can enhance the flexibility of social–environmental resource commitments and, as such, supports its capability of reconfiguring its (hard and soft) asset base in response to evolving customer requirements and dynamic stakeholder expectations. A key learning from the study is the salience of a long-term orientation to truly value future flexibility and allow shadow options and learning-based options to emerge, which cannot be foreseen ex ante. Relatedly, the study exemplifies that an MNE's ability to act and execute on its real asset flexibility is a complementary option in itself that supports effective responsiveness. The study demonstrated how investments in stakeholder goodwill and reputation underpinned this qualitative aspect behind real option execution.

Similarly, relational and trust-based stakeholder engagement capabilities contribute to the MNE's adaptive capacity and ability to access and influence stakeholder resources. Internally, this was exemplified in UP's swift response during COVID-19, where its extensive goodwill enabled it to draw on its employees' resources and creativity to emerge from this shock as more efficient and competitive. Externally, the study showed that through early signal scanning from interaction with customers, NGOs, and various stakeholders at the RSPO, the MNE can proactively address emergent social–environmental issues before they materialize into formal regulation.

In responding to the regulation for sustainable supply chains, collaborative stakeholder engagement capabilities are a valuable relational asset and a potential source of competitive advantage. By capitalizing on this relational capability and its absorptive capacity, the responsive commodity MNE may leverage its advantageous network position to mediate pragmatic sustainability solutions between downstream customers and its upstream developing country supplier network. This requires recognizing and assimilating new demands for traceability and verifiability and adapting them to commercial ends through collaborative solutions across its supply chain. The study suggested that proactively responding to the Deforestation Regulation requires the MNE to take a leading role in handling what might be a wicked problem. It involves addressing a collective action problem in establishing shared traceability systems, finding a solution to the uneven distribution of costs and benefits associated with full supply chain compliance, and mitigating potential host-country political risks induced by regulatory changes abroad. The study demonstrated how continuous investments in responsible behavior may enhance corporate reputation and, over time, extend the MNE's political influence in support of pragmatic solutions to mitigate such risks.

The theory triangulation and derivative propositions offered a multitude of tools, approaches, and perspectives supportive of responsiveness to regulatory uncertainty. Although the study provides evidence for the value of the individual response strategies, the overarching conclusion is that their effective application is amplified by the core organizational values that drive internal sensemaking processes. The core values of integrity and a genuine commitment to social and environmental care act as the bedrock for an ethical leadership style and trust-based, relational stakeholder engagement. It also accentuates top management's critical role in cultivating the "right" organizational climate by exemplifying ethical behavior and encouraging open communication. This facilitates sensing, ongoing learning, and sustainability-driven innovation and supports congruence between corporate-espoused and practiced values. These findings may nuance Porter and Kramer's (2011) CSV concept and contribute to the ongoing debate on the business case for CSR. Is the presence or absence of certain core values enacted authentically through ethical leadership an explanatory factor to why CSR only under some circumstances improves corporate performance and responsiveness, as otherwise indicated by the inconclusiveness of many prior studies on CSR's performance-enhancing effects? Learnings from this study suggest that core internal values have a conducive, possibly even pre-conditioning, role in the MNE's effective application of CSR and CSV programs. These "softer" organizational attributes constitute a competitive advantage and may, in fact, be the MNE's strongest asset in its responsiveness to uncertainty and the "secret sauce" to its organizational resilience in facing emergent sustainability regulation.

Moving ahead on the sustainability transition agenda and responding to the multilayered uncertainties discussed in this chapter is, without doubt, a daunting task. At many firms globally, it is addressed through a compliance orientation, driven by a natural inclination to change uncertainty into risk and deal with it in a control-based manner (Andersen & Young, 2020). Such a control-based approach resembles a series of sprints, in which firms play catch-up with emergent regulation, for example, by mapping out known risks and preparing road maps for sustainability compliance against specified KPIs and reporting requirements. This was observed as the predominant initial response to the EU Taxonomy among 275 firms in a 2022 KPMG survey, showing that most companies are yet to explicitly link their broader ESG strategy to the EU Taxonomy and remain mostly focused on immediate compliance and short-term reporting

(McCalla-Leacy et al., 2022). Given its novelty, compliance with the immediate is an expected and natural first step to address evolving regulation. A compliance-oriented response does, however, lean toward short termism and attempting to control what is predictable, measurable, and foreseeable within the realm of existing business models. In aggregate, this is unlikely to suffice in truly moving the needle on corporate contributions to Taxonomy objectives and in developing meaningful solutions to the social and environmental challenges characterized as wicked problems. This issue is captured by Mercer (2015) in their distinction between firms passively waiting for regulatory changes to unfold before acting – *future takers* – and companies actively preparing for sustainability transition by being part of the solution – *future makers* – proactively responding to emergent regulation through experimentation and ongoing learning.

UP may serve as inspiration for MNEs who seek a shift in focus from mere compliance toward strategic responsiveness founded on adaptivity and renewability. Thus, key takeaways of the study mainly speak to boards and executives prepared to embrace the challenges of sustainability transition as a marathon and evolutionary process rather than a series of catch-up sprints. The study illustrates the possible long-term merits of wholeheartedly committing to a sustainability culture based on core values, which are authentically adopted not only in management's words but consistently demonstrated in how the organization thinks and acts over longer periods of time.

## Managerial Implications and Future Research

This chapter concluded that internal core values are pivotal for the effectiveness of the response strategies proposed to regulatory and stakeholder uncertainty. Few organizations are, however, already enriched with a long history of corporate responsibility or embody an organizational culture highly supportive of resilient response strategies similar to that observed at UP. A viable path toward enhanced responsiveness will, for most firms, begin with a consciousness of the pre-conditions that enable adaptivity and embracing the mindset of adaptive organizations. This has much to do with leadership's attitude, the way it acts, and the room executives give to open conversation. A willingness to listen to updated information from the organization's frontline and its stakeholders appears fundamental in establishing feedback loops and discussing solutions in an open and dynamic way.

An overarching implication for MNEs seeking enhanced responsiveness is for decision-makers to pay greater attention to the *strategic processes* underlying their social–environmental initiatives. Rather than through the ESG outcome or EU Taxonomy alignment itself, it is through the interactive processes underlying it that the seeds are sowed for expanded horizon scanning, input flows, and collaborative solutions from joint learning – enabling the MNE to swiftly adapt under evolving conditions. Senior management, therefore, ought to engage all levels of the organization in its sustainability agenda rather than it being a task exclusively dealt with by a siloed sustainability department. Furthermore, decision-makers should consider how interactive forums, platforms, and networks can proactively be established to better engage the MNE with its various external stakeholders. Promoting an open dialogue with inputs from multiple constituents is also an important risk management consideration to avoid the often-seen pitfalls of cognitive biases in decision-makers when acting under contexts of high uncertainty.

Another managerial takeaway is the importance of sufficient resource allocation toward explorative activities, both to bolster the organization's capacity for continued renewal and to extend its maneuverability in coping with unforeseen events or evolving trends. This process may be guided by scenario planning and is practically facilitated through structural ambidexterity – such as by establishing matrix teams separately tasked to explore sustainability innovation independent of formal organizational structures. Due to path dependencies, however, decision-makers must also be cautious to avoid early resource overcommitments under uncertain or changing conditions. Where possible, it is advisable to build in flexibility for adjustments since uncertainty (in technology, regulation, and stakeholder expectations) often means that the optimal ESG strategy or sustainability solution cannot be developed at once but instead through a process of guided experimentation and adaptation as you go along.

In expanding the *process perspective* on sustainability responsiveness, future research could examine how decision-makers can adjust and leverage particular organizational attributes that would facilitate the very processes conducive to adaptivity and ongoing renewal. This may include empirical research on how firms practically establish and nurture interactive platforms and stakeholder networks supportive of collaboration and joint learning. Further research examining the role of reward and recognition programs in promoting collaboration and a long-term orientation, power distance, and the role of ownership structures and boards in securing shareholder buy-in on sustainability agendas would add valuable insights of relevance to academics and managers alike. Finally, future research could also explore MNEs' receptivity to sustainability regulation and the extent to which it is effective at influencing corporate behavior from the perspective of EU policymakers seeking to accelerate sustainability transition. Research into specific policies that may encourage a broader movement of MNEs going beyond mere short-term compliance to embracing the marathon analogy required for substantive long-term sustainability advancement would support pragmatic refinements to this evolving regulatory framework.

## Acknowledgements

My profound gratitude goes to United Plantations, without whose collaboration this chapter would not have been possible. Everyone's openness and contributions are truly appreciated. A sincere thank you to Martin Bek-Nielsen and Rasmus Frederiksen for their outstanding support to the project. My gratitude is extended to Torben Juul Andersen for the valuable input and academic feedback provided throughout the process.

# References

Ali, W., Yu, D., Latif, B., Kouser, R., & Baqader, S. (2021). Corporate social responsibility and customer loyalty in food chains – Mediating role of customer satisfaction and corporate reputation. *Sustainability*, *13*(16), 8681. https://doi.org/10.3390/su13168681

Andersen, T. J. (2006a). *Global derivatives: A strategic risk management perspective.* Prentice Hall.

Andersen, T. J. (2016). Corporate responsible behavior in multinational enterprise. *International Journal of Organizational Analysis*, *25*(3), 485–505. https://doi.org/10.1108/ijoa-12-2016-1098

Andersen, T. J., & Torp, S. (2019). *Achieving adaptive responsiveness through strategic planning, autonomous strategic actions, and interactive controls.* Emerald Insight. www.emerald.com/insight/content/doi/10.1108/978-1-78973-011-120191005/full/html

Andersen, T. J., & Young, P. C. (2020). *Strategic risk leadership: Engaging a world of risk, uncertainty, and the unknown.* Routledge.

Aragón-Correa, J. A., Marcus, A. A., & Hurtado-Torres, N. (2016). The natural environmental strategies of international firms: Old controversies and new evidence on performance and disclosure. *Academy of Management Perspectives*, *30*(1), 24–39. https://doi.org/10.5465/amp.2014.0043

Aragón-Correa, J. A., Marcus, A. A., & Vogel, D. (2020). The effects of mandatory and voluntary regulatory pressures on firms' environmental strategies: A review and recommendations for future research. *Academy of Management Annals*, *14*(1), 339–365. https://doi.org/10.5465/annals.2018.0014

Aragón-Correa, J. A., & Sharma, S. (2005). *Corporate environmental strategy and competitive advantage.* Edward Elgar.

Arora, S., Sur, J. K., & Chauhan, Y. (2022). Does corporate social responsibility affect shareholder value? Evidence from the Covid-19 crisis. *International Review of Finance*, *22*(2), 325–334. https://doi.org/10.1111/irfi.12353

Asmussen, C. G., Chi, T., & Narula, R. (2022). Quasi-internalization, recombination advantages, and global value chains: Clarifying the role of ownership and control. *Journal of International Business Studies*, *53*(8), 1747–1765. https://doi.org/10.1057/s41267-022-00551-5

Asmussen, C. G., & Fosfuri, A. (2019). Orchestrating corporate social responsibility in the multinational enterprise. *Strategic Management Journal*, *40*(6), 894–916. https://doi.org/10.1002/smj.3007

Barnett, M. L. (2008). An attention-based view of real options reasoning. *Academy of Management Review*, *33*(3), 606–628. https://doi.org/10.5465/amr.2008.32465698

Basu, K., & Palazzo, G. (2008). Corporate social responsibility: A process model of sensemaking. *Academy of Management Review*, *33*(1), 122–136. https://doi.org/10.5465/amr.2008.27745504

Becchetti, L., Ciciretti, R., & Hasan, I. (2009). *Corporate social responsibility and shareholder's value: An empirical analysis.* ResearchGate, Feb. 2009.

Benito, G. R., Petersen, B., & Welch, L. S. (2019). The global value chain and internalization theory. *Journal of International Business Studies*, *50*(8), 1414–1423. https://doi.org/10.1057/s41267-019-00218-8

Blyler, M., & Coff, R. W. (2003). Dynamic capabilities, social capital, and rent appropriation: Ties that split pies. *Strategic Management Journal*, *24*(7), 677–686. https://doi.org/10.1002/smj.327

Bosch-Badia, M.-T., Montllor-Serrats, J., & Tarrazon-Rodon, M.-A. (2015). Corporate social responsibility: A real options approach to the challenge of financial sustainability. *PLoS One*, *10*(5), e0125972. https://doi.org/10.1371/journal.pone.0125972

Boutilier, R. G. (2009). *Stakeholder politics: Social capital, sustainable development, and the corporation*. Stanford University Press.

Bowman, E. H., & Hurry, D. (1993). Strategy through the option lens: An integrated view of resource investments and the incremental-choice process. *Academy of Management Review, 18*(4), 760–782. https://doi.org/10.5465/amr.1993.9402210157

Brach, M. A. (2003). *Real options in practice*. Wiley.

Brown, L. W., Goll, I., Rasheed, A. A., & Crawford, W. S. (2020). Nonmarket responses to regulation: A signaling theory approach. *Group & Organization Management, 45*(6), 865–891. https://doi.org/10.1177/1059601120963693

Burt, R. S. (1992). *Structural holes: The social structure of competition* (p. 323). Harvard University Press.

Busch, T., & Hoffmann, V. H. (2009). Ecology-driven real options: An investment framework for incorporating uncertainties in the context of the natural environment. *Journal of Business Ethics, 90*(2), 295–310. https://doi.org/10.1007/s10551-009-0043-y

Chain Reaction Research. (2022). *EU deforestation regulation: Implications for the palm oil industry and its financers*. Chain Reaction Research. chainreactionresearch.com/report/eu-deforestation-regulation-implications-for-the-palm-oil-industry-and-its-financers/

Chapple, W., & Moon, J. (2005). Corporate social responsibility (CSR) in Asia. *Business & Society, 44*(4), 415–441. https://doi.org/10.1177/0007650305281658

Cheng, B., Ioannou, I., & Serafeim, G. (2011). Corporate social responsibility and access to finance. *Strategic Management Journal, 35*(1), 1–23. https://doi.org/10.1002/smj.2131

Cohen, W. M., & Levinthal, D. A. (1990). Absorptive capacity: A new perspective on learning and innovation. *Administrative Science Quarterly, 35*(1), 128. https://doi.org/10.2307/2393553

Conner, K. R., & Prahalad, C. K. (1996). A resource-based theory of the firm: Knowledge versus opportunism. *Organization Science, 7*(5), 477–501.

Copeland, T., & Antikarov, V. (2011). *Real options: A practitioner's guide*. Texere.

Cottrell, E., et al. (2015). Defining the benefits and challenges of stakeholder engagement in systematic reviews. *Comparative Effectiveness Research*, p. 13. https://doi.org/10.2147/cer.s69605

Crane, A., Palazzo, G., Spence, L. J., & Matten, D. (2014). Contesting the value of 'creating shared value.' *California Management Review, 56*(2), 130–153. https://doi.org/10.1525/cmr.2014.56.2.130

Dahlsrud, A. (2008). How corporate social responsibility is defined: An analysis of 37 definitions. *Corporate Social Responsibility and Environmental Management, 15*(1), 1–13. https://doi.org/10.1002/csr.132

Darendeli, I. S., & Hill, T. L. (2015). Uncovering the complex relationships between political risk and MNE firm legitimacy: Insights from Libya. *Journal of International Business Studies, 47*(1), 68–92. https://doi.org/10.1057/jibs.2015.27

De los Reyes, G., Scholz, M., & Smith, M. C. (2017). Beyond the 'win–win.' *California Management Review, 59*(2), 142–167. https://doi.org/10.1177/0008125617695286

Donaldson, T., & Dunfee, T. W. (1994). Toward a unified conception of business ethics: Integrative social contracts theory. *Academy of Management Review, 19*(2), 252–284. https://doi.org/10.2307/258705

Donaldson, T., & Preston, L. E. (1995). The stakeholder theory of the corporation: Concepts, evidence, and implications. *Academy of Management Review, 20*(1), 65–91. https://doi.org/10.5465/amr.1995.9503271992

Dyllick, T., & Muff, K. (2015). Clarifying the meaning of sustainable business. *Organization & Environment, 29*(2), 156–174. https://doi.org/10.1177/1086026615575176

Eisenhardt, K. M. (1989a). Agency theory: An assessment and review. *Academy of Management Review, 14*(1), 57–74. https://doi.org/10.5465/amr.1989.4279003

Eisenhardt, K. M. (1989b). Building theories from case study research. *Academy of Management Review, 14*(4), 532–550. https://doi.org/10.5465/amr.1989.4308385

European Commission. (2022). Proposal for a regulation on prohibiting products made with forced labour on the Union market, COM(2022) 453.

European Commission. (2022c). Regulation on deforestation-free products. *Environment.* environment.ec.europa.eu/topics/forests/deforestation/regulation-deforestation-free-products_en

Freeman, R. E. (1984). *Strategic management: A stakeholder approach.* Pitman.

Freeman, R. E. (1999). Divergent stakeholder theory. *Academy of Management Review, 24*(2), 233–236. https://doi.org/10.5465/amr.1999.1893932

Friedman, M. (1970). A Friedman doctrine – The social responsibility of business is to increase its profits. *The New York Times,* September 13. www.nytimes.com/1970/09/13/archives/a-friedman-doctrine-the-social-responsibility-of-business-is-to.html

Gajadhur, R. (2022). Corporate social responsibility in developed as opposed to developing countries and the link to sustainability. *Athens Journal of Law, 8*(2), 189–216. https://doi.org/10.30958/ajl.8-2-6

Galant, A., & Cadez, S. (2017). Corporate social responsibility and financial performance relationship: A review of measurement approaches. *Economic Research-Ekonomska Istraživanja, 30*(1), 676–693. https://doi.org/10.1080/1331677x.2017.1313122

Garcia, A. S., Mendes-Da-Silva, W., & Orsato, R. J. (2017). Sensitive industries produce better esg performance: Evidence from emerging markets. *Journal of Cleaner Production, 150,* 135–147. https://doi.org/10.1016/j.jclepro.2017.02.180

Garelli, S. (2016). Why you will probably live longer than most big companies. *IMD.* www.imd.org/research-knowledge/disruption/articles/why-you-will-probably-live-longer-than-most-big-companies/

Gereffi, G., Humphrey, J., & Sturgeon, T. (2005). The governance of global value chains. *Review of International Political Economy, 12*(1), 78–104.

Ghardallou, W., & Alessa, N. (2022). Corporate social responsibility and firm performance in GCC countries: A panel smooth transition regression model. *Sustainability, 14*(13), 7908. https://doi.org/10.3390/su14137908

Gottlieb, C. (2022). *The corporate sustainability due diligence directive* (pp. 1–6). EC.

Gustafsson, J. (2017). *Single case studies vs. multiple case studies: A comparative study.* Halmstad University, School of Business, Engineering and Science.

Hancock, A., Terazono, E., & Ruehl, M. (2023). EU deforestation law triggers ire of its trading partners. *Financial Times,* February 6. www.ft.com/content/c2f2eea9-1eb5-478f-ac53-5666776c0a35

Harrison, J. S., & Wicks, A. C. (2013). Stakeholder theory, value, and firm performance. *Business Ethics Quarterly, 23*(1), 97–124. https://doi.org/10.5840/beq20132314

Hart, S. L. (1995). A natural-resource-based view of the firm. *Academy of Management Review, 20*(4), 986–1014. https://doi.org/10.5465/amr.1995.9512280033

Hennart, J.-F. (1993). Explaining the swollen middle: Why most transactions are a mix of 'market' and 'hierarchy.' *Organization Science, 4*(4), 529–547. https://doi.org/10.1287/orsc.4.4.529

Hörisch, J., Schaltegger, S., & Freeman, R. E. (2020). Integrating stakeholder theory and sustainability accounting: A conceptual synthesis. *Journal of Cleaner Production, 275*(1), 124097. https://doi.org/10.1016/j.jclepro.2020.124097

Husted, B. W. (2005). Risk management, real options, corporate social responsibility. *Journal of Business Ethics, 60*(2), 175–183. https://doi.org/10.1007/s10551-005-3777-1

Ingram, V., van den Berg, J., van Oorschot, M., Arets, E., & Judge, L. (2018). Governance options to enhance ecosystem services in cocoa, soy, tropical timber and palm oil value chains. *Environmental Management, 62*(1), 128–142. https://doi.org/10.1007/s00267-018-0996-7

Jones, T. M. (1995). Instrumental stakeholder theory: A synthesis of ethics and economics. *Academy of Management Review, 20*(2), 404–437. https://doi.org/10.5465/amr. 1995.9507312924

Jong, H. N. (2023). Indonesia and Malaysia assail new EU ban on 'dirty commodities' trade. *Mongabay Environmental News*, January 31. news.mongabay.com/2023/01/ indonesia-and-malaysia-assail-new-eu-ban-on-dirty-commodities-trade/

Kogut, B. (1991). Joint ventures and the option to expand and acquire. *Management Science, 37*(1), 19–33. https://doi.org/10.1287/mnsc.37.1.19

KPMG International Entities. (2022). *The EU's corporate sustainability due diligence.* KPMG.   kpmg.com/xx/en/home/insights/2023/02/the-eu-corporate-sustainability-due-diligence-directive.html#:~:text=The%20European%20Commission%2C%20 via%20its,the%20environment%20and%20human%20rights

Luehrman, T. A. (1998). Investment Opportunities as Real Options: Getting Started on the numbers. *Harvard Business Review, 76*(4), 51–67.

Martin, S. M. (2004). *The UP saga* (2nd ed.). NIAS Press.

McCalla-Leacy, J., Shulman, J., & Threlfall, R. (2022). *Big shifts, small steps – KPMG.* KPMG International. assets.kpmg.com/content/dam/kpmg/se/pdf/komm/2022/ Global-Survey-of-Sustainability-Reporting-2022.pdf

McGrath, R. G. (1997). A real options logic for initiating technology positioning investments. *Academy of Management Review, 22*(4), 974–996. https://doi.org/10.5465/ amr.1997.9711022113

McKinsey & Company. (2016). Our research. www.mckinsey.com/mgi/our-research/all-research

McWilliams, A., & Siegel, D. (2001). Corporate social responsibility: A theory of the firm perspective. *Academy of Management Review, 26*(1), 117–127. https://doi. org/10.5465/amr.2001.4011987

Menghwar, P. S., & Daood, A. (2021). Creating shared value: A systematic review, synthesis and integrative perspective. *International Journal of Management Reviews, 23*(4), 466–485. https://doi.org/10.1111/ijmr.12252

Mercer. (2015). Investing in a time of climate change. Mercer. www.mercer.com.au/ content/dam/mercer/attachments/asia-pacific/australia/investment/sustainable-growth/mercer-climate-change-study-2015.pdf.

Mitchell, R. K., Agle, B. R., & Wood, D. J. (1997). Toward a theory of stakeholder identification and salience: Defining the principle of who and what really counts. *Academy of Management Review, 22*(2), 275–314. https://doi.org/10.3138/9781442673496-014

Moon, H.-C., & Parc, J. (2019). Shifting corporate social responsibility to corporate social opportunity through creating shared value. *Strategic Change, 28*(2), 115–122. https://doi.org/10.1002/jsc.2252

Neslen. (2023). EU ban on Deforestation-linked goods sets benchmark, say US lawmakers. *The Guardian*, January 5, 2023.

Orlitzky, M., & Benjamin, J. D. (2001). Corporate social performance and firm risk: A meta-analytic review. *Business & Society, 40*(4), 369–396. https://doi.org/ 10.1177/000765030104000402

Ortiz-de-Mandojana, N., & Bansal, P. (2015). The long-term benefits of organizational resilience through sustainable business practices. *Strategic Management Journal, 37*(8), 1615–1631. https://doi.org/10.1002/smj.2410

Panda, S. S., & Sangle, S. (2019). Stakeholder engagement as a dynamic capability. *Business Strategy & Development, 3*(2), 204–212. https://doi.org/10.1002/bsd2.89

Parks, C. D. (2005). Tan Sri Dato' Seri Bek-Nielsen ... a great man and mentor has passed away. *Scandasia*, October 4. scandasia.com/1851-tan-sri-dato-seri-bek-nielsen-a-great-man-and-mentor-has-passed-away/

Pedersen, E. R., & Andersen, M. (2006). Safeguarding corporate social responsibility (CSR) in global supply chains: How codes of conduct are managed in buyer-supplier relationships. *Journal of Public Affairs, 6*(3–4), 228–240. https://doi.org/10.1002/pa.232

Peters, R. C., Waples, E. P., & Golden, P. (2014). A real options reasoning approach to corporate social responsibility (CSR): Integrating real option sensemaking and CSR orientation. *Business and Society Review, 119*(1), 61–93. https://doi.org/10.1111/basr.12025

Porter, M. E. (1991). America' green strategy. *Scientific American*, April 1. www.scientificamerican.com/article/essay-1991-04/

Porter, M. E., & Kramer, M. R. (2006). Strategy and society: The link between competitive advantage and corporate social responsibility. *Harvard Business Review*, October 22. hbr.org/2006/12/strategy-and-society-the-link-between-competitive-advantage-and-corporate-social-responsibility

Porter, M. E., & Kramer, M. R. (2011). Creating shared value. *Harvard Business Review*, February. hbr.org/2011/01/the-big-idea-creating-shared-value

Porter, M. E., & Van Linde, C. (1995). Toward a new conception of the environment-competitiveness relationship. *Journal of Economic Perspectives, 9*(4), 97–118. https://doi.org/10.1257/jep.9.4.97

Ring, P., & Rands, G. (1989). Sensemaking, understanding, and commitment: Emergent interpersonal transaction processes in the evolution of 3M's microgravity research program. In A. H. Van de Ven, H. L. Angle, & M. S. Poole (Eds.), *Research on the management of innovation: The Minnesota studies* (pp. 337–366). Ballinger.

Ritchie, H., & Roser, M. (2021). Drivers of deforestation. *Our World in Data*, February 9. ourworldindata.org/drivers-of-deforestation

Rugman, A. M., & Verbeke, A. (1998). Corporate strategies and environmental regulations: An organizing framework. *Strategic Management Journal, 19*(4), 363–375. https://doi.org/10.1002/(sici)1097-0266(199804)19:4<363::aid-smj974>3.0.co;2-h

Sachs, S., & Rühli, E. (2011). *Stakeholders matter – A new paradigm for strategy in society*. Cambridge University Press.

Salancik, G. R., & Pfeffer, J. (1978). A social information processing approach to job attitudes and task design. *Administrative Science Quarterly, 23*(2), 224–253. https://doi.org/10.2307/2392563

Schein, H. E. (1990). Organizational culture. *American Psychologist, 45*(2), 109–119. https://doi.org/10.1037/0003-066X.45.2.109

Scholten, K., & Schilder, S. (2015). The role of collaboration in supply chain resilience. *Supply Chain Management: An International Journal, 20*(4), 471–484. https://doi.org/10.1108/scm-11-2014-0386

Schouten, G., Leroy, P., & Glasbergen, P. (2012). On the deliberative capacity of private multi-stakeholder governance: The roundtables on responsible soy and sustainable palm oil. *Ecological Economics, 83*, 42–50. https://doi.org/10.1016/j.ecolecon.2012.08.007

Spitzeck, H., & Chapman, S. (2012). Creating shared value as a differentiation strategy – The example of BASF in Brazil. *Corporate Governance: The International Journal of Business in Society, 12*(4), 499–513. https://doi.org/10.1108/14720701211267838

Story, J., Castanheira, F., & Hartig, S. (2016). Corporate social responsibility and organizational attractiveness: Implications for talent management. *Social Responsibility Journal, 12*(3), 484–505. https://doi.org/10.1108/srj-07-2015-0095

Strand, R., & Freeman, R. E. (2015). Scandinavian cooperative advantage: The theory and practice of stakeholder engagement in Scandinavia. *Journal of Business Ethics, 127*(1), 65–85. https://doi.org/10.1007/s10551-013-1792-1

Teece, D. J. (2007). Explicating dynamic capabilities: The nature and microfoundations of (sustainable) enterprise performance. *Strategic Management Journal, 28*(13), 1319–1350. https://doi.org/10.1002/smj.640

Teece, D. J., Pisano, G., & Shuen, A. (1997). Dynamic capabilities and strategic management. *Strategic Management Journal, 18*(7), 509–533. https://doi.org/10.1002/(sici)1097-0266(199708)18:7<509::aid-smj882>3.0.co;2-z

Think Tank European Parliament. (2023). *Proposal for a ban on goods made using forced labour*. Think Tank European Parliament. www.europarl.europa.eu/thinktank/en/document/EPRS_BRI(2023)739356

Trigeorgis, L., & Reuer, J. J. (2016). Real options theory in strategic management. *Strategic Management Journal, 38*(1), 42–63. https://doi.org/10.1002/smj.2593

Tushman, M. L., & O'Reilly, C. A. (1996). Ambidextrous organizations: Managing evolutionary and revolutionary change. *California Management Review, 38*(4), 8–29. https://doi.org/10.2307/41165852

United Plantations Berhad. (2021a). *Annual report 2021* (pp. 1–210).

United Plantations Berhad. (2021b). *Sustainability report 2021* (pp. 1–73).

United Plantations Berhad. (2022a). *Annual report 2022* (pp. 1–220).

United Plantations Berhad. (2022b). *Sustainability report 2022* (pp. 1–79).

UP Anniversary Booklet. (1967). *United Plantations' 50 years anniversary booklet*. United Plantations Berhad. https://unitedplantations.com/wp-content/uploads/2020/09/AR1967-2.pdf

Visser, W. (2009). *Corporate social responsibility in developing countries* (pp. 473–500). Oxford Academic.

Weick, K. E. (1995). *Sensemaking in organizations*. Sage Publications.

Weigelt, C., & Shittu, E. (2016). Competition, regulatory policy, and firms' resource investments: The case of renewable energy technologies. *Academy of Management Journal, 59*(2), 678–704. https://doi.org/10.5465/amj.2013.0661

Wieland, J. (2017). Shared Value: Theoretical implications, practical challenges. In J. Wieland (ed.), *Creating Shared Value: Concepts, Experience, Criticism* (pp. 9–22). Springer.

Yin, R. K. (1994). Discovering the future of the case study method in evaluation research. *American Journal of Evaluation, 15*(3), 283–290. https://doi.org/10.1177/109821409401500309

Yin, R. K. (2009). *Case study research: Design and methods*. Sage Publications.

Zaheer, S. (1995). Overcoming the liability of foreignness. *Academy of Management Journal, 38*(2), 341–363. https://doi.org/10.5465/256683

Zhao, D., & Zhou, Y. M. (2022). A real options perspective on corporate social responsibility: Evidence using causal forest. *SSRN Electronic Journal*. https://doi.org/10.2139/ssrn.4084084

## Appendix: UP's Awards and Recognitions

### 2021

- Awards received from the Edge Billion Ringgit Club for the Highest Return on Equity over three years and the Highest Growth in profit after tax in three years.

### 2020/2021

- Significant Achievement Award for Land Use and Biodiversity under the Sustainable Business Awards Malaysia (SBAM) 2020/2021.

### 2019

- Sustainable Business Award Malaysia (SBAM) presented by Global Initiatives.

### 2018

- Biodiversity Award by the SBAM 2018 presented by Global Initiatives.
- Winner of the Best Sustainability Reporting by Europa Awards for Sustainability organized by EUMCCI2018 MSPO Certification (for all UP's Malaysian operations).

### 2017

- Awarded third place out of 184 companies (Plantations) – sectoral award based on two financial performance indicators by the Edge Billion Ringgit Club: Highest Return on Equity over three years.
- Highest return to shareholders over three years.
- Awarded the ACCA MaSRA Commendation Award for Biodiversity.

### 2016

- Winner of the Best CSR Initiatives category by the Edge Billion Ringgit Club (Below RM 10 billion market cap).

### 2014

- Awarded second place out of 178 companies under the Best CSR Initiatives category by the Edge Billion Ringgit Club.

### 2013

- Awarded third place out of 144 companies under the Best CSR Initiatives category by the Edge Billion Ringgit Club.

## 2011

- Winner of the Commodity Industry Award 2011 under the CSR Category to Jendarata Estate by the Malaysian International Commodity Conference and Showcase (MICCOS).

## 2010

- Winner and sectoral winner under the Agriculture and Fisheries Sector by KPMG Shareholder Value Award 2009.

## 2009

- Winner of the Best Managed Estate (Jendarata Estate) by MICCOS.

## 2008

- RSPO Certification – the world's first certified producer of sustainable palm oil by the RSPO.
- Malaysian Palm Oil Board (MPOB) Award for the highest oil extraction rate (OER) in Peninsular Malaysia and the second highest in Malaysia 2007 to Jendarata Palm Oil by MPOB.

## 2007

- Prime Minister's Hibiscus Award 2006/2007 for Notable Achievement in Environmental Performance.
- Joint winner for the Malaysian Business CSR Award 2007 for Environmental Performance.
- Certificate for Excellence Award for Occupational Safety and Health in the Agriculture Category.

## 2006

- Second prize winner in the Corporate Governance Survey from the Minority Shareholders Watchdog Group (MSWG).

## 2005

- Winner of the Palm Oil Mill Industry Mill Practices and Innovation to Ulu Bernam Engineering Department by MPOB.

## 2004

- Winner of the National Occupational Safety and Health Award to Jendarata Estate by Ministry of Human Resources, Malaysia.

- Winner of the higher OER in the Northern Peninsular Region to Jendarata Engineering Department by **MIPOB**.
- Winner of **MPOB**'s Milling Certificate of Competency – 96% UIE(M) Sdn. Bhd.

## 2003

- KPMG Shareholder Value Award.
- Best Commercial Nursery Award from **MPOB**.
- Approved supplier to Swiss Supermarket Chain, **MIGROS**, based on their criteria on sustainable palm oil by Proforest Consultants (United Kingdom).

*Source*: https://unitedplantations.com/awards-recognitions/

Chapter 8

# When Supply Chain Sustainability Means Supply Chain Resilience: The Case of Dr. Bronner's

*Hannah Stolze[a], Jon Kirchoff[b] and Alexis Bateman[c]*

[a]*Baylor University, USA*
[b]*East Carolina University, USA*
[c]*Massachusetts Institute of Technology, USA*

## Abstract

Interest in the intersection of sustainability and supply chain resiliency has grown in recent years by managers and scholars. However, examples of how sustainability can improve resiliency are rare. The purpose of this article is to address this dearth of evidence by investigating how sustainable strategies and practices can create more robust supply chains that are resilient to global disruptions. A strategic model of resiliency is introduced based on the supply chain management practices at Dr. Bronner's, a rapidly growing personal care product company. The case study data explores the relationship between sustainability and resiliency and reveals a potential pathway for companies to merge the two.

*Keywords*: Corporate values; dynamic systems; operating principles; resilience; strategy–structure–performance; sustainable value chain

## Introduction

The expansion of global supply chains has made them increasingly more susceptible to global risk and disruptions. A potential key to managing risk, supply chain sustainability strategies, and initiatives have been part of business school,

Sustainable and Resilient Global Practices:
Advances in Responsiveness and Adaptation, 193–215
doi:10.1108/978-1-83797-611-920241008

and boardroom agendas for decades and by all accounts are not a new discussion. Indeed, both scholars and managers have expressed the importance and the rational for firms and managers to move sustainability beyond emerging and into the realm of critical strategy in order to preemptively address rising challenges with social and environmental issues around the globe. One potential resource to manage these challenges may be adopting supply chain sustainability strategies and practices. However, incorporating supply chain sustainability into business operations remains an emerging discussion. This designation is due, in part, to continued, prevailing attitudes toward sustainability among many global firms. While some firms have integrated sustainability strategies into their overall corporate focus, most notably Unilever, Nike, and Intel, most struggle to understand not only how sustainability should fit into their business model but also why resources should be spent on sustainability initiatives. These concerns are fueled by what many managers express as general skepticism of a positive cost/benefit trade-off between resource commitment and reward, a risk they may not be willing to take (Kirchoff et al., 2016). These concerns are particularly acute when resources become scarce or unavailable, for example, during an economic downturn.

An area of strategy development and business continuation that is currently garnering considerable attention is concerned with how firms operate during disruptions and more extreme business cycles, both of which have been more acute with the effects of COVID-19 on the global economy. Specific to sustainability, managers, and academics grapple with what happens to supply chain sustainability strategies and initiatives during economic disruptions and downturns (Kano et al., 2022). Is sustainability an expendable strategy when resources are tight? Do firms remain committed? Are supply chain sustainability strategies considered to be core to a firms' overall operations or more as an ancillary discussion in the boardroom?

The answers to these inquiries may lie in asking a different question, namely, why wouldn't firms commit resources to supply chain management sustainability strategies and initiatives, especially during economic downturns, if these strategies help them be more resilient to disruptions? Research suggests that resiliency as a benefit can help to answer why firms should consider implementing sustainability strategies and why these should be integrated into their overall corporate strategies. Some scholars and managers have floated the idea that the implementation of sustainable practices is as important to establish a resiliency to economic downturns as innovation and adaptation (Wieland & Durach, 2021). Furthermore, going against some prevailing notions, evidence suggests that firms may be able to create a more permanent barrier to disruption through resiliency by integrating sustainability strategies into their overall corporate strategies. Indeed, sustainability may act as a buttress and build more robust supply chains by overcoming disruptions and trade-offs (e.g., scarce sustainable raw materials vs more plentiful non-sustainable materials) and through long-term planning.

## Materials and Methods

### *Sustainability and Resilient Supply Chain Literature*

*Sustainability as a Corporate Strategy*

The essence of strategy is being unique and differentiating from competitors (Porter, 1987). Today, strategic thinking among managers has evolved into a suite of strategies that include elements of innovation, differentiation, and efficiency and effectiveness. As a result, firms often pursue two or more strategies simultaneously to maintain or increase competitiveness in the global business environment. For example, Amazon has achieved significant success by combining multiple strategies from rapid innovation to create a consumer centric strategy. Integrating sustainability into the overall corporate strategy emerged in the 1990s as a way for firms to highlight social and environmental strategies they were already pursuing (energy-efficient lighting, packaging optimization, and optimal routing) but also have those efforts be recognized by their stakeholders. Some early adopters saw it as a precautionary approach to address emerging environmental regulation but also as an opportunity for innovation and competitive differentiation.

Core strategies are less likely to change or lose dedicated resources during economic downturns or other business disruptions while peripheral or untested strategies and initiatives are more likely to lose support. This is consistent with the ideas of "slack" and resource "stickiness" where strategies with sunk resources will remain dedicated, despite any volatility in the business (Voss et al., 2008).

The challenge many companies face when attempting to implement sustainability strategies and ensuring that sustainability resources remain dedicated or "sticky" often lies in overcoming how outcomes of these strategies are measured. The triple bottom line (TBL) of sustainability considers economic, social, and environmental dimensions of performance is one way in which firms have sought to incorporate differing strategies to produce positive outcomes. However, using the TBL framework, these three dimensions are supposed to be equally weighted, which can potentially lead to conflict in profit-first business models and in trade-off decision models. But strategies that may not lead to cost savings but instead avoid potential risks and enable a more resilient enterprise can be evaluated differently. Thus – with sustainability as a potential contributor strategy – we need shift thinking about sustainability from a short-term loss to a long-term preparation of resiliency for managing disruption.

*Resilience*

Research finds that resiliency is critical for managing global supply chains and the resulting strategies of specialization, location decisions, supply base reductions, and technological innovation (Pettit et al., 2019). There are a myriad of definitions and models to describe the concept of resilience, with any number of factors included. Some of the most common outline key preparations in place include levers that help firms withstand disruption and allow them to return to normal operations (Carpenter et al., 2001) or emerge stronger, post-disruption (Sheffi & Rice, 2005). At its core, resiliency captures the ability of a firm to bounce back and emerge from disruption both profitably and competitively. Thus, for the purposes of this discussion, resiliency in the context of supply chain management is both "the ability of a supply chain to both resist disruptions and recover operational capability after disruptions occur" (Melnyk et al., 2014, p. 36) and "the capacity for an enterprise to survive, adapt, and grow in the face of turbulent change" (Fiksel, 2006; Pettit et al., 2019, p. 57). By combining the two definitions, a more complete picture of organizational resiliency is established.

Before resiliency emerged as a major component of risk management, Bettis and Hitt (1995) introduced the concept of a strategic response capability, capturing the ability of a firm to respond to unexpected disruptions, an early predecessor to the concept of resilience. Twenty years ago, they argued that with increasing disruption on the horizon, firms would need to sense change in the environment, conceptualize a response, and reconfigure resources to execute the response (Bettis & Hitt, 1995). Today, all firms can expect to experience a shock to their operations and systems when a disruption occurs. For example, in the years between 2020 and 2022, the disruption caused by COVID-19 had an initial impact on supply chains that was then escalated through a continued series of disruptions over the following years (i.e., port bottlenecks, railroad strikes, volatile oil prices, inflation, etc.). The "triangle" of resilience represents the standard way most organizations respond when confronted with a major risk occurrence due to disruption (Fig. 8.1). Firms typically follow one of four observed courses of behavior after a risk shock. These range from firms that return or exceed pre-shock levels of performance (adaptive and robust behavior) to those that return to a lower pre-shock level or those that cease to exist (ductile and collapsing behavior).

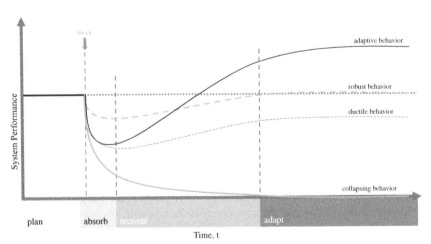

Fig. 8.1.   The Triangle of Resilience. *Source*: Inspired by Bevilacqua et al. (2017).

*Sustainability, Risk Management, and Resilience*

The traditional concepts of risk management and resilience have merged in recent years as the complexity of global supply chains has demanded risk management capabilities to be coupled with supply chain resilience (Linkov & Florin, 2016). As firms recognize their vulnerabilities and capabilities, they are better able to predict vulnerability to resilience gaps and to improve recovery strategies. However, there is a growing recognition that traditional risk management techniques lack the capacity to inspire a truly resilient enterprise, leading managers to explore other strategies to manage risk (Pettit et al., 2019). One area to emerge from resilience research is the link between supply chain risk management and sustainability practices and operations. The link between risk and sustainability initiated from the contention that firms can avoid fines, bad publicity, supplier issues, and product recalls (all risks) by incorporating sustainability into overall corporate strategies (Eggert & Hartmann, 2022).

In recent years, investors have started to take note of the impact of environmental, social, and governance (ESG) and sustainability strategies on the long-term resiliency and financial performance of firms. This has driven financial and investment stakeholders to focus on building portfolios of companies that are actively pursuing supply chain sustainability strategies as it increases their likelihood of resilience in the face of disruption overtime. Leading investment company, BlackRock (2022), states that "Sustainable investing is the practice of analyzing a company's ESG *risk*, as well as assessing its opportunities and progress, using ESG data and fundamental insights, to inform the allocation of capital." Further, accounting services from Price Waterhouse Cooper (PWC) highlight the importance of sustainability strategies, ESG disclosures now required by the SEC, and leveraging ESG requirements as a competitive advantage through value created sustainability initiatives (PWC, 2022). This requires firms to adopt both a strategic view of sustainability and a risk assessment of environmental, social, and economic operations and practices.

The merging of sustainability and risk has provided opportunities for organizations to view resilience from an "eco"-systems perspective. The Fiksel model of "triple value" illustrates an approach to understanding the global supply chain system from a vantage point that includes vulnerabilities and strategic capabilities that are linked to human societies, industrial economies, and ecosystems in the natural environment (Fiksel, Bruins, et al., 2015).

The model in Fig. 8.2 integrates the fields of industrial ecology and systems thinking to explore the interconnectedness between human and biological systems, industrial systems (energy, transportation, manufacturing, and agriculture), and societal systems (urbanization, mobility, and communication). The industrial system, or the economic strategies, of a company will drive investments in infrastructure, energy, and coordination of information across the organization. The industrial system then drives the physical and human capital investments that will create effective efficiencies for the organization. These investments in turn directly impact the human and biological systems and the societal systems. Raw material inputs and waste outputs of manufacturing created by the industrial system will

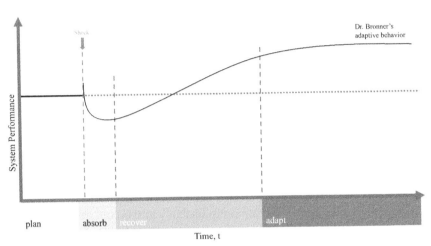

Fig. 8.2.  Resilience and Dynamic Systems. *Source*: Adapted from Fiksel, Bruins, et al. (2014).

have a direct effect on resource availability and the natural environment in which the surrounding community resides.

System thinking is a leading way of exploring the intersection of risk, resilience, and sustainability. Traditional risk assessments do not deal effectively with unforeseeable events, whereas supply chain resilience strategies, with a system perspective, enable supply chains to adapt to unforeseen circumstances. Sustainability-driven resilience impacts transformative innovation (focused on well-being) (Fiksel et al., 2015; Mollenkopf et al., 2020), agility and robustness (Wieland & Wallenberg, 2013), connectivity and visibility (Brandon-Jones et al., 2014), flexibility and adaptability (Ivanov et al., 2014), and supply chain relationships and collaboration (Tukamuhabwa et al., 2015).

Risk assessments that include elements of sustainability can create a strategic outlook that builds solutions for both short- and long-term disruptions. Considerable mainstream risk assessment focuses on short-term risks and too small a scope of vulnerability (in house vs system thinking) with less attention to long-term risk assessments that are necessary for supply chain sustainability strategies to develop across multiple firms (Fiksel et al., 2015). For instance, a risk assessment with the goal to explore the likelihood and impact of a disruption in the short term may focus on demand spikes and weather disruptions. Whereas a long-term risk assessment may also assess the likelihood and impact of natural resources scarcity over time, of global political unrest, and human rights issues with suppliers over time. Research notes that sustainability is essential for risk management and resilience as it enhances the viability of the enterprise as a whole while also conserving critical resources (Fiksel, Goodman, et al., 2014).

### Research Approach and Case Selection

Despite the attention and importance placed on sustainability in today's global business discussions, sustainability remains a nebulous concept for most companies. Furthermore, the connection between sustainability and supply chain resilience is typically not made by top management. As such, many aspects of the link between sustainability and resilience are not well understood by both managers and scholars, which calls for a more exploratory approach to research. We use a single-case approach to inductive research methodology as case studies can be used to facilitate an in-depth examination of sustainability and resilience, a complex phenomenon with multiple facets and layers (Daghar et al., 2022).

The sample case is the Dr. Bronner's organization and was chosen for several reasons. First, Dr. Bronner's was founded on a strong corporate culture of commitment to sustainability and the company continues to follow this culture today. It is part of the company's DNA and informs all decisions and operations. At the same time, Dr. Bronner's has seen significant year after year growth since its inception and saw increased growth during economic downturn cycles over the last 20 years. The growth has been on a global scale, with more than 20% of sales coming from outside of the United States. Finally, Dr. Bronner's has successfully integrated its sustainability culture with a strong business acumen that has helped fuel growth.

The case study was informed by three sources of information: company interviews, company specific data, and content analysis of available materials in the form of Corporate Social Responsibility (CSR) reports, media coverage, and other publicly available information about the company. Semi-structured, in-depth interviews were conducted with 13 line-staff, senior managers, and executives from across the Dr. Bronner's organization (Table 8.1). Participants were chosen based on purposive sampling techniques and snowballing, as the interviews progressed. Interviews were conducted over a number of years beginning in 2012, but most heavily in 2020 and 2021 during the height of the COVID-19 pandemic. Several participants were interviewed more than once to get a better sense of changing strategies over time. The selection process was also based on participant position within the organization, knowledge of supply chain management, and experience. The sample size may be comparatively small but is nonetheless robust because of the size of the company and because of the participants' critical involvement in the company's operations.

### Company Background

Dr. Bronner's is a small ethical soap company out of Vista, California, based on a 150-year-old heritage of German soap making. The company started formally in the United States in 1948 by Emmanuel Bronner who used the soap to distribute his manifesto proclaiming a globally inclusive religion (Moralez, 2020). While the soap was used as a vehicle to distribute his spiritual message. The soap became hugely popular with the counterculture of the 1960s because of the soap's ability to be used for many purposes from body to household.

Table 8.1.   Participant Description.

| #     | Position                                              | Primary Emphasis                  |
|-------|-------------------------------------------------------|-----------------------------------|
| 1     | CEO                                                   | Executive                         |
| 2     | President                                             | Executive                         |
| 3     | CFO                                                   | Finance                           |
| 4     | COO                                                   | Operations                        |
| 5     | VP of special operations                              | Supplier and subsidiary operations |
| 6     | Logistics director                                    | Transportation and logistics      |
| 7     | Director of operational sustainability and innovation | Certification and sustainability  |
| 8     | Production manager                                    | Production                        |
| 9-12  | Production line workers                               | Productions                       |
| 13    | Fair trade intern                                     | Certification                     |

With its growing popularity, in the 1980s, the Dr. Bronner's brand expanded into domestic health food stores. From its conception, the product was designed with a simple set of natural ingredients. In the 1990s and early 2000s, the company started to make more formal strides in its sustainability journey. In 2003, they became one of the largest personal care companies to get a product certified United States Department of Agriculture (USDA) organic. The same year they pioneered 100% post-consumer recycled plastic bottles for its liquid soaps, which is still almost unheard of today. In 2006, they started a comprehensive effort to source all of their major materials organically and through fair trade. This included palm, olive, hemp, and coconut oils. This vertically integrated effort has been enabled through several sister companies they launched to operate locally where each material is sourced to ensure visibility to source, production verification, and certification.

The company has grown steadily in the last 20 years, growing approximately 2,963% in 20 years from 2008 to 2018 (Kirwin, 2020). Their sales grew from $4 million in 2008 to $122.5 million in sales in 2018 (Concepcion, 2019). Further, according to key staffers, the demand for certain key products, such as their hand sanitizer, has grown over 400% since the start of the COVID-19 pandemic. Importantly, sustainability is part of Dr. Bronner's DNA and is ingrained in their corporate culture. This is exemplified in their six "cosmic" operating principles which can be categorized into the three dimensions of the TBL.

Economic:

• Work hard and grow;
• Do right by the customers.

Social:

- Treat employees like family;
- Be fair to suppliers.

Environmental:

- Treat the Earth like home;
- Fund and fight for what's right.

Interestingly, the Dr. Bronner's interviewees rarely used terms like "sustainable" or "triple bottom line" when describing the six operating principles or the company's operations. Instead, management refers to a moral culture embedded in the corporate culture, in the model of operations, in their strategic decision-making, and in global their supply chain and operations. This culture recognizes the challenges of adhering to the six principles. Therefore, people within the organization understands that the inherent trade-offs that might exist among the principles and works to reconcile them through least-harm strategies.

### Data Analysis

Analysis of the data collected from Dr. Bronner's followed Eisenhardt's recommendations for within-case analysis (Eisenhardt, 1989). First, each researcher analyzed the case data independently, where interview transcriptions allowed for the emergence of insights into each interview of the case. During and after the interviews, the research team reviewed the data to recognize and begin to code patterns across the interviews. This initial analysis of the data served as a commentary of what was happening throughout the case supply chain operations and allowed the researchers to probe emergent themes and to design specific questions for future interviews. Second, as the researchers began to recognize themes in the data, patterns emerged that connected the interviews. Next, the themes from the data were grouped into first-order codes (i.e., terms used by the informants), after which axial coding was conducted wherein relationships among first-order codes were assembled into higher-order themes. This process yielded the three key areas that were then refined based on the literature and continued analysis of the data. Finally, examples from the interviews were used to map supply chain sustainability to resilience, creating a model based on the strategy–structure–performance (SSP) theoretical concept. The next section details the findings, the theoretical model, and the application of the model to the case.

## Findings

### Resilient to Disruption

Dr. Bronner's commitment to sustainability has cultural and moral underpinnings, yet the findings from the data analysis suggest that the company has also found the commitment to be strategic in terms of market differentiation and resiliency, leading to brand loyalty among stakeholders. As a family-owned business, Dr. Bronner's has top management that have literally grown into being savvy business players in the increasingly competitive consumer packaged goods (CPG) industry. But while different brands have fluctuated in terms of market share and growth during economic growth, and recession periods, Dr. Bronner's growth has gone in one direction – up.

Research indicates that firms with more established and proactive sustainability initiatives and strategies fared better during the COVID-19 pandemic than those who did not (Eggert & Hartmann, 2020). More specifically, Ding et al. (2021) found that global firms with lower debt, less social exposure, and higher sustainability-related activities had stronger stock performance during the COVID-19 disruption. In these studies, sustainability activities include strong relationships with stakeholders and communities in which the firms operate, employee health and safety, environmental protection, and environmental supply chain management. Interestingly, one of the key practices found in both studies pointed to the level of commitment to collaboration and cooperation with members of the supply chain before, during, and after disruptions.

Many businesses struggle to remain solvent during economic downturns, increased global competition, supply disruptions, and, most recently, the global pandemic. Why some businesses succeed during these events and others fail can be related to a number of factors: how well they partner with their suppliers, the willingness of employees to adapt and change in crisis, the ability to listen and respond to the changing needs and demands of customers, access to resources, and a reputation for ethical decision-making. Importantly, all of these factors are in line with sustainability supply chain strategies, and the key driver of each factor is the resiliency of the relationship and parties involved. Without deep relationships that foster resiliency, many companies succumb to failure without enough or the right product to meet demand profitably. The following discussion explores what factors have allowed the sustainable soap company to continue to grow amidst multiple recessions and, most recently, the COVID-19 pandemic.

### The 2008 Recession

The recession of the late 2000s created significant challenges for firms, especially small- and medium-sized enterprises (SMEs), as they experienced large losses in sales, investment, and employment between early 2008 and 2010 (Sahin et al., 2011). The ability for SMEs to survive recessions is often related to several factors including labor issues and workforce viability, cash flow loss due to increased costs and lower demand, liquidity shortages, and supply limitations. However, SMEs with resiliency strategies and initiatives have a greater chance of overcoming many of the inherent limitations due to their size. Sustainable strategies along with marketing positioning helped Dr. Bronner's do just that.

During the recession, Dr. Bronner's benefited from the *lipstick effect*. This is the concept that during difficult economic times, demand for small indulgences goes up, which coincided with Dr. Bronner's expansion into Target. However, the lipstick effect was only one benefit to the company. More significantly, Dr. Bronner's fair trade label helped propel their business into markets that previously bought almost exclusively from their larger and better known competitors. Dr. Bronner's brand of sustainability was a strong marketing point that helped them gain customers seeking to increase sustainability in their own supply chains. When they were brought onboard, Dr. Bronner's gave Target legitimacy and sustainable supply chain information that they were then able to pass along to consumers, shareholders, and other interested stakeholders. The fair trade label also gave Dr. Bronner's greater access to international markets in Europe even during the 2008 recession.

### The COVID-19 Pandemic

The COVID-19 significantly shocked global supply chains, with the bulk of the challenges and negative effects falling on SMEs (Sarkis, 2020). Nearly 40% of SME manufacturing businesses were considered highly to moderately vulnerable to closure because of COVID (McKinsey, 2020). An estimated 11 million SME jobs were lost between 2008 and 2010, along with significant revenue loss (OECD, 2020).

For a company that has little to no spend on advertising, Dr. Bronner's had grown significantly in the 15 years leading up to the pandemic, with overall sales increasing 11-fold to $135 million in sales in 2019. In 2020, due to the COVID-19 pandemic, demand for hand sanitizers has resulted in a 550% increase in production and a 70% increase in the rest of their soap lines (CNN, 2020). The result of the increased demand pushed the company's average growth of 10% per year to an expected 45% growth in 2020. The growth is welcomed at Dr. Bronner's but has come with several challenges and juxtapositions to meet the increase in demand. These include packaging shortages, the need to increase production lines and run additional shifts, add personnel, and expedite new supplier approvals. As one interviewee looked forward to the end of 2020, they reflected on the events of the last year and contemplated how the company had managed the changes. They also understood the need to consider the dynamic business environment that awaited Dr. Bronner's in the new year.

### Mapping Sustainability to Resilience Through the SSP Paradigm

Sarkis (2020) suggests that sustainability strategies and initiatives can contribute to supply chain resilience. Themes across the participant interviews and corporate reports demonstrated that Dr. Bronner's principles and culture form the core of their sustainability practices and provides the company with a strategic barrier to economic downturns. This barrier has allowed them to capitalize on increasing demand through company expansion fueled by loyal stakeholders, strong relationships, careful planning, waste reduction, and a strong culture of responsibility. These ideas go beyond the strict definition of economic value. As one interviewee stated:

[...] the fallacy of the idea of value is that you're measuring (just) economically ... supplier relationships, our customer base, worker treatment, really our principles ... they support growth in a very resilient way.

Ultimately, Dr. Bronner's ability to map sustainability to resilience can be explained by using the SSP framework. SSP suggests that a firm's operational structure is driven by strategy, created in consideration of the external business environment, which leads to some performance outcome. The framework relies on the "fit" between the strategy and structure to determine the outcome, and the extent to which it is realized in relation to the competition (Lim et al., 2022). SSP has been used extensively to help explain supply chain management phenomena and is applicable to situations where specific strategies have been used to establish supply chain operations and tactics, with positive performance outcomes. Importantly, organizational resiliency is not a static attribute, but rather one that is malleable by organizations in response to change, disruptions, and impacts from the external environment (Ortiz-de-Mandojana & Bansal, 2016). Therefore, the fit requirement in SSP is necessary not only in the relationship between strategy and structure but also between these components and the external business environment.

In the case of Dr. Bronner's, the SSP framework is useful to show how the company's supply chain operations are couched in the moral strategy of six cosmic principles, which lead to the structure of their global operations, with an outcome of firm resiliency. The two antecedent components of strategy and structure are built and formed as contingent responses to the business environment in which the firm operates (Defee & Stank, 2005). The concept of the ecosystem thinking is also evident in the framework with the entire model operating as a system with bidirectional relationships and a feedback loop between performance and strategy. In this way, Dr. Bronner's strategy (moral calculus), structure (central nervous system), and performance (resilience) are interrelated and where linear causality is emphasized less than a system perspective that allows the company to deal effectively with unforeseen events and disruptions. The three main components along with the related structure subcomponents are discussed in the following sections and are illustrated in Fig. 8.3.

### *Strategy*

The expression attributed to Peter Drucker in 2006 and made famous by Mark Fields, CEO of Ford Motor Company is that "culture eats strategy for breakfast." At Dr. Bronner's, the moral culture embedded in the corporate culture is certainly the driver of the sustainability strategy of the company. Dr. Bronner's overarching business strategy can be summed as the "moral calculus" of sustainability, based on the six cosmic principles. The moral calculus was a term used consistently by interviewees to explain how the company adheres to these principles to keep the company viable. However, the data seem to indicate the term has an even deeper

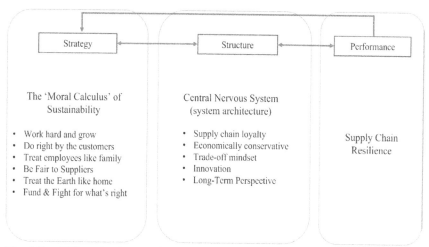

Fig. 8.3.   SSP at Dr. Bronner's.

meaning than this. The term "moral calculus" was described as a strategic direction for the company in terms of corporate culture that adheres to forward-thinking long-term viability and growth through conservative financial management, the ability to adjust to market demands, and flexibility in making supply chain operations sustainable. Furthermore, the term indicates that there is an inherent trade-off among the three dimensions of the TBL that results in strategic growth.

The idea of the moral calculus couched in the six principles aligns with what Wu and Pagell (2011) call "balancing priorities" in sustainable supply chain management (SCM) decision-making. Trade-off decisions are necessary, but when coupled with continuous improvement, these decisions can lead to long-term gains to TBL performance (Wu & Pagell, 2011). The use of the moral calculus strategy in practice at Dr. Bronner's when sourcing issues surfaced during the COVID-19 pandemic. Their sustainable bottle manufacturer did not have enough of the raw material post-consumer recycled (PCR) and could not keep up with demand, so the Dr. Bronner's had to source elsewhere, with a non-certified supplier. The result, however, was that Dr. Bronner's was able to meet the growing demand and expand the company's reach in terms of new markets, sales, and overall financial growth. This, in turn, benefited the workforce, furthered the company's mission, and ensured long-term viability. Ultimately, the moral calculus strategy has helped Dr. Bronner's become a more resilient organization. One interviewee summed up the idea of moral calculus as the idea "growth without selling our soul" and looking to the future:

> […] I guess the moral calculus is that you play the long game. And that if we're not around, we can't operate in the future. And we can't innovate in the future. And so I will (make trade-offs) when I have to. Yeah.

This moral calculus is the foundation for the six cosmic principles that capture the supply chain sustainability strategy of Dr. Bronner's. Balancing the six principles allows employees within Dr. Bronner's to build an operating structure that will enable them to achieve their strategic goals.

### Structure

The structure through which Dr. Bronner's has been able to implement their strategy is referred to as the central nervous system, which was also described by participants as the "system architecture." The architecture terminology reflects the six pillars that enable employees to achieve their goals with the moral calculus as the strategic foundation. SSP research explains that a firm's strategy drives the development of an organization-wide structure to implement that strategy (Stock et al., 1998). For example, a firm with a proactive quality strategy should integrate quality concerns into the firm's organizational structure and in the decision-making processes. Structure also refers to structure as the configuration of resources to support the strategy (Hall & Saias, 1980) and intra- and inter-firm relationships (Dai et al., 2017). Resources and relationships are evident in the Dr. Bronner's practices and processes that enable employees to assess "doing what is right" and to engage fairly and effectively with customers, other employees, and suppliers in order to operationalize the six cosmic principles.

Firms establish and implement a structure to ensure congruent implementation of firm strategy across the supply chain in order to achieve performance and competitive advantage outcomes. One interviewee discussed Dr. Bronner's central nervous system as:

> Here at Dr. Bronner's, we have a kind of central system ... call
> it like a central nervous system, where everyone is encourage to
> help implement the vision of the company, our strategy for being
> a good company. For following the six principles.

Dr. Bronner's central nervous system disseminates the moral calculus strategy throughout the company's supply chain operations through five primary structure components. These include supply chain loyalty, economically conservative orientation, trade-off mindset, innovation, *risk management,* and long-term orientation.

### Supply Chain Loyalty

Dr. Bronner's has created supply chain relationships that focused on shared risk and reward, respect, and, in some cases, governance. This allows greater visibility into production, closer business ties, and cooperation. Strong relationships with key suppliers engenders loyalty and ensures adherence to supplier codes of conduct and business terms. One practice that engenders strong supplier loyalty came about when the company helped support their raw material suppliers in India who couldn't work because of the pandemic. Dr. Bronner's provided resources and aid for these mostly small farmers until the economy opened back up. As one executive stated:

> We reaped what we sowed (in terms of supplier relationships).
> And in these relationships, people then wanted to help us out …

Similarly, Dr. Bronner's has relationships tailored for their customers in a way that simultaneously focuses on high customer service and fairness. For example, during the pandemic, the company made sure a share of high-demand product was given to small retailers, especially those that are in underserved areas. End consumers are loyal to Dr. Bronner's brand because of their commitment to sustainability and because the company actions to improve the company as a brand rather than as a commodity.

*Economically Conservative Orientation*

The TBL concept has gained respect among researchers and managers in recent years as evidence accumulates for increased performance when firms focus on all three dimensions simultaneously. Some critics, however, insist that most companies using TBL performance either place emphasis on the economic dimension only and include the other two dimensions to enhance legitimacy or place emphasis on the environmental and social dimensions at the cost of financial performance (Rambaud & Richard, 2015). Dr. Bronner's manages to move beyond these criticisms by adhering to conservative economic principles, which has allowed to realize strong financial growth, while excelling at social and environmental performance. Indeed, the company's focus on all three dimensions of TBL performance sustained symbiotic relationships among the three. For example, financial and resource support for their workforce, smaller suppliers, and community initiatives during the economic downturns helped fuel loyalty to the Dr. Bronner's as a customer and as a brand. One interviewee summed it up:

> why do we run the company in such a conservative financial way?
> So we can give away insane amounts of money.

Not surprisingly, Dr. Bronner's extends being economically conservative to the general processes of decision-making within the firm. In the context of decision-making under pressure, Dr. Bronner's management describes the process in five steps: Don't Panic, Communicate, Assess the Facts, Decide on the Plan, and Post-Mortem. These steps help guide the company on routine decisions, such as determining optimal safety stock levels, to more strategic decisions, such as new market expansion. Importantly, managers state that adhering to the five steps has helped to guide the company through challenging situations and build a resilient operation.

*Trade-off Mindset*

Dr. Bronner's strong commitment to sustainability has created trade-offs in upfront costs and opportunities for growth that many other companies see as non-negotiables. For instance, in the early 2000s, Dr. Bronner's chose to not to sell to Walmart because they disagreed with some of Walmart's operating principles (Harkinson, 2014). The company has since reversed that decision, as Walmart has become more committed to sustainability broadly but will sometimes make a choice on whether to sell or how to prioritize deliveries to customers, based on sustainability performance. The choice by a supplier to avoid doing business with a potential large customer because of value misalignment is rare in principle, with few other exemplars than Dr. Bronner's. Similarly, like Dr. Bronner's, Patagonia has refused to sell logoed products to firms they deemed socially or environmentally irresponsible (Cerullo, 2019). One manager summed up the issue by stating "… it doesn't matter where you buy our (responsibly made) products, it's that you buy them and support our cause."

The implementation of the moral calculus strategy is clear in these examples and through assessing the issues and making decisions based on how to navigate potential conflicts among the different dimensions of the TBL. The non-certified bottle supplier discussion in the "Strategy" section illustrates how trade-offs as a component of structure supports the company's moral calculus strategy. The decision to meet growing demand propelled the company forward, creating a stronger force of sustainability and allowing Dr. Bronner's to continue implementing the six cosmic principles throughout their global supply chains. As one interviewee stated:

> "But here are times when there are not enough of what we need … we do have to go outside of (sustainability)" In these situations, "we set aside a certain percentage … into what we call a fair trade fund … for projects."

*Innovation*

Dr. Bronner's has a strong entrepreneurial culture, which is not surprising given that it is an SME and family owned and run. However, the innovative ideas and processes that management and rank-and-file employees implement could almost be considered unique to the company. For example, the sourcing team actively looks for and finds forward-thinking suppliers who support sustainability and corporate responsibility, even when the supplier does not offer materials Dr. Bronner's needs in their products. The company then works with the suppliers to innovate and develop new products that use the suppliers' offerings. This kind of reverse engineering has led to new markets and customers and is akin to the idea of radical innovation process success, but one that does not disrupt the ongoing operations of the company (Hahn, 2020).

Innovation is also apparent through the principles of the company. One interviewee discussed the relationship between innovative ideas and strengthening the company's ability to fund important sustainability-related initiatives. The connection was described as innovating to overcome financial and ideological barriers that are present in the global business environment. In one case, when faced with supplier worker challenges in India during the height of both the 2008 economic downturn and during the pandemic, Dr. Bronner's designed a new process in a few days that helped bring needed resources to their supplier's workforce. As one interviewee stated:

> But honestly, there were no backup systems (for the employees).
> So, for us to go in there and do that within a couple of days over in
> India, that was pretty rewarding and guerrilla style. And that, we
> were only able to do because we were already on the ground, and
> we knew how to innovate quickly.

### Long-Term Orientation

One of the key components of the moral calculus, a long-term orientation is perhaps the key component of the structure that is most directly tied to Dr. Bronner's strategy. The definition of moral calculus is the concept of looking at the long term, considering how the decisions today will benefit the company into the future. As one interviewee put it, "… always looking 10 years ahead vs. the next quarter." The long-term perspective is evident in the company's policies and throughout their supply chain operations. For example, how and where Dr. Bronner's chooses to invest resources mirrors the long-term perspective in planning through supplier sustainability programs. Management collaborates with suppliers that are "growing into the cultural similarities to Dr. Bronner's" and provides needed resources to enhance that growth. The timeframe has been years, but the long-term investment has created a more resilient organization and a more resilient supply chain and supply base.

A strong connection between long-term thinking about sustainability and resilience is discussed by Ortiz-de-Mandojana and Bansal (2016), who contend that the relationship is critical because short-term approaches to sustainability will only address one-time or limited disruptions, rather than continuous anticipation and adjustment to the future. The long-term approach to sustainability supports the moral calculus strategy and allows Dr. Bronner's supply chain operations to behave as a dynamic structure that can recognize disruptive cues and act accordingly to be *capability* resilient.

### Performance

SSP predicts the performance outcome of the proper fit between strategy and structure. The moral calculus strategy at Dr. Bronner's is disseminated throughout the firm's supply chain operations via the central nervous system. Evidence of the fit between strategy and structure is seen through consistent performance or in the case of Dr. Bronner's, sustained performance through consistent growth.

The fit is also evident in the performance outcome of resilience. Nearly every interviewee expressed how the company was resilient in the face of not only economic downturn during the recession of 2008 and the pandemic but also toward other challenges to the company's business.

As one interviewee described it:

> What part of that business model helped (us) ... supplier relationships ... worker treatment and benefits and safety and these things that we had in place that were never questioned. They just – they supported our growth in a very resilient way, right? So making that connection between sustainability and resilience, right?

Critically, Dr. Bronner's implements their own recommendations and principles because they are looking to become more resilient. As one manager described it, "... these are things to put in place now. They're always good operating principles, and they will help (us) in future disruptions ... that's one – that's the element we are seeking."

## Conclusion

### *Overcoming the Triangle of Resilience*

Dr. Bronner's was able to minimize the resilience triangle with continued upward growth for both the 2008 recession and COVID disruptions (see Fig. 8.4). This is because the central nervous system moves the moral calculus throughout the companies' supply chain operations and was critical to helping Dr. Bronner's avoid dipping too deep into the triangle of resiliency by using sustainability to create a shock absorber. The result has been a nearly imperceptible dip, followed by strong growth in both the shocks discussed by the case, the 2008 recession and the global pandemic (Fig. 8.4). Dr. Bronner's "triangle" contrasts with the examples shown in Fig. 8.1, succinctly illustrating how the company mapped sustainability to resilience.

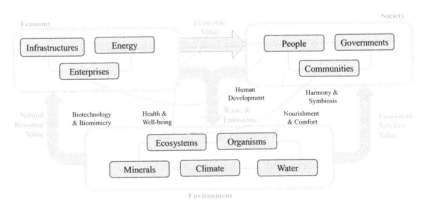

Fig. 8.4.    Dr. Bronner's Triangle of Resilience.

This research has connected sustainability and supply chain resilience through the case of Dr. Bronner's through the lens of SSP theory. Importantly, the findings distill the mechanisms through which the company has spread the culture of sustainability throughout the organization and supply chain. By exploring how Dr. Bronner's uses its supply chain management sustainability strategies and initiatives to help them be more resilient to disruptions, this research uncovers the importance of a strategy based on strong cultural underpinnings that drive the structure of corporate operations and ultimate performance of the firm. It is important to note that the culture and strategy of Dr. Bronner's has created opportunity for growth during normal times and in times of disruption.

Many firms exist without a centering moral calculus like that of Dr. Bronner's. The model for resilience of a firm or organization that has a strategy built on the alignment of a core competency and market opportunity (sustainability laggards) may look very different than that of a social enterprise or an organization with a social purpose beyond profit like that of Dr. Bronner's (a sustainability leader). For similar companies that strive to be sustainability leaders, to have purpose beyond profit and a centering moral calculus, there are some key lessons to be learned from the Dr. Bronner's case that could inform corporate strategies and structures that drive resilient performance throughout economic cycles and global disruption. For companies that may be evolving from an initial profit focus to a strategic sustainability model of organization, there are also lessons that can be learned from Dr. Bronner's.

## Questions That Must Be considered When Emulating the Dr. Bronner's Model

### What Sustainability Initiatives Mean for Growth?

Dr. Bronner's core moral calculus reflected the three components of sustainability with a focus that included growth and profitability, people and relationships, and environmental impact on the planet. While the moral compass might have led to a slow start for Dr. Bronner's, the company achieved 2,963% growth over 20 years. Dr. Bronner's did not initially jump in markets that would have compromised its moral calculus only to find that its consistency of brand built a reputation that did not require advertising in order to provide credibility for the sustainability laggards. Sustainability laggards recognized the importance of sustainability initiatives to the consumer market and leaned on Dr. Bronner's for product and brand recognition.

### How Are Supply Chain Relationships Altered as New Suppliers Are Brought on Board?

As any company grows, the share of revenue that is captured by supply chain partners shifts over time. While Dr. Bronner's initially sold their soaps and products through more organic and sustainability-oriented smaller organizations, as they scaled, their product distribution shifted to include big box retailers (sustainability laggards) who needed to shift into sustainability strategies to meet market/consumer demands.

## How Do Sustainability Strategies Support Resiliency as Supply Chain Disruptions Change?

Dr. Bronner's strategy and structure are adaptable to changes in a dynamic external environment. The five components are supported by the moral calculus but are mailable to specific changes and threats. For example, product innovation has been important to replace difficult to obtain ingredients (recipe for one product was changed) and packaging (bottle lids design was changed). With these changes, however, the moral calculus of the company was maintained because this strategy is akin to core competencies of the firm and are adaptable.

### Theoretical Implications

The SSP theory offers good insights into the outworking of the moral calculus at Dr. Bronner's. Previous research has demonstrated that organizational culture can impact structure and performance in many ways. At Dr. Bronner's, organizational culture impacts all three components of the SSP paradigm. While previous supply chain research on SSP has seen culture as a part of firm structure (Defee & Stank, 2005), this research demonstrates how important culture is to create competitive advantage for firms that are early adopters of a moral calculus versus profitability as the driving reason for being in business. Also referred to in supply chain literature as an orientation, the philosophy of the firm that determines the reason for the firm's existence will also drive the strategy, structure, and ultimate performance outcomes of the organization, including profitability.

### Managerial Implications

This research has implications for two different types of managers, those who work for organizations with a sustainability leadership strategy and those who work for organizations with a sustainability laggard position that recognize the strategic importance of sustainability for the future. For the managers in organizations with sustainability leadership, this research demonstrates the importance of sustainability initiatives in creating an operating structure of resilience to global disruptions. Supply chain sustainability not only meets the growing demands of the marketplace but also creates a strategic culture that looks beyond short-term gains to create strategies that mitigate risk and help organizations to bounce back quickly. For managers at organizations lagging in supply chain sustainability, this research demonstrates the importance of a centering core of values to drive sustainability throughout the organization. Without a centering core, sustainability strategies may seem periphery in the face of trade-offs. However, the Dr. Bronner's case demonstrates the strategic benefits and the resilience possible from a moral culture that drives SSP.

# References

Bettis, R. A., & Hitt, M. A. (1995). The new competitive landscape. *Strategic Management Journal, 16*(S1), 7–19.

Bevilacqua, M., Ciarapica, F. E., & Marcucci, G. (2017). Supply chain resilience triangle: The study and development of a framework. *World Academy of Science, Engineering and Technology, International Journal of Social, Behavioral, Educational, Economic, Business and Industrial Engineering, 11*(8), 2046–2053.

Blackrock. (2022). *Sustainable investing at BlackRock*. https://www.blackrock.com/ch/individual/en/themes/sustainable-investing#:~:text=Sustainable%20investing%20is%20the%20practice,inform%20the%20allocation%20of%20capital

Brandon-Jones, E., Squire, B., Autry, C. W., & Petersen, K. J. (2014). A contingent resource-based perspective of supply chain resilience and robustness. *Journal of Supply Chain Management, 50*(3), 55–73.

Carpenter, S., Walker, B., Anderies, J. M., & Abel, N. (2001). From metaphor to measurement: Resilience of what to what?. *Ecosystems, 4*(8), 765–781.

Cerullo, M. (2019). Patagonia will no longer sell vests with finance firms logos on them. CBS News. https://www.cbsnews.com/news/midtown-uniform-patagonia-will-no-longer-sell-vests-with-finance-firms-logos-on-them/

CNN. (2020). *Dr. Bronners' coronavirus hand sanitizer bottles*. https://www.cnn.com/2020/04/10/business/dr-bronners-coronavirus-hand-sanitizer-bottles/index.html

Concepcion, M. (2019). Dr. Bronner's magic sops has prescription success. *San Diego Business Journal*. https://www.sdbj.com/news/2019/may/29/dr-bronners-magic-soaps-has-prescription-success/#:~:text=The%20Numbers-,In%202018%2C%20Dr.,David%20Bronner%2C%20who%20runs%20Dr

Daghar, A., Alinaghian, L., & Turner, N. (2022). The role of cognitive capital in supply chain resilience: An investigation during the COVID-19 pandemic. *Supply Chain Management, 28*(3), 576–597.

Dai, J., Cantor, D. E., & Montabon, F. L. (2017). Examining corporate environmental proactivity and operational performance: A strategy-structure-capabilities-performance perspective within a green context. *International Journal of Production Economics, 193*, 272–280.

Defee, C. C., & Stank, T. P. (2005). Applying the strategy-structure-performance paradigm to the supply chain environment. *The International Journal of Logistics Management, 16*(1), 28–50.

Ding, W., R. Levine, Lin, C. & Xie, W. (2021). Corporate immunity to the COVID-19 pandemic. *Journal of Financial Economics, 141*(2), 802–830.

Eggert, J., & Hartmann, J. (2022). Sustainable supply chain management: A key to resilience in the global pandemic. *Supply Chain Management, 28*(3), 486–507.

Eisenhardt, K. M. (1989). Building theories from case study research. *Academy of Management Review, 14*(4), 532–550.

Fiksel, J. (2006). Sustainability and resilience: Toward a systems approach. *Sustainability: Science, Practice, and Policy, 2*(2), 14–21.

Fiksel, J. (2014). An interview with David Bresch. *Solutions, 5*(5), 17–18.

Fiksel, J. (2015). *Resilient by design: Creating businesses that adapt and flourish in a changing world*. Island Press.

Fiksel, J., Bruins, R., Gatchett, A., Gilliland, A., & ten Brink, M. (2014). The triple value model: A systems approach to sustainable solutions. *Clean Solutions Technologies and Environmental Policy, 16*(4), 691–702.

Fiksel, J., Goodman, I., & Hecht, A. (2014). Resilience: Navigating toward a sustainable future. *Solutions, 5*(5), 38–47.

Hahn, G. J. (2020). Industry 4.0: A supply chain innovation perspective. *International Journal of Production Research, 58*(5), 1425–1441.

Hall, D. J., & Saias, M. A. (1980). Strategy follows structure! *Strategic Management Journal*, *1*(2), 149–163.

Harkinson, J. (2014). *How Dr. Bronner's soap turned activism into good clean fun*. Mother Jones. https://www.motherjones.com/environment/2014/05/dr-bronners-magic-soap-david-bronner-gmo-hemp/

Ivanov, D., Sokolov, B., & Dolgui, A. (2014). The ripple effect in supply chains: Trade-off 'efficiency-flexibility-resilience' in disruption management. *International Journal of Production Research*, *52*(7), 2154–2172.

Kano, L., Narula, R., & Surdu, I. (2022). Global value chain resilience: Understanding the impact of managerial governance adaptations. *California Management Review*, *64*(2), 24–45.

Kirchoff, J. F., Omar, A., & Fugate, B. S. (2016). A behavioral theory of sustainable supply chain decision making in non-exemplar firms. *Journal of Supply Chain Management*, *52*(1), 41–65.

Kirwin, P. (2020). *Dr. Bronner's grew revenue 2963% in 20 years with no advertising*. Channel Signals. https://channelsignal.com/blogs/dr-bronners-grew-revenue-2963-in-20-years-with-no-advertising/#:~:text=Bronner's%20Grew%20Revenue%202963%25%20in,With%20No%20Advertising%20%2D%20Channel%20Signal

Lim, J. J., Dai, J., & Paulraj, A. (2022). Collaboration as a structural aspect of proactive social sustainability: The differential moderating role of distributive and procedural justice. *International Journal of Operations & Production Management* (forthcoming).

Linkov, I., & Florin, M. (Eds.). (2016). *IRGC resource guide on resilience*. International Risk Governance Center. https://www.irgc.org/riskgovernance/resilience/

Ortiz-de-Mandojana, N., & Bansal, P. (2016). The long-term benefits of organizational resilience through sustainable business practices. *Strategic Management Journal*, *37*(8), 1615–1631.

McKinsey. (2020). Nearly 40% of SME manufacturing businesses were considered highly to moderately vulnerable to closure because of COVID.

Melnyk, S. A., Closs, D. J., Griffis, S. E., Zobel, C. W., & Macdonald, J. R. (2014). Understanding supply chain resilience SCMR resilience oriented investments and their relationship with sustainability.

Mollenkopf, D. A., Ozanne, L. K., & Stolze, H. J. (2020). A transformative supply chain response to COVID-19. *Journal of Service Management*, *32*(2), 190–202.

Moralez, M. (2020). In a time where soap has become a coveted product, Dr. Bronner's hasn't lost its values. *Supply & Demand Chain Executive*. https://www.sdcexec.com/warehousing/article/21134641/dr-bronners-washes-away-uncertainties-in-the-sustainable-supply-chain

OECD. (2020). An estimated 11 million SME jobs were lost between 2008 and 2010, along with significant revenue loss.

Pettit, T. J., Croxton, K. L., & Fiksel, J. (2019). The evolution of resilience in supply chain management: A retrospective on ensuring supply chain resilience. *Journal of Business Logistics*, *40*(1), 56–65.

Porter, M. (1987). From competitive advantage to corporate strategy. *Harvard Business Review*. https://hbr.org/1987/05/from-competitive-advantage-to-corporate-strategy

Price Waterhouse Coopers. (2022). *SEC climate disclosures and your company: How you can prepare today for investor-grade, tech-enabled reporting*. https://www.pwc.com/us/en/services/esg/library/sec-climate-disclosures.html?WT.mc_id=CT3-PL300-DM1-TR1-LS3-ND30-PRG7-CN_ESG-Google&gclid=Cj0KCQjw-2aBhD5ARIsALiRlwBtE7tHC80JAIHwRuE9NLCP_9AWu01cyKfvPq-K3IUU6XPvLxKW18caAtjAEALw_wcB&gclsrc=aw.ds

Rambaud, A., & Richard, J. (2015). The "triple depreciation line" instead of the "triple bottom line": Towards a genuine integrated reporting. *Critical Perspectives on Accounting*, *33*, 92–116.

Sahin, A., Kitao, S., Cororaton, A., Laiu, S. (2011). Why Small Businesses Were Hit Harder by the Recent Recession. *Current Issues in Economics and Finance, 17*(4), 1–7.

Sarkis, J. (2020). Supply chain sustainability: Learning from the COVID-19 pandemic. *International Journal of Operations & Production Management, 41*, 63–73.

Sheffi, Y., & Rice, J. B., Jr. (2005). A supply chain view of the resilient enterprise. *MIT Sloan Management Review, 47*(1), 41.

Stock, G. N., Greis, N. P., & Kasarda, J. D. (1998). Logistics, strategy and structure: A conceptual framework. *International Journal of Operations & Production Management, 18*(1), 37–52.

Tukamuhabwa, B. R., Stevenson, M., Busby, J., & Zorzini, M. (2015). Supply chain resilience: Definition, review and theoretical foundations for further study. *International Journal of Production Research, 53*(18), 5592–5623.

Voss, G. B., Sirdeshmukh, D., & Voss, Z. G. (2008). The effects of slack resources and environmental threat on product exploration and exploitation. *Academy of Management journal, 51*(1), 147–164.

Wieland, A., & Durach, C. F. (2021). Two perspectives on supply chain resilience. *Journal of Business Logistics, 42*(3), 315–322.

Wieland, A, & Wallenburg, C. M. (2013). The influence of relational competencies on supply chain resilience: A relational view. *International Journal of Physical Distribution & Logistics Management, 43*(4), 300–320.

Wu, Z., & Pagell, M. (2011). Balancing priorities: Decision-making in sustainable supply chain management. *Journal of Operations Management, 29*(6), 577–590.

# Chapter 9

# Justice in a Cooperative Enterprise: The Case of Brazilian Justa Trama

*Italo Anderson Taumaturgo dos Santos and Victor Pessoa de Melo Gomes*

*University of São Paulo, Brazil*

## Abstract

Justice appears as an important strategic concept for promoting sustainability. Among the sustainable development goals established by the United Nations (UN), Goal 16 is about providing access to justice for all and building effective, accountable, and inclusive institutions. In the stakeholder theory perspective, the perception of fair treatment in the stakeholder management allows the organization to value fairness, impartiality, and morality among all stakeholders. The purpose of this chapter is to analyze the influence of justice in the organizational processes of a network of solidarity economy cooperatives. We used semi-structured interviews and desk research on documents made available by the network. The results point to a series of values and processes based on justice throughout the production and managerial chain, providing relationships understood as fair, which can be replicated in organizations that pursue the same ideals.

*Keywords*: Case study; Justa Trama; justice; stakeholder theory; sustainable development; UN development goals

## Introduction

The topic of justice has been the focus of many studies, in a wide variety of subjects in the management field, such as human resources (e.g., Bies & Moag, 1986; Tyler & Bies, 1990), marketing (e.g., Jordan et al., 2019; Laczniak & Murphy, 2007;

Sustainable and Resilient Global Practices:
Advances in Responsiveness and Adaptation, 217–235

Saleem et al., 2018), and strategic management (e.g., Kim & Mauborgne, 1998; Luo, 2007; Migacz et al., 2018). Following this trend, stakeholder management sees the perception of justice as an essential component of its models and a requirement for effective implementation of managerial activity (Freeman, 1984; Freeman et al., 2020; Harrison et al., 2010).

Furthermore, the notion of justice is presented as a component of Goal 16 of the sustainable development goals (SDG) devised by the UN. According to the UN, the goal's definition is to promote peaceful and inclusive societies for sustainable development; provide access to justice for all; and build effective, accountable, and inclusive institutions at all levels (UN, 2015). Although the concept of justice has been consolidated in the literature – including Stakeholder Theory – the notion of what is considered fair, from the stakeholders' point of view, is not clear (Bridoux & Stoelhorst, 2016; Freeman et al., 2020).

Every stakeholder wants to be treated ethically and fairly (Crul & Zinkhan, 2007; Harrison et al., 2010). Managers should pay special attention to the stakeholders' perception of justice, as this can be decisive for the stakeholder to decide to cooperate or punish the company. Stakeholders support organizational decisions when they perceive fair treatment by the corporation, while unfair treatment generates punitive behavior (Hayibor & Collins, 2016).

In this sense, the theoretical and practical investigation of the vision of justice in the organizational context becomes necessary. The present study aims to analyze the influence of justice in the organizational processes of a network of solidarity economy cooperatives. The organization chosen for this purpose is Justa Trama, a network formed by workers organized around solidarity economy enterprises, which have constituted a productive chain that starts from the planting of agroecological cotton to the commercialization of garments produced from this input. We show that several aspects of fairness are considered throughout the production and management of the cooperative, which are promoted in the justice and stakeholder theory literature.

This study is structured as follows: initially, the theoretical approach that supports this research is presented, followed by an explanation of the chosen method. Next, the research findings are presented, relating them to the addressed theory. This chapter concludes with an overview of the research, main contributions, and limitations.

## Theoretical Background

### *Justice as a Pillar for Sustainable Development*

Sustainable development is designed to meet the needs of the present without compromising the ability of future generations to fulfill their own needs (WCED, 1987). This definition refers to the view that sustainability reaches different dimensions and involves multiple stakeholders (Giovannini & Kruglianskas, 2008). While companies focus on the ecological discussion of sustainability, narrower aspects have been emphasized in the path toward sustainability (Klewitz & Hansen, 2014).

Among the specific themes, the term justice appears as an important strategic concept for promoting sustainability. The UN has established 17 SDGs for the year 2030. Among these, Goal 16 addresses promoting peaceful and inclusive societies for sustainable development, providing access to justice for all, and building effective, accountable institutions at all levels (UN, 2015).

Even though the idea of justice has gained prominence in the context of sustainability, this concept is still misinterpreted and misunderstood in different literatures (Ikeme, 2003). Historically, Aristotle was the first to adopt the term distributive justice, contrasted with the term corrective justice. This vision of justice suffered a rupture at the end of the 18th century, with the ideas coming from Smith, who first drew attention to the damage that poverty causes in the lives of the poor. In the 1950s and 1960s, John Rawls began to develop his theory of justice, in which he argued that the plurality of distinct persons, with separate systems of ends, constituted an essential characteristic of human societies (Fleischacker, 2005).

According to Rawls (1971), justice in its modern sense can be defined in two principles: (1) each person should have an equal right to the most extensive system of equal basic liberties, consistent with a similar system of liberty for all; (2) social and economic inequalities should be arranged so that both (a) are to the maximum benefit of the least advantaged, consistent with the principle of just savings, and (b) are linked to offices and positions open to all under conditions of equal opportunity (the principle of difference).

Based on the perspective proposed by Rawls, justice is recurrently mentioned in the management literature under three dimensions: distributive justice, procedural justice, and interactional justice. Distributive justice deals with the equity of outcomes (Folger & Konovsky, 1989). At the organizational level, it is concerned with the relationship of outcomes, behavior, and employee expectations (Cohen-Charash & Spector, 2001; Folger & Konovsky, 1989).

Procedural justice, on the other hand, considers the process by which outcomes are achieved. Thus, the outcome is relegated to a less important aspect of the process (Cropanzano et al., 2007; De Cremer & Tyler, 2005). There are six rules that help guide a fair process in an organization: (1) consistency, (2) suppression of bias, (3) accuracy, (4) correctness, (5) representativeness, and (6) ethics (Leventhal, 1980).

Interactional justice is concerned with how managers behave toward employees throughout the communication process. It deals with the communication process and examines the way in which managers address employees, such as courtesy, honesty, and respect (Bies & Moag, 1986; Tyler & Bies, 1990).

While these three dimensions of justice are the most commonly used in management literature, other approaches of the concept can be found. For example, environmental justice (Berry, 2003) and the nonhuman nature approach (Kortetmäki et al., 2023) highlight the concern with the environment and ecological issues, referring to the distribution of environmental impacts, power relations, discourses, policymaking, and mobilization in local and specific ways.

The applicability of justice in different contexts demonstrates the importance of the topic in sustainable development. Debates in the political field of sustainability increasingly highlight the issue of justice. Exploring the dimension of justice in sustainability also means advancing theoretical and philosophical discussions in this regard. As sustainability relations connect complex economic, technological, and scientific systems, these structures require an adapted vision of justice, necessitating changes at a normative-legal level (instruments of justice) and attention to the different claims of different stakeholders involved (Freudenreich et al., 2020; Stumpf et al., 2015).

### *Justice in Stakeholder Theory*

For stakeholder theory, the business is a set of value-creating relationships among the stakeholders that make up the market. Business is about how customers, suppliers, employees, financiers, communities, and managers interact and create value. The manager's responsibility is therefore to manage and shape these relationships to maximize value for every stakeholder involved (Freeman, 1984; Freeman et al., 2020; Miles, 2017).

Three attributes are important when discussing the prioritization of stakeholders' interests: power, legitimacy, and urgency (Mitchell et al., 1997). Power is related to the probability that an actor, within a social relationship, is able to carry out his/her own will. Legitimacy is the general perception that an entity's actions are desirable, appropriate, or proper within some socially constructed system of norms, values, and beliefs. Urgency is a demand for immediate attention or pressure, based on the time sensitivity or criticality of the relationship with the stakeholder (Mitchell et al., 1997).

The stakeholder theory presents certain problems with the prioritization of certain stakeholders to the detriment of others who have less influence on the organization, and the identification of who is or is not a stakeholder (Phillips, 1997). This view refers to the discussion of justice, which prompts the quest for equal – and therefore fair – treatment among different stakeholders (Freeman, 1984; Hayibor, 2017). It is possible to identify who is or is not a stakeholder for the organization through the interpretation of justice (Phillips, 1997).

To manage stakeholders, it is necessary to understand that all actions of an organization influence different stakeholders and that the needs of each must be identified (Harrison et al., 2010). The vision of fair treatment in stakeholder management allows the organization to value fairness, impartiality, and morality among all stakeholders (Bridoux & Stoelhorst, 2014). They must perceive that their needs are being met and that everyone is being treated fairly and with respect (Harrison et al., 2010). Behaviors considered fair are rewarded, while unfair behaviors are punished (Phillips, 1997).

Justice-based obligations arise when stakeholders, individually or in groups, engage in voluntary exchanges that bring benefits to both parties, being an important factor for improving stakeholder's utility function (Harrison & Wicks, 2013; Phillips, 1997). The perceived fairness of a stakeholder occurs over time and is influenced by the relationship the organization has with other stakeholders. If the organization is unfair to one stakeholder, it may influence the perceived fairness of other stakeholders of the organization (Bosse et al., 2009). Stakeholders are aware that it is not possible to serve all stakeholders at the same time, so the return will only be seen in the long term (Harrison et al., 2010). Furthermore, the stakeholder profile is relevant. Some stakeholders respond better to actions and perceived fairness (fairness approach) than others, who favor power and bargaining relations (arms-length approach), emphasizing the importance of correctly identifying stakeholders (Bridoux & Stoelhorst, 2014).

In stakeholder theory, justice is discussed in its dimensions of distributive, procedural, and interactional justice (Bosse et al., 2009; Hosmer & Kiewitz, 2005). Distributive justice is present through active stakeholder participation, such as employees' active participation in the success of the organization; with the community, through the company's commitment to the environment; and with customers, through loyalty (Bosse et al., 2009; Donaldson & Preston, 1995). Procedural and interactional justice happen when the organization interacts with stakeholders by giving them a voice and presenting its decisions for stakeholder evaluation (Harrison et al., 2010; Hosmer & Kiewitz, 2005).

Companies that maintain distributive, procedural, and interactional justice in their actions are able to create more value over time (Bosse et al., 2009; Bridoux & Stoelhorst, 2022). For value creation, organizations must establish fairness-based contracts with their respective stakeholders according to their interests (Freeman, 1984). However, if certain stakeholders have more value to the organization, there may be differences. In general, fairness can contribute to firm performance, value creation, and competitive advantage (Bridoux & Stoelhorst, 2014; Donaldson & Preston, 1995; Harrison & Wicks, 2013; Harrison et al., 2010; Jones et al., 2018), resulting in more resources, tangible or intangible, for the firm and its customers (Bosse et al., 2009). Table 9.1 shows a compilation of the concept of justice found in the stakeholder theory literature.

Justice in stakeholder theory comprises a broad discussion and brings together themes concerned with the organization's moral and ethical aspects, which concerns the standards of how people or organizations act toward others based on the notions of human well-being, law and justice (Bauman & Skitka, 2012). It is also important to highlight that, in the last case, there is a financial motivation that allows the organization to consider justice as an important strategic variable. Stakeholders' perceptions of the justice practiced by the organization affect financial performance through the impact on behavior arising from stakeholders. In addition, justice is considered a means to generate trust (or not) of the stakeholder with the organization, which affects the formation of the company's reputation in the long term and, consequently, influences the company's sustainability in several aspects (Greenwood & Van Buren, 2010; Harrison et al., 2010).

## Methodology

The present research has a qualitative and exploratory nature. It followed the orientation of an instrumental case study (Stake, 2000), having as a unit of analysis the justice relations identified in the organization studied.

The case selected for the study is the Cooperativa Central Justa Trama. It was chosen because of its representativeness in the garment sector of organic inputs.

Table 9.1   Definitions and General Concepts of Justice in the Stakeholder Theory Literature.

| Authors | Definitions and Concepts |
| --- | --- |
| Greenberg (1990) | The theory of justice is composed of two general areas: distributive justice and procedural justice. Distributive justice refers to perceptions about the fairness of the actual distribution of outcomes or ends achieved. Procedural justice, on the other hand, focuses on the fairness of the process used to distribute outcomes or achieve goals |
| Phillips (1997) | Whenever people or groups of people voluntarily accept the benefits of a mutually beneficial cooperative scheme that requires sacrifice or contribution on the part of the participants and there is the possibility of free riding, obligations of fairness are created among the participants of the cooperative scheme in proportion to the benefits accepted |
| Berry (2003) | Environmental justice has traditionally been concerned with the distribution of environmental impacts, power relations, discourses, policy formulation, and mobilizations [...] the environmental justice movement combats specific and local environmental issues but is generally concerned with social justice and perceived patterns of institutional discrimination |
| Brink and Eurich (2006) | Stakeholder management can no longer rely on a distributive justice approach to benefit its stakeholders. It is necessary to adopt a social justice perspective, with the aim of recognizing legitimate groups and ensuring fair treatment |
| Crul and Zinkhan (2007) | The principle of distributive justice concerns a fair distribution of outcomes in the economic system. Procedural justice, on the other hand, deals with fair procedures in decision-making. These two types of justice are fundamental to avoiding conflict and assessing shared benefits among stakeholders |
| Bosse et al. (2009) | Distributive justice refers to the material outcomes of a system of distribution. Procedural justice refers to the fairness of the rules and procedures that make up that system. Interactional justice refers to the way in which actors treat each other |
| Brink and Eurich (2006) | It is necessary to adopt a social justice perspective, with the aim of fairly recognizing legitimate stakeholder groups and ensuring fair treatment |

Table 9.1  (*Continued*)

| Authors | Definitions and Concepts |
|---|---|
| Goodstein and Butterfield (2010) | Distributive justice refers to individuals' reactions to unfair distributions of outcomes. Procedural justice focuses on the fairness of the procedures used to achieve those outcomes, such as taking into account the views of affected parties and making decisions without undue bias. Interactional justice refers to the perceived quality of interpersonal treatment used by decision-makers, including respectful behavior, truthfulness of communication, and showing appropriate concern for affected parties |
| Harrison et al. (2010) | Distributive justice suggests that stakeholders are fully cooperative only when they perceive that the value they receive is fair compared to the value received by other stakeholders. Procedural justice refers to stakeholders' perception of how fair a decision-making process is. Interactional justice refers to fairness in the way stakeholders are treated in transactions with the company |

*Source*: Based on De Melo et al. (2020).

Cooperativa Central Justa Trama is the largest production chain in the garment segment of the solidarity economy, articulating 600 cooperative members in five Brazilian states: Rio Grande do Sul, Mato Grosso do Sul, Minas Gerais, Ceará and Rondônia, taking charge from the planting of agroecological cotton to the commercialization of garments produced with it (FAO, 2017).

Data collection was conducted from primary and secondary sources. For the collection of primary data, the semi-structured interview technique was applied in November 2019 with the cooperative's project coordinator. The script used in the interview was developed based on the studies of Brashear et al. (2004) and Mai et al. (2014).

The interview was conducted by telephone and recorded with the interviewee's (I1) permission, having a total duration of 48 minutes. Afterward, the recording was transcribed and translated for further analysis. In total, nine pages were compiled, with 1.5 spacing and Times New Roman font size 12. It is important to emphasize that the transcriptions were made and translated *ipsis litteris* to the interviewee's speech.

Regarding secondary sources, desk research was carried out (Lehmann, 1989) based on documents from the network's institutional site, class associations, and research institutes, in addition to reports, advertising materials, and academic research involving the Cooperativa Central Justa Trama, all available online.

Other two interviews with participants of Justa Trama (I2 and I3), recorded and available on the internet, were used for the analysis.

The qualitative data generated by the interviews and the documents were segmented into metacategories for analytical treatment, inspired by the textual analysis proposed by Flores (1994). Faced with the compilation of primary and secondary data, a corpus of analysis was constituted with information related to Justa Trama.

In the first analysis, these documents were narrowed down to information directly linked to the object of the study. Subsequently, elements that fit into the categories of analysis emerging from the literature review were identified. The categories used for classification and organization of the analyzed documents were summarized as (1) Conceptual aspects of the organization, in which the characteristics that explain Justa Trama as an organization were highlighted; (2) Stakeholder Management, which sought to identify organizational practices consistent with the management philosophy focused on stakeholders; and (3) Principles of justice at Justa Trama, in which practices and ideals adopted by the organization that reflect the search for ethical management based on justice among the network's stakeholders were highlighted. In this sense, the categories should contribute to the understanding of the influence of justice in the organizational processes of Justa Trama.

After distributing the cataloged data among the categories, an in-depth analysis was initiated, developing meanings and associations regarding the phenomenon of organizational justice in the context of cooperative networks. The results of this analysis are reported and discussed in the subsequent section.

## Results and Discussion

The analysis of the results is presented in three parts. Initially, the organization studied is presented, followed by an explanation of how the organization considers and manages its stakeholders. Finally, the analysis of how the organization seeks to develop its actions based on the principles of justice is described.

### *Justa Trama*

Justa Trama is a network composed of three cooperatives, two associations, and two informal groups, which mobilizes a production chain formed from the union of these institutions, responsible for a process that begins with the planting of agroecological cotton and ends with the commercialization of garments. At the time this research was carried out, the organization articulated 600 cooperative members/associates in five states: Rio Grande do Sul, Mato Grosso do Sul, Minas Gerais, Ceará, and Rondônia.

The network emerged in 2005, in a scenario of incentive to cooperativism policies in Brazil, supported by UNISOL Brasil (Central of Cooperatives and Solidarity Enterprises). That year, the World Social Forum was held in Porto Alegre (RS), Brazil. To meet the demand of this event, 45 clothing manufacturing enterprises were brought together. Coordinated by the cooperative Univens, the group was challenged to produce 60,000 eco-bags for the forum.

After the success of the event, the participants believed that the chain could continue. In this context, Justa Trama emerges as an organization. Supported by the National Secretariat of Solidarity Economy (SENAES) of the Ministry of Labor in Brazil, the network was registered as a legal entity in 2008.

The following enterprises have joined Justa Trama as informal groups: the cooperative of artisans Açaí (natural ornaments), the Associação de Desenvolvimento Educacional e Cultural de Tauá-ADEC (production of cotton lint), Coopertêxtil (spinning and weaving), the Associação da Escola Família Agrícola da Fronteira (AEFAF), Cooperativa Fênix (accessories and footwear).

The network works from links, aggregating each activity that is part of the chain. Production starts at ADEC (Tauá-CE) and AEFAF (Pontaporã-MG). The products and inputs are directed between the cooperatives along the chain as the production steps are carried out. The Justa Trama chain is represented in Fig. 9.1. Among the products commercialized are shirts, eco-bags dresses, dolls, bedding sets, and accessories. The products are sold in partner stores and through the organization's own e-commerce.

The central cooperative is in Porto Alegre (RS), responsible for all the administration of the network, communication, and relationship between cooperatives and associations. It is important to note that the institutions that are part of Justa Trama also work individually, with activities and marketing outside the network.

### Stakeholder Management at Justa Trama

Justa Trama assumes, as its organizational mission, to articulate and integrate enterprises of the production chain of ecological fiber through planting, transformation, production, and commercialization, promoting solidarity economy, sustainability, agroecology, fair trade, conscious consumption, environmental preservation, and fair income distribution for its associates and society in general.

To achieve this mission, a series of principles and values are adopted and considered in the management of the organization's stakeholders. The primary stakeholders, considered by Clarkson (1995) as those crucial to the survival of the organization, are identified in Justa Trama as the cooperatives that make up the network, their members, consumers, and the environment, which gains importance since it is incorporated into the philosophy of the organization.

Fig. 9.1   Production Chain of the Justa Trama Network. *Source*: Based on FAO (2017).

Because it is a solidarity enterprise, only collective institutions can be part of the network. This premise contributes to the dissemination and understanding of the organizational philosophy by the member institutions of Justa Trama. To manage the chain, the central cooperative establishes a hierarchical structure formed by traditional administrative positions of the cooperative regime, contemplating members of the different links of the productive chain:

> [To be part of the chain] you must be an association or a cooperative and understand this collectivity and what this foundation of the solidarity economy is. So it is either a cooperative or an association to be part of the network. There is no way individual people can get in, nor companies, because it would run away from the proposal, because they have another methodology, other ideas, which is corporativism. We have a team of assistants, secretaries, treasurer, all from a cooperative. It changes every three years. (I1)

The fact that the organization works with cooperatives contributes to the engagement of employees, most of whom are also cooperative members. Thus, the feeling of "owning the business" and participating in the decisions of the organization has a positive effect on the performance of employees:

> [...] being a cooperative member you don't have that constant fear that you might leave the following month. They are the ones who coordinate the business, let's say. (I1)

> When I get the cotton seed, in November or December I already know how much I'll sell the arroba for. For me it is important to strive to produce because I know what I will earn. (I2)

The products created at Justa Trama are designed according to the consumer profile that the organization aims to reach: the socially and ecologically conscious consumer. According to the organization, the responsible and solidary consumer is a fundamental part of the process of Justa Trama. The network, thus, appropriates the goal of meeting the expectations of this consumer who values conscious consumption and supplies the demand for environmentally friendly products (FAO, 2017).

Considering the needs of its consumers and the organizational philosophy, Justa Trama sees the environment as one of its priority stakeholders. There is a special focus on the treatment of inputs and environmental preservation:

> The other cotton, conventional, is planted and I don't know how many tons, but it is actually a lot of agrochemicals dumped on it. I know that we have research that says that conventional cotton carries 68% of agrotoxins in the fabric, so it's a very large amount and we don't realize it. So, to have organic cotton, our work is intense [...]. (I1)

IBD certification, Latin America's largest organic product certification, reaffirms Justa Trama's commitment to adopt processes effectively based on organic agriculture and environmental concern, denoting the organization's proper treatment of this stakeholder.

### Principles of Justice Applied to Justa Trama Management

The business concept of Justa Trama demonstrates that the principles of justice are the foundation for the organization and are used to underpin a sustainable development of the network. A series of activities incorporate the vision of justice as a factor intrinsic to the process. This fact can be reported mainly under three perspectives: the treatment of employees, the prices applied, and environmental sustainability.

Regarding fair trade, this is the central concept that classifies Justa Trama as a solidarity enterprise. Fair trade is characterized as a way of organizing the production chain, based on commercial relationships that meet criteria of justice, solidarity, and environmental sustainability (FAO, 2017). Justa Trama adopts fair trade standards when articulating production, connecting organized family farmers to the socially and ecologically conscious consumer. This vision permeates the entire chain.

From the point of view of normative justice, some laws and decrees have enabled the articulation and development of the organization: Decree 48688 of December 15, 2011, which regulated the state council of solidarity economy; Law 13.874 of December 28, 2011, which instituted differentiated Brazilian Tax on Circulation of Goods and Services (ICMS) taxation for cooperatives; Law 13.922 of January 17, 2012, which determines public purchases coming from the solidarity economy; Law 12.690 of July 19, 2012, which provides for the organization and operation of Work Cooperatives; Decree 50,285 of April 30, 2013, which institutes the policy of certification of solidarity enterprises; and, finally, Decree 50,459 of July 3, 2013, which regulates the popular and solidarity economy program in Rio Grande do Sul.

There is a concern for fairness in relations between the participating cooperatives. The organizational structure of Justa Trama has a president, secretaries, and treasurers democratically elected every three years. All participating associations and cooperatives have equal chances to occupy the positions on the board, which corroborates Rawls' idea of equal rights (Fleischacker, 2005) and the vision of procedural justice (Leventhal, 1980).

The organization is also concerned with gender equality in decision-making positions throughout the chain. This concern of the central cooperative has caused some cooperatives that participate in the network to change their bylaws to ensure the participation of women in the management of the entities, requiring the involvement of at least 30% women in managerial positions (FAO, 2017). Studies in stakeholder theory have posited the need to consider gender diversification in decision-making positions in order to reach multiple stakeholders within the organization (Greenwood & Mir, 2019), with gender diversity offering advantages in defining business strategies (Amorelli & García-Sánchez, 2021).

Communication within Justa Trama is designed to happen transparently, which reaffirms the vision of interactional justice in the organization (Bies & Moag, 1986; Bosse et al., 2009; Tyler & Bies, 1990). Major decisions are made democratically in an annual assembly that always takes place in different cities that have participation in the network:

> [...] every assembly that Justa Trama holds is in some link – we call the associations and cooperatives a link, so that other people can see the needs or successes, achievements of others. [...] the assemblies are for us to always correct, fix or redirect what is not working. (I1)

The costs and prices adopted annually are also decided at the annual meeting. The pricing issue is a point that highlights the organization's concern about fairness with its workers and consumers. The fair price is one of the main mechanisms that guarantee the equal distribution of income in the chain and includes both production costs and an additional margin that incorporates environmental and social costs to ensure respect for the norms of the organic production system and decent work in the numerous segments of the production chain.

Justa Trama pays its producers a value above what is paid for conventional cotton, not only for being an organic product but also the fair price that covers the production costs. Moreover, the price passed on to the consumer is also considered a fair price:

> An assembly is held at the beginning of the year with all the links to decide how much can apply readjustment to not be onerous to anyone, because the motto is that the cooperative member of Justa Trama can also buy the clothes that she makes. So I see in other brands, that we also do the commercialization here in Porto Alegre, then we have requests for fabrics for other brands and in these other brands a ready-made garment is 200–300% above the value that Justa Trama practices in a garment that it makes. (I1)

When it comes to distributive justice, which concerns the sharing of the results generated by the organization (Folger & Konovsky, 1989), some aspects of this are questioned inside Justa Trama. This occurs because apparently egalitarian decisions may be seen as unfair. This is the case with the distribution of the surplus (excess profits) at the end of the year. After the closing of the annual results, the surplus is distributed equally among the cooperatives. However, some institutions participate more proactively in the results than others, which may lead to the understanding that equal distribution is not fair to them:

> [...] since we are a central, at the end of the year we close the year and the surplus or no surplus. If the year ends well, we all receive the same amount of surplus. What we were questioning is that there are cooperatives that don't comply or don't do everything

they are supposed to do, or don't make the same effort as the other cooperative did, or didn't do all the work that another cooperative did, and up to this moment all of them have the same number, the same amount of surplus. It is thought, based on this, even because it happened this year only, that one cooperative was less active than another, that we really have to have these criteria to determine how much surplus can be left if all are met. However, it is very difficult to classify these criteria, so I think that is why it hasn't been done until today. (I1)

In this aspect, the concern with fair play and distribution – in this case, the surplus – according to the contribution, advocated by Phillips (1997), helps explain the situation of injustice created. On the other hand, the central cooperative is concerned about the sustainability and individual characteristics of the enterprises that are part of Justa Trama, which is related to the principle of difference mentioned by Rawls (Fleischacker, 2005). When an enterprise has trouble in a given year, the central cooperative offers support from a reserve fund created for this purpose:

[…] we had crises that lasted six years without rain in Ceará. So you can imagine that for some years we had problems, right? There is a reserve fund, one of the funds that Justa Trama has, which is exactly for this. There was no harvest, but the farmer needs resources. We usually talk to the president, the whole staff, about what we can really do. They decide if it is to pay for inputs, or to pay a part of what they would harvest. (I1)

The environment, in turn, is one of the main stakeholders of the organization and every care is taken to ensure the correct treatment of the environment, which is related to environmental justice and nonhuman nature (Berry, 2003; Kortetmäki et al., 2023). In the production stage, the production processes are ensured to be environmentally sustainable. The non-use of pesticides reverberates in fair working conditions for cotton producers, ensuring better health for families and communities.

The planting is in an agro-ecological way, which is more than organic, because it is the intercropping. When you don't do monoculture you also guarantee the necessary substances so that you don't take away all the fertility of the land. (I3)

Thus, there is concern not only with the production but also with the continuity and safety of the environment from which the cotton is extracted. The cotton fiber is naturally dyed, avoiding the use of chemical products and consequently reducing the environmental impact caused. Throughout the chain, there is environmental awareness, combating waste and full use of inputs, exemplified by the use of fabric scraps to cover buttons and other details of the pieces in the manufacturing stage (FAO, 2017). All the smoothness of this process is reaffirmed and ensured by IBD certification, which the organization discloses and makes available on its website.

Despite these precautions, situations of environmental injustice cannot be fully mitigated due to the need for transportation along the chain:

> Between the cooperatives, in the cooperativism, you can do the inter-cooperative transport. So we use this to make it cheaper, because otherwise it would be really expensive. (I1)

Since parts of the network are located in different regions, the organization ends up having high logistics costs to connect the productive links. Therefore, the use of road transportation is a polluting and environmentally damaging mechanism. This aspect becomes a barrier in the pursuit of total fair management for the organization, corroborating the difficulty in serving all stakeholders fairly at the same time (Freeman et al., 2020; Harrison et al., 2010).

Finally, all the processes that the Justa Trama network mobilizes return in benefits related to the quality of life of those involved, which demonstrates the generation of social justice as defined by Brink and Eurich (2006) and fair contribution proposed by Phillips (1997). In addition, there is an increase in the utility function of those involved as a result of the actions perceived as fair by the organization, pointed out as one of the factors of value creation for stakeholders (Bridoux & Stoelhorst, 2022; Harrison & Wicks, 2013).

The opportunities created by the network were able to generate better working conditions for employees, in addition to the positive change in the reality of families impacted by the activities of Justa Trama:

> [...] as long as you can have a better chair to sew, it improves your quality of life, right? So not only your professional life, but also your personal life. So there are many cooperative members that have finished their houses working here, their children in day care, they can give a better study. [...] There are testimonials of people here, who improved and grew up here. [...] The working conditions were very difficult. Now they have a building that they work in, a schedule determined by them. In this case, we close here at 11 o'clock because most of them are from the area and go to lunch with their families and come back. Then it reopens at 1 pm. They eat, sleep, so there is a quality of life that they chose that is better at this time. So I do think there was an advance, and if God wants, we will progress, thinking about people, about the whole. (I1)

> When you pay a seamstress fairly, it has repercussions because she will spend most of her money here in the community. When we improve our earnings, the earnings improve for everyone. It improves the artisans' earnings, the farmers' earnings, the

seamstresses' earnings. You improve the lives of everybody, and the results are exactly the same, improving the lives of the community where each one of us is. (I3)

By establishing fair relationships throughout the process of production, management, and trade, Justa Trama demonstrates an understanding of how its stakeholders respond to its actions. This process of identifying and managing priority stakeholders follows the fairness approach model proposed by Bridoux and Stoelhorst (2014) and yields concrete results for the organization.

The principles of justice applied throughout the chain and the impact generated on the families involved show that the example of Justa Trama is a model of organization guided by social justice goals indicated in the SDGs of the UN 2030 Agenda, especially with regard to the development of effective, accountable, transparent, inclusive, and fair institutions.

## Conclusions

The present study aimed to analyze the influence of justice in the organizational processes of a network of solidarity economy cooperatives. The topic of justice has been gaining more and more notoriety in the field of organizational ethics and stakeholder management, being seen as an important strategic variable for organizational sustainability.

Being treated fairly is a common desire of all stakeholders. They use their perceptions of justice, in the distributive, procedural and interactional dimension, to positively repay the company when they perceive fair treatment or punish the organization when they perceive unfair treatment (Crul & Zinkhan, 2007; Harrison et al., 2010; Hayibor & Collins, 2016). In this sense, companies that adopt unfair behavior can compromise their reputation with stakeholders, affecting their sustainability in different aspects.

The case covered in this study was Justa Trama, a network of cooperatives that generates a productive chain of agroecological cotton production for making products. The organizational model based on fair trade and solidarity and the numerous actions and processes based on the principles of justice show that the organization is a concrete example when it comes to the vision of fair treatment of multiple stakeholders.

Among the relationships observed in the chain, the following stand out: the way information is disseminated (interactional justice); how decisions are made through the annual assembly and the way the cooperatives participate (procedural justice); how the results are shared among the cooperatives (distributive justice) – although in this aspect feelings of injustice were identified; how the environment is considered in an agroecological production (environmental justice); and how the whole process generates quality of life for the families involved (social justice).

It is important to highlight that the organization chosen for the study operates in the cooperative format and prioritizes the philosophy of fair and solidary trade, allowing the principles of justice to be more easily adopted (Novkovic,

2008). Thus, making comparisons between social organizations and private companies in the prism of justice can be a limiting factor in this research. However, we argue that Justa Trama's organizational practices, based on principles of justice, can inspire private organizations to improve their processes, leading to a more ethical and fair approach to stakeholders.

The use of the single case method based on secondary information and an interview are other limitations seen in the research, given the difficulty in establishing generalizations regarding the themes addressed. Finally, this study provides insights for further future research.

Researchers can take a deeper approach to the vision of justice from the cooperative members' perspective, seeking to validate the information found in this chapter and provide a more comprehensive look at the justice relationships established by Justa Trama. A quantitative approach can also be used, based on the use of justice scales already validated in the stakeholder literature (e.g., Brammer et al., 2007) to analyze the cooperative members' perception of the dimensions of distributive, procedural, and interaction of Justa Trama.

# References

Amorelli, M. F., & García-Sánchez, I. M. (2021). Trends in the dynamic evolution of board gender diversity and corporate social responsibility. *Corporate Social Responsibility and Environmental Management*, *28*(2), 537–554.

Bauman, C. W., & Skitka, L. J. (2012). Corporate social responsibility as a source of employee satisfaction. *Research in Organizational Behavior*, *32*, 63–86

Berry, G. R. (2003). Organizing against multinational corporate power in cancer alley: The activist community as primary stakeholder. *Organization & Environment*, *16*(1), 3–33.

Bies, R. J., & Moag, J. F. (1986). Interactional justice: Communication criteria of fairness. In R. J. Lewicki, B. H. Sheppard, & M. H. Bazerman (Eds.), *Research on negotiations in organizations* (Vol. 1, pp. 43–55). JAI Press.

Bosse, D. A., Phillips, R. A., & Harrison, J. S. (2009). Stakeholders, reciprocity, and firm performance. *Strategic Management Journal*, *30*, 447–456.

Brammer, S., Millington, A., & Rayton, B. (2007). The contribution of corporate social responsibility to organizational commitment. *The International Journal of Human Resource Management*, *18*(10), 1701–1719.

Brashear, T. G., Brooks, C. M., & Boles, J. S. (2004). Distributive and procedural justice in a sales force context: Scale development and validation. *Journal of Business Research*, *57*(1), 86–93.

Bridoux, F., & Stoelhorst, J. W. (2014). Microfoundations for stakeholder theory: Managing stakeholders with heterogeneous motives. *Strategic Management Journal*, *35*(1), 107–125.

Bridoux, F., & Stoelhorst, J. W. (2016). Stakeholder relationships and social welfare: A behavioral theory of contributions to joint value creation. *Academy of Management Review*, *41*(2), 229–251.

Bridoux, F., & Stoelhorst, J. W. (2022). Stakeholder theory, strategy, and organization: Past, present, and future. *Strategic Organization*, *20*(4), 797–809.

Brink, A., & Eurich, J. (2006). Recognition based upon the vitality criterion: A key to sustainable economic success. *Journal of Business Ethics*, *67*(2), 155–164.

Clarkson, M. E. (1995). A stakeholder framework for analyzing and evaluating corporate social performance. *Academy of Management Review*, *20*(1), 92–117.

Cohen-Charash, Y., & Spector, P. E. (2001). The role of justice in organizations: A meta-analysis. *Organizational Behavior and Human Decision Processes*, *86*(2), 278–321.

Cropanzano, R., Bowen, D. E., & Gilliland, S. W. (2007). The management of organizational justice. *Academy of Management Perspectives*, *21*(4), 34–48.

Crul, L., & Zinkhan, G. M. (2007). A theory of the firm perspective on marketing and distributive justice. *Journal of Macromarketing*, *28*(1), 12–23.

De Cremer, D., & T. R. Tyler. 2005. Managing group behavior: The interplay between procedural justice, sense of self, and cooperation. In M. Zanna (Ed.), *Advances of experimental social psychology* (Vol. 38, pp. 151–218). Academic Press.

De Melo, V. P., Taumaturgo, Í., Jhunior, R. D. O. S., & Uchôa, M. T. (2020). The concept of justice in stakeholder theory: A systematic literature review. *BASE-Revista de Administração e Contabilidade da Unisinos*, *17*(3), 429–455.

Donaldson, T., & Preston, L. E. (1995). The stakeholder theory of the corporation: Concepts, evidence, and implications. *Academy of management Review*, *20*(1), 65–91.

FAO. (2017). *Justa Trama, a cadeia solidária do algodão agroecológico*. FAO.

Fleischacker, S. (2005). *A short history of distributive justice*. Harvard University Press. https://doi.org/10.4159/9780674036987

Flores, J. G. (1994). *Análisis de datos cualitativos: Aplicaciones a la investigación educativa*. Promociones y Publicaciones Universitarias.

Folger, R., & Konovsky, M. A. (1989). Effects of procedural and distributive justice on reactions to pay raise decisions. *Academy of Management Journal*, *32*(1), 115–130.

Freeman, R. E. (1984). *Strategic management: A stakeholder approach*. Pitman.

Freeman, R. E., Phillips, R., & Sisodia, R. (2020). Tensions in stakeholder theory. *Business & Society*, *59*(2), 213–231.

Freudenreich, B., Lüdeke-Freund, F., & Schaltegger, S. (2020). A stakeholder theory perspective on business models: Value creation for sustainability. *Journal of Business Ethics*, *166*(1), 3–18.

Giovannini, F., & Kruglianskas, I. (2008). Fatores críticos de sucesso para a criação de um processo inovador sustentável de reciclagem: Um estudo de caso. *RAC-Revista de Administração Contemporânea*, *12*(4), 931–951.

Goodstein, J., & Butterfield, K. D. (2010). Extending the horizon of business ethics: Restorative justice and the aftermath of unethical behavior. *Business Ethics Quarterly*, *20*(3), 453–480.

Greenberg, J. (1990). Organizational justice: Yesterday, today, and tomorrow. *Journal of Management*, *16*, 399–432.

Greenwood, M., & Mir, R. (2019). Critical management studies and stakeholder theory. In J. S. Harrison, J. B. Barney, R. E. Freeman, & R. A. Phillips (Eds.), *The Cambridge handbook of stakeholder theory* (pp. 35–52). Cambridge University Press.

Greenwood, M., & Van Buren, H. J. (2010). Trust and stakeholder theory: Trustworthiness in the organisation–stakeholder relationship. *Journal of Business Ethics*, *95*(3), 425–438.

Harrison, J. S., Bosse, D. A., & Phillips, R. A. (2010). Managing for stakeholders, stakeholder utility functions, and competitive advantage. *Strategic Management Journal*, *31*(1), 58–74.

Harrison, J. S., & Wicks, A. C. (2013). Stakeholder theory, value, and firm performance. *Business Ethics Quarterly*, *23*(1), 97–124.

Hayibor, S. (2017). Is fair treatment enough? Augmenting the fairness-based perspective on stakeholder behaviour. *Journal of Business Ethics*, *140*(1), 43–64.

Hayibor, S., & Collins, C. (2016). Motivators of mobilization: Influences of inequity, expectancy, and resource dependence on stakeholder propensity to take action against the firm. *Journal of Business Ethics, 139*(2), 351–374.

Hosmer, L. T., & Kiewitz, C. (2005). Organizational justice: A behavioral science concept with critical implications for business ethics and stakeholder theory. *Business Ethics Quarterly, 15*(1), 67–91.

Ikeme, J. (2003). Equity, environmental justice and sustainability: Incomplete approaches in climate change politics. *Global Environmental Change, 13*(3), 195–206.

Jones, T. M., Harrison, J. S., & Felps, W. (2018). How applying instrumental stakeholder theory can provide sustainable competitive advantage. *Academy of Management Review, 43*(3), 371–391.

Jordan, S. L., Ferris, G. R., & Lamont, B. T. (2019). A framework for understanding the effects of past experiences on justice expectations and perceptions of human resource inclusion practices. *Human Resource Management Review, 29*(3), 386–399.

Kim, W., & Mauborgne, R. (1998). Procedural justice, strategic decision making, and the knowledge economy. *Strategic Management Journal, 19*(4), 323–338.

Klewitz, J., & Hansen, E. G. (2014). Sustainability-oriented innovation of SMEs: a systematic review. *Journal of Cleaner Production, 65*, 57–75

Kortetmäki, T., Heikkinen, A., & Jokinen, A. (2023). Particularizing nonhuman nature in stakeholder theory: The recognition approach. *Journal of Business Ethics, 185*(1), 17–31.

Laczniak, G. R., & Murphy, P. E. (2007). Distributive justice: Pressing questions, emerging directions, and the promise of Rawlsian analysis. *Journal of Macromarketing, 28*(1), 5–11.

Lehmann, D. R. (1989). *Market research and analysis* (Vol. 3). Irwin.

Leventhal, G. S. (1980). What should be done with equity theory? New approaches to the study of fairness in social relationships. In K. J. Gergen, M. S. Greenberg, & R. H. Willis (Eds.), *Social exchange: Advances in theory and research* (pp. 27–55). Plenum.

Luo, Y. (2007). The independent and interactive roles of procedural, distributive, and interactional justice in strategic alliances. *Academy of Management journal, 50*(3), 644–664.

Mai, N. T. T., Rahtz, D. R., & Shultz, C. J. (2014). Tourism as catalyst for quality of life in transitioning subsistence marketplaces: Perspectives from Ha Long, Vietnam. *Journal of Macromarketing, 34*(1), 28–44.

Migacz, S. J., Zou, S., & Petrick, J. F. (2018). The "terminal" effects of service failure on airlines: Examining service recovery with justice theory. *Journal of Travel Research, 57*(1), 83–98.

Miles, S. (2017). Stakeholder theory classification: A theoretical and empirical evaluation of definitions. *Journal of Business Ethics, 142*(3), 437–459.

Mitchell, R. K., Agle, B. R., & Wood, D. J. (1997). Toward a theory of stakeholder identification and salience. *Academy of Management Review, 22*(4), 853–886. https://doi.org/10.2307/259249

Novkovic, S. (2008). Defining the co-operative difference. *The Journal of Socio-Economics, 37*(6), 2168–2177.

Phillips, R. A. (1997). Stakeholder theory and a principle of fairness. *Business Ethics Quarterly, 7*(1), 51–66.

Rawls, J. (1971). *A theory of justice.* The Belknap Press of Harvard University Press.

Saleem, M. A., Yaseen, A., & Wasaya, A. (2018). Drivers of customer loyalty and word of mouth intentions: Moderating role of interactional justice. *Journal of Hospitality Marketing & Management, 27*(8), 877–904.

Stake, R. E. (2000). Case studies. In N. Denzin & Y. Lincoln (Eds.), *The SAGE handbook of qualitative research* (pp. 435–455). Sage.

Stumpf, K., Baumgärtner, S., Becker, C., & Sievers-Glotzbach, S. (2015). The justice dimension of sustainability: A systematic and general conceptual framework. *Sustainability*, *7*(6), 7438–7472.

Tyler, T. R., & Bies, R. J. (1990). Beyond formal procedures: The interpersonal context of procedural justice. In J. S. Carroll (Ed.), *Applied social psychology and organizational settings* (pp. 77–98). Erlbaum.

United Nations. (2015). *Transforming our world: The 2030 agenda for sustainable development.* https://sdgs.un.org/sites/default/files/publications/21252030%20Agenda%20for%20 Sustainable%20Development%20web.pdf

World Commission on Environment and Development (WCED). (1987). *Report of the World Commission on Environment and Development: "Our Common Future"* [General Assembly Document A/42/427]. http://www.wbcsd.org

Printed and bound by CPI Group (UK) Ltd, Croydon, CR0 4YY

21/11/2024

14596800-0003